TREATMENT OF SUICIDAL PEOPLE

TREATMENT OF SUICIDAL PEOPLE

Edited by

Antoon A. Leenaars, John T. Maltsberger,
and Robert A. Neimeyer

Taylor & Francis

Publishers since 1798

USA	Publishing Office:	Taylor & Francis
		1101 Vermont Avenue, N.W., Suite 200
		Washington, DC 20005-3521
		Tel: (202) 289-2174
		Fax: (202) 289-3665
	Distribution Center:	Taylor & Francis
		1900 Frost Road, Suite 101
		Bristol, PA 19007-1598
		Tel: (215) 785-5800
		Fax: (215) 785-5515
UK		Taylor & Francis Ltd.
		4 John St.
		London WC1N 2ET
		Tel: 071 405 2237
		Fax: 071 831 2035

TREATMENT OF SUICIDAL PEOPLE

Some chapters in this book were originally published in the journal *Death Studies*, Volume 18, Numbers 4 and 5, © 1994 Taylor & Francis.

1 2 3 4 5 6 7 8 9 0   B R B R   9 8 7 6 5 4

This book was set in Times Roman by Harlowe Typography, Inc. The editor was Deborah Klenotic; the production supervisor was Peggy M. Rote. Cover design by Michelle M. Fleitz. Cover photo by Lee Worley. Printing and binding by Braun-Brumfield, Inc.

A CIP catalog record for this book is available from the British Library.
∞ The paper in this publication meets the requirements of the ANSI Standard Z39.48-1984 (Permanence of Paper)

Library of Congress Cataloging-in-Publication Data
Treatment of suicidal people / edited by Antoon A. Leenaars, John T. Maltsberger, Robert A. Neimeyer.
   p.   cm.
   Includes index.

    1. Suicide—Prevention. 2. Crisis intervention (Psychiatry) 3. Suicidal behavior. I. Leenaars, Antoon A. II. Maltsberger, John T. III. Neimeyer, Robert A.
RC569.T74   1994
362.2'88—dc20

ISBN 1-56032-287-X   94-12025
ISSN 0275-3510   CIP

To our patients

Contents

PART III: THERAPEUTIC APPROACHES

PART IV: PSYCHIATRIC ISSUES

PART V: CLINICAL AND LEGAL ISSUES

PART VI: APPLICATIONS TO THE CASE

Contributors

Alan L. Berman, Ph.D., is director of the National Center for the Study and Prevention of Suicide at the Washington School of Psychiatry and maintains a private practice at the Washington Psychological Center, Washington, DC. He is a past president of the American Association of Suicidology and is co-author of *Adolescent Suicide: Assessment and Intervention*.

Bruce Bongar, Ph.D., is associate professor in the doctoral program in clinical psychology, Pacific Graduate School of Psychology, Palo Alto, California, and clinical associate professor of psychiatry at Stanford University School of Medicine, Palo Alto, California. He is author of *The Suicidal Patient: Clinical and Legal Standards of Care*.

Silvia Sara Canetto, Ph.D., is assistant professor in the department of psychology at Colorado State University, Fort Collins, Colorado. She is a prominent researcher in gender and suicide and is co-editor of *Women and Suicidal Behaviors*.

C. James Frankish, Ph.D., is assistant director and research associate with the Institute of Health Promotion Research, and clinical assistant professor in the Department of Health Care and Epidemiology at the University of British Columbia, Vancouver, British Columbia. He is president of the board of directors of the Vancouver Distress Centre.

Mark J. Goldblatt, M.D., is an instructor in psychiatry in the Department of Psychiatry at Harvard Medical School and a psychiatrist in the affective disease program at McLean Hospital, Belmont, Massachusetts. He is currently co-editing a volume of the classical psychoanalytic papers on the topic of suicide.

Sheila A. Greaney, M.B.A., is a doctoral candidate in clinical psychology at Pacific Graduate School of Psychology, Palo Alto, California.

David A. Jobes, Ph.D., is associate professor of psychology at the Catholic University of America (CUA), Washington, D.C., and associate director of the CUA Counseling Center. He is co-author of *Adolescent Suicide: Assessment and Intervention*.

Michael J. Kral, Ph.D., C.Psych., is assistant professor of psychology at the University of Windsor, Windsor, Ontario. He is a past vice-president of the Canadian Association for Suicide Prevention (CASP), co-founder of the Suicide Prevention/Intervention Network in Winnipeg, Manitoba, and he is currently co-editing *Suicide in Canada*.

Antoon A. Leenaars, Ph.D., C.Psych., is a clinical psychologist in private practice in Windsor, Ontario. He is the first past president of the Canadian Association for Suicide Prevention; is president-elect of the American Association of Suicidology; is active in international aspects of suicide prevention; and is editor of the recent volume *Suicidology: Essays in Honor of Edwin S. Shneidman*.

David Lester, Ph.D., is executive director at the Center for the Study of Suicide, Blackwood, New Jersey. He is president of the Intenational Association for Suicide Prevention (IASP) and is the field's most prolific researcher. He is author of the reference book, *Why People Kill Themselves* (3rd Ed.), and is currently co-editing *Suicide and the Unconscious*.

John T. Maltsberger, M.D., is a lecturer at the Harvard Medical School, a member of the faculty of the Boston Psychoanalytic Society and Institute, and a senior consultant at McLean Hospital, Belmont, Massachusetts. He is a past president of the American Association of Suicidology, author of *Suicide Risk*, and co-editor of *Assessment and Prediction of Suicide*.

Peter M. Marzuk, M.D., is assistant professor of psychiatry at the Payne Whitney Psychiatric Clinic at Cornell University Medical College, New York, New York. He is a prominent researcher on HIV illness and suicide and is currently active in the study of homicide and suicide.

Peter McLean, Ph.D., is professor of psychiatry at the University of British Columbia, Vancouver, British Columbia. He is a prominent researcher in depression and its treatment, and is currently active in the application of family therapy for distressed patients.

Robert A. Neimeyer, Ph.D., is professor in the Department of Psychology, Memphis State University, Memphis, Tennessee. He is editor of the journal *Death Studies*, and is a prominent researcher on suicide intervention skills. He is co-editor of *Dying: Facing the Facts*, now in its third edition.

Angela M. Pfeiffer, M.A., is a graduate student in the Department of Psychology, Memphis State University, Memphis, Tennessee.

Joseph Richman, Ph.D., is in private practice in New York and is professor emeritus at Albert Einstein College of Medicine, New York, New York. He is a prominent scholar in gerontological suicidology and the author of *Family Therapy for Suicidal People* and *Preventing Elderly Suicide: Overcoming Personal Despair, Professional Neglect, and Social Bias*.

Isaac Sakinofsky, M.B., Ch.B., M.D., D.P.M. (London), FRCP(C), FRCPsych(UK), is professor of psychiatry at the University of Toronto and head of the Suicidology Program at the Clarke Institute of Psychiatry, Toronto, Ontario.

Lloyd I. Sederer, M.D., is associate general director for clinical services at McLean Hospital and a faculty member of the Harvard Medical School, Belmont, Massachusetts. He is editor of *Inpatient Psychiatry: Diagnosis and Treatment*, now in its third edition.

Edwin S. Shneidman, Ph.D., is professor of thanatology emeritus at the University of California of Los Angeles School of Medicine, Los Angeles, California. He was the founder, in 1968, and the first president of the American Association of Suicidology, the founding editor of the journal *Suicide and Life-Threatening Behavior*, and the author of *Definition of Suicide*.

Andrew Edmund Slaby, M.D., Ph.D., M.P.H., is an epidemiologist and psychiatrist in private practice in New York City and New Jersey and clinical professor of psychiatry at New York University and New York Medical College, New York, New York. He is a past president of the American Association of Suicidology, a board member of the American Suicide Foundation, and author of *Handbook of Psychiatric Emergencies* and *Aftershock*.

Steven Taylor, Ph.D., is assistant professor of psychiatry at the University of British Columbia, Vancouver, British Columbia.

Preface

Because of their incidence, severity, and universality, suicide and sublethal forms of life-threatening behavior constitute major public health problems throughout the world. As such, they call for an informed response on the part of physicians and mental health professionals, who represent the front line in the defense against this tragic but often avoidable loss of human life. Ironically, however, even these professional helpers are insufficiently trained in the essentials of suicide prevention with vulnerable populations, and even fewer are sophisticated in the plethora of clinical, pharmacological, legal, and ethical issues that such preventive efforts entail. Our aim in editing this book was to provide an authoritative handbook for professionals of many disciplines—including psychiatrists, psychologists, counselors, social workers, family therapists, nurses, crisis interventionists, and pastoral counselors—whose work involves them in the assessment of suicide and its prevention.

The classical approach to the prevention of mental health problems and public health problems is that of Caplan, who in *Principles of Preventive Psychiatry* (New York: Basic Books, 1942) distinguished among primary, secondary, and tertiary prevention. The more commonly used terms for these activities are *prevention, intervention,* and *postvention,* respectively. All have a place in the treatment of suicidal people.

Deriving from the Latin roots for "to come" and "before," *prevention* refers to the principle of good mental hygiene in general. Suicide prevention consists of strategies to ameliorate the conditions that lead to suicide. Preventing suicide is best accomplished through primary prevention, an inherently educational activity. People must be educated about suicide. Such education—given that suicide is a multidimensional malaise—is enormously complicated, almost tantamount to preventing human misery.

Intervention, or secondary prevention, refers to the treatment and care of a suicidal crisis or suicidal problem. Suicide is an event with biological (including biochemical), neuropsychological, sociocultural, interpersonal, psychological, and personal philosophical or existential aspects. Obviously, suicide is not solely a medical problem, and a layperson can serve as a life-saving agent. Nonetheless, psychologists, psychiatrists, social workers, psychiatric nurses, and other professionals continue to play the primary roles in intervention. A great deal has been learned about how to intervene with suicidal people.

Postvention—a term introduced by Shneidman in 1971—refers to those things done after the event has occurred. Postvention deals with the traumatic aftereffects in the survivors of a person who has committed suicide (or in those close to someone who has attempted suicide). It includes working with all those who are in need: spouses, siblings, parents, teachers, friends, and so on.

The chapters in this book, drawn in part from articles published in *Death Studies*, examine the state of the art in suicide intervention. Although some attention is given to suicide prevention in the context of health promotion programs and to the role of postvention in risk management, the focus of this book is on direct intervention with the suicidal person. Intervention is emphasized because it is generally agreed that suicidal people are in need of such treatment as crisis intervention, psychotherapy, medication, and hospitalization. Intervention demands great skill and long-term commitment of resources. We are not suggesting that prevention and postvention have no place in treatments; rather, we are proposing that we need to better understand how we can intervene with the person who is standing at the suicidal abyss.

The intervention techniques described in this book have evolved gradually, beginning scientifically at the turn of the century with Freud's struggle to find an effective way to help distressed and melancholic patients. That tradition has evolved over the last hundred years to include important contributions not only from psychiatry and psychology but also from ethnography, public health, and legal studies. Today, a multitude of complementary strategies are used in the treatment of suicidal people, including crisis centers, crisis intervention, psychotherapy, psychopharmacology, and hospitalization. Special consideration must be given to an array of patient factors: age, sex, health status, cultural issues, and more. Intervention today is further complicated by a host of clinical, legal, and ethical issues. Not only is this the state of the art, but it is also in keeping with our perspective: We embrace all sound and humane methods of blocking the unnecessary final exit of a suicidal person.

To enhance the utility of this book as a learning experience, we have organized it as follows. In Part I, Shneidman presents a special case study of Arthur Inman, a fascinating publicly available case of "a warped and deeply troubled man" who chronicled his own long trajectory toward suicide in an equally lengthy personal diary, briefly excerpted here. Throughout the book we then explore different aspects of suicide and treatment possibilities, and at the end we return to Inman's case to reflect on interventions that possibly could have helped him.

Effective intervention requires efficient clinical assessment in the midst of crisis. For this reason, Part II includes a troika of chapters by Kral and Sakinofsky, Frankish, and Leenaars that provide complementary guidelines for the evaluation of suicide risk and crisis intervention. Successful assessment and directive management of the initial crisis set the stage for more sustained efforts in psychotherapy, the theme of Part III. Like contemporary psychotherapy in general, modern approaches to the treatment of suicidal people are multifaceted and specialized, a diversity that is reflected in the six chapters in Part III. After a general exposition of psychodynamic and cognitive–behavioral approaches to treatment by Lester, McLean and Taylor outline a specific model of family therapy for the life-threatening patient, placing a concern with individual dynamics in a broader systemic context. The remaining chapters in this part examine issues of central relevance to special populations, including suicidal adolescents (Berman and Jobes), older adults (Richman), women (Canetto), and the seriously ill (Marzuk).

Part IV extends this predominantly psychological emphasis by taking up a cluster of psychiatric issues that are essential to the treatment of highly perturbed and lethal patients. Slaby considers the specific psychopharmacological needs of potentially suicidal individuals, focusing on classes of medication appropriate for patients with different clinical presentations. Goldblatt discusses the matrix of considerations involved in the decision to hospitalize a suicidal patient, and Sederer provides practical guidelines for inpatient management.

A common core of clinical and legal issues transcends any one population of suicidal people and all treatment approaches and contexts. These issues are examined in Part V. Such issues include strategies for minimizing the risk of litigation without compromising standards of care, as discussed by Bongar and Greaney, and the need to balance the restraint required for patient safety against the greater degree of freedom required for eventual patient recovery, as articulated by Maltsberger. Neimeyer and Pfeiffer conclude this part by offering remedies for the most frequent errors committed by both medical and nonmedical suicide interventionists, as identified by their research with more than 200 would-be helping professionals.

Finally, in Part VI, Leenaars and Maltsberger return to the case of Arthur Inman, providing two alternative perspectives on his treatment. In case consultations, each draw on themes woven throughout the book to conceptualize this challenging case. It is hoped that the reader will be stimulated to develop his or her own perspective of the case.

In closing, we believe that suicide and related forms of self-injurious behavior can often be prevented, if the professionals who are charged with doing so approach their work with a humane and informed perspective. Although the chapters contained in this volume define the state of the art in suicide assessment and intervention, there is much that professionals have yet to learn about the causes, consequences, and cure of this uniquely human tragedy. We hope that this book will serve as a prolegomenon for future directions.

Antoon A. Leenaars
John T. Maltsberger
Robert A. Neimeyer

Part I

The Case

Personal case histories have a significant place in suicidological treatment. Case documents, letters, notes, and diaries contain special revelations of the human mind, and there is much one can glean from them that may be used to refine both clinical theory and practical strategies for intervention. Perhaps one of the most fascinating kinds of case histories left by suicidal people is the suicide diary. It is generally a lengthy, literate document kept over a fairly long period of time, often years. Of the available documents in this genre, the diaries kept by Arthur Inman are likely the most fascinating and are publicly available. In Chapter 1, Shneidman outlines all references to suicide made by this "warped and deeply troubled man," whose aberrations call for clinical analysis. Readers are warned that Inman's racist paranoia is offensive. Inman's constriction and perturbation are typical of the difficulties experienced by highly lethal suicidal people, at times leading to rejection by others.

Throughout the book, we explore the different treatment options that may be used with suicidal patients. In the last chapter, we attempt to apply that knowledge to the intriguing case of Arthur Inman.

Chapter 1

The Inman Diary: Some Reflections

Edwin S. Shneidman

Upon his suicide in 1963 at the age of 68, Arthur Crew Inman left more than 200 boxes of his typed diary and a will bequeathing them to the Harvard Library. Subsequently, Daniel Aaron, professor of American Studies at Harvard, spent 7 years editing this prodigious 17 million word typescript into 1,600 tightly printed pages—the two-volume *The Inman Diary: A Public and Private Confession* (Aaron, 1985). The book is distinguished by Aaron's high scholarship; the man, Inman, was characterized by a number of repellent attributes: He was a sexual molester, a hypochondriac, an anti-Semite, an admirer of Hitler and an opponent of Franklin Roosevelt, an opium addict, an abusive husband, an imperious employer, and a generally wretched human being.

What, then, are the possible virtues of having *The Inman Diary* available? Simply put, it is the most thorough, candid, and accessible set of 20th century autobiographical materials we have of an individual who documented his suicidal thoughts over a number of years and then committed suicide. As such, the Inman volumes provide a fully explicated case history that is easily available (from the Harvard University Press or any good university library) to any serious student and can thus serve as the common case history for multidisciplinary studies by any number of investigators.

Inman had excessively high aspirations for his diary. Professor Aaron tells us that early in the 1920s, when Inman was about 25 years old, he "decided that the only way for him to win fame, perhaps even immortality, would be to write a diary unlike any ever written, an absolutely honest record of himself and his age" (p. 1). Well into the diary, at the end of one of his volumes, Inman states these goals explicitly:

> I have striven to portray myself. I have endeavored to give to posterity a true picture of American life and times. I have labored to turn out each entry with the utmost workmanship at my command. I have been honest. . . . I have held as my inspiration the inexorable judgment of an ideal posterity, the elite among them. It has been my wish to amuse, to instruct, to foster thought, to encourage action, to inspire men of genius to the full stature of their greatness (May 1927, age 32, p. 338).

The extent to which Inman remained faithful to his creed is impressive. If nothing else, at the end of his life, just before he committed suicide, he had earned the right to say, "I have been honest." This is a diary that laypersons may decide tells more than they really want to know but that professionals welcome as a richness of personal and historical insights, albeit distorted by Inman's warped personality and idiosyncratic view of his world.

The number of published extended diaries or autobiographical case histories of individuals who committed suicide is not large. In this century, the only serious rival to the Inman diary, in my opinion, is the published diary of the prize-winning Italian writer, Cesare Pavese (Shneidman, 1979, 1982). The Pavese diaries are available in English under the title *The Burning Brand* (Pavese, 1961). Other published diaries of suicidal persons exist (Cavan, 1928), but they are inferior in their psychological richness. Allport's monograph on the use of personal documents in psychological science (1942) is the indispensable theoretical piece in this field—although, inexplicably, Allport failed even to mention suicide notes or suicide diaries in his otherwise comprehensive treatment of diaries, autobiographies, memoirs, letters, and logs.

How trustworthy are these diary materials to give us the real goods about suicide? There are, of course, differences between the veridicality—the essential truthfulness, what is really so—of a case history, which is generated by an other, and that of an anamnesis, which is generated by the self. Nor can we adequately deal with the question of how truthful, after all, a single autobiography or diary can be, given the fact that individuals are capable of generating several different more or less truthful accounts of their lives.

I shall also try to avoid the vexing questions of why people keep diaries, publish their autobiographies, leave suicide notes, and in general write about themselves at all. I can say with some confidence that there are no definitive answers to any of these questions.

Are suicidal diaries such as Inman's and Pavese's atypical and misleading in that, by virtue of their having been kept over a period of years, they tell only of individuals who are characterologically suicidal and have lived "suicidal careers" (Maris, 1981), rather than of individuals who are suicidal only briefly, in a transient episode of unbearable pain? Does a full suicide note tell more about suicide than a lengthy suicidal diary?

My current preference among the personal documents of suicide is neither the suicide diary nor the suicide note, but the lengthy detailed accounts by individuals who attempted suicide—actually shooting themselves, immolating themselves, or jumping from a high place—but miraculously survived and are able to give us an account of what it was like to be inside those lethally intended suicidal scenarios (Shneidman, 1980).

There is stuff in the Inman diary to capture the interest of a pharmacologist, geneticist, genealogist, biochemist, physician, sociologist, political scientist, social historian, psychologist, psychoanalyst, linguist, logician, and philosopher. Certainly, as I have stated before (Shneidman, 1992), every suicidologist should own a copy of *The Inman Diary*. The ability of suicidologists and other social and behavioral scientists to refer to the same case, citing pages and paragraphs, would make for more lucid communication in our field.

For me, two aspects of Inman's diary made ploughing through it difficult: his unattractive personal attributes—he stands for almost everything I am against—and the vast amount of psychological pain that he suffered, which, even in this loathsome person, aroused some compassion in me. And no one can fail to be impressed by the tenacious honesty of his self-reporting.

One need only dip into the diary to sense immediately the alert, restless, self-centered, opinionated, intensely curious, candid, authoritarian, querulous mind at work. The man was filled with hate, as his opinions of Jews, Negroes, and Franklin Roosevelt, for example, showed. To convey the bitterness of this individual's mind, I have chosen some excerpts on some of Inman's pet social–political topics: Jews (for whom there are 120 separate entries, "Negroes" (60 entries), Hitler (80 entries), and Franklin Roosevelt (140 entries).

Jews: "They are the hyenas of the world. They are an incredible people, the Jews. They are made of mental and spiritual rubber. They bend but never break. They are physical cowards. . . . And their purpose? It is, I believe, to rule the world as Hebrew overlords. Are they not God's chosen people? . . . Perhaps I sound rabid on the subject of Jews. Well I am, rather. I do not trust a one of them. I am repelled by their personalities. They are liars, thieves, cowards, rotten sentimentalists, voluptuaries. . . . The race disgusts me individually and in toto. Parasites they are" (May 1926, age 31, pp. 306–307).

"It is impossible to blame Hitler for his attitude toward the Jews. . . . I feel (with a qualm as to the wisdom of my feelings) that I wish to God every Jew and every Irishman and every negro and every Mediterranean and every Mexican could by some means be forced to leave this fair broad land of ours to us Nordics. . . . If Hitler can restore to the Germans a Germanic culture and a Germanic religion, the outright killing of the six hundred thousand Jews in Germany would be worth the price . . . and so I say, all luck to Herr Hitler" (April 1933, age 37, pp. 525–527).

"Negroes": "On a low type of man, such as the African negro, the coccyx sticks out horizontally; on the average man it sticks straight down; and on a highly sensitized type like me it sticks in horizontally. . . . On the average their reasoning is simply that of a child. Their emotions are the emotions of a child. . . . They are, above all, without self-controlled mental balance" (November and December 1919, age 24, p. 163).

"I have been devoting some additional thought to the negro question. . . . I love the race as a whole. I grew up enough with them to realize how their minds and their emotions function. . . . I feel in their presence a peace that eminates [sic] from no other humans. . . . You will find that those negroes who have progressed the furthest in our civilization have been those with the largest amount of white blood. The negro claims that he fails to better his condition because he isn't given a chance to do so. I don't agree with that for a moment. The negro remains as he is because of lack of certain innate traits, not because of lack of opportunity. . . . The destiny of negroes for decades to come will be to plow the land, to clean up civilization's messes, to wait on other people, to make night-club whoopee, to stevedore and tote" (November 1935, age 40, pp. 665–666).

Roosevelt: Roosevelt . . . has been travelling across the Northwest inspecting Government dam projects, visiting national parks, making speeches that cause stocks to shiver downward. I had not realized until pictures of his smirking mug began again to appear on the front page of every newspaper just what an obnoxious person he strikes the eye as being. I would on no account trust that face. It is weak, stubborn, cruel, the face of a scoundrel and a bigot. I cannot reconcile his expressed altruism with his physiognomy. It may be that I misjudge the man. However, I do not think so. So many hundreds and thousands of pictures cannot lie. . . . The face of Roosevelt is that of a bigoted and hypocritical minister of the gospel (July 1934, age 39, p. 581).

"The demonstration that is being put on about Roosevelt's death seems to me, rank sentimentalist though I am, sickeningly mawkish. . . . The volatile American people are wallowing in an emotional orgasm. . . . Well, Roosevelt is to be buried tomorrow at his estate at Hyde Park by the Hudson River, and I, for one, shall be glad to have him underground" (April 1945, age 50, p. 1269).

Whew!

For suicidologists and thanatologists, the most interesting items in Inman's diary are the documentations of his slide toward suicide. One major personal theme in the often dissonant and tortured music of the diary is the constant drum roll of Inman's suicidal ideation, the siren call of death as an escape from pain. We can see, over the years, how the leitmotif of general perturbation increases as Inman becomes older and genuinely more ill and realistically more helpless. The following is a chronological listing of some of the 50-odd diary entries on death and suicide, covering half a century from 1912, when he was 17, through three serious suicide episodes (one by chloroform and two by overdose), to 1963, when he shot himself to death at age 68.

Not growing in stature, I was painfully aware of how offsized for my age I looked and how artificial and sissy I seemed. . . . It estamped me as outside my class, a scorned thing to myself and to others, a blasted tree. I felt then a failure, a person confined within himself (1913, age 17, p. 98).

As I watched the receding campus through the rear window of a shaky old station cab, I felt very small, very tired, very lonely. If I could have foreseen ahead, I would have killed myself. Or would I have? (reflecting back to 1915, when he was 19; written in 1923, age 28, pp. 130–131).

Exactly what is life worth to me? I hate life with a consuming and virulent hatred. I have always hated life, yet have never sought immediate and self-inflicted death for the very reason, I suspect, that to kill oneself were so vastly easy. But now I am weary. Under certain circumstance I feel I would take my own life and end all this (April 1925, age 30, p. 272).

Last day of another year. One year after another. I count them, for each one that is passed shortens the time until death. What a comfort it is that death is assured to each one of us impartially (December 1925, age 30, p. 290).

Someday when things become too difficult, I shall go under. I am resolved that whenever affairs force me too hard against the wall I shall kill myself. But not yet (November 1926, age 31, p. 327).

Another birthday. I am thirty-two. . . . It seems as though I have lived an eternity. Is there no end? Why do I not kill myself? Well, I do not. I live on and year creeps laboriously after year (May 1927, age 32, p. 336).

You cannot realize the physical wreck I am, how lugubriously sensitive to every disturbance. I want to be dead. I am a craven to keep on living. . . . If I don't get away from noise soon I'll plain pop. It never ends. Getting nearer and nearer to shooting myself. A finger on the trigger—then the end. . . . A slight readjustment in the atomic balance and the earth and all its petty schemes may be blown to dissolution. In such event, what would my work count? (August 1927, age 32, p. 341).

I am practically crazy with my eyes. I cannot even see to write legibly any longer. I wake up every morning about four and lie awake trying to muster the guts to kill myself. I'll do it yet. I must. The horror goes on and on without end. I can't stand it. If only I possessed the courage to put a gun to my head and shoot. But it seems I am a coward. Will life never end? (July 1928, age 33, p. 375–376).

I lay awake last night and thought. I concluded, although not decisively enough to please me, that were my back to fall to pieces in an agonizing way, I would kill myself (December 1931, age 36, p. 464).

It has been two weeks since my heart commenced to go haywire, and I am as yet sitting up not two hours a day. Yesterday was the first day for three weeks that my bowels acted without an enema. My heart still pains grievously at times. Thoughts of doing away with myself were in my head. I wanted the pistol on the bureau. But how to get it? . . . Next morning I went after the pistol. My heart nearly collapsed in the effort, or so it felt. Anyway, I secured the weapon and put it in bed with me. I felt reassured and fell asleep (February 1932, age 37, p. 473).

It is only by some mental or spiritual fluke that there is an entry today. I came closer to killing myself last night than ever before. I had the door locked, the cork on the chloroform bottle extracted, notes written avowing my responsibility, cotton for the chloroform. Then I backslid, and here I am. But was closer to the act than ever before, regardless of failure. My philosophy is changing. I feel certain that sooner or later I shall resort to death at my own hand. If so, why not at the least cause, and why not now rather than later? If horror lies ahead, I might as well meet it at once rather than to procrastinate. I cannot stop the horror, if there be such, by dwelling upon it and enlarging its proportions and dreadfulness. I can see nothing ahead in this life save link after link in a chain of misery. So why not die quietly with resignation toward the future, whatever it might be? A little courage and less imagination is what I need. . . . Leave life I will, I must, some day, by some means. . . . I tore up the notes into small pieces, opened the window, threw them out in groups. They fluttered and swirled and flew away down the alley, into backyards, over rooftops (November 1934, age 39, p. 602).

Stormed all day yesterday. Snowing now. . . . I am sitting in my chair and, as is evident, am writing. My back is in torture. Ever since it was twisted last winter it has been set up wrongly. All the pressure comes on the sacrum, which is becoming inflamed. I have tried to put thought of self-destruction out of my head. Since I lack the guts to end it all, am striving to exist as best I may with the knowledge of cowardice at my heart. Someday, somehow, I shall collect nerve enough to kill myself. Until then I am trying not to dwell on the possibility as I used to (April 1935, age 40, p. 626).

I wish I were not so terrified of the inexorable vengeance of a cruel God meted out to those who take their own lives, of ill luck that would cause me to mangle myself if I attempted suicide (June, 1935, age 40, p. 633).

I feel that it is no wonder that I fear death. For aught I know, eternal underworld dementia exists for the frenzied mind to wander in and never escape (July 1936, age 41, p. 700).

Billy nailed a rug across the window side of the room last evening. I guess I was frantic, to put it mildly, more at the speed of the noise than at the noise. I thought a lot about death. I tried strangling myself to find out how it felt until I hurt my gullet and stopped. I rehid my pistol so that no one would abscond with it. . . . I suppose there are people who feel in their spirits the same consuming human emotions and their inability to cope with them. Each one of us, it seems, must exist within a cocoon of adjusted habit, wrappings for the assailable individual consciousness, delicately and tremblingly fragile at best (November 1941, age 46, pp. 1041–1042).

Nearly went wild yesterday. . . . My intelligence tells me that living here, with my sensitivity to noise, may become impossible. In simplest terms, the matter resolves to a choice between two decisions—either to kill myself and get out of all the woe that is ahead for me in life, or move. . . . As to killing myself, I'm still debating that. I don't think I could bear to shoot myself in the head; it would have to be the heart. If I took sleeping pills, they wouldn't work. A pistol, the only way. Still dread a miscarriage of the act, resulting in injury. I should not be afraid of killing myself. It is, I suppose, the crucial pulling of the trigger that disturbs every natural instinct to remain alive and functioning as much as the fear of the possibility of a continued conscious existence. No it isn't. I know it isn't. What's the pulling of a trigger? A final gesture requiring a certain nugatory bravery of the kind I possess. When you look at it calmly, there's no reason why I can't aim calmly and pull the trigger firmly. I'm tired of evading life like a panicked rabbit (November 1941, age 46, p. 1042).

So much has transpired during this last seven days that I scarcely know where or how to begin. . . . I think I finally made up my mind last Saturday at about 8:45 in the evening, told Mrs. Cash I didn't want to read longer, kissed Evelyn good night. At 9:45 I commenced taking sleeping pills. I can remember swallowing with water at five minute intervals seven 3-grain nembutal tablets and three 5-grain Veronal tablets. The schedule called for at least two more of the latter, but whether I took them or not I am unable to determine. Billy found me the next morning with an undissolved tablet in my mouth. I was out for forty hours. I regained consciousness (and a realization, vague but certain, that my efforts at self-destruction had failed) in a walled bed in what I was aware was a hospital. The first contact with the life I had striven to leave was Billy's moist hand which, I do not know how, I recognized. . . . All in all, I have come out of this experience with a new respect for myself as a man and as a person (November 1941, age 46, pp. 1042–1044).

I don't wonder I tried to bump myself off. This noise is almost unendurable to me. Less than three hours sleep last night. Am inside out with wildness this morning. . . . Almost anything at this juncture seems preferable to being kept awake from two to eight in the mornings, thus becoming conscious of a daytime noise I otherwise might forget. . . . It would be good to vanish from all consciousness forever. I wish I were dead. . . . The whole affair, save for the hospital part, was no worse than a bad illness. I shouldn't be afraid to try it again one day, should I? (December 1941, age 46, p. 1047).

To come to my worst woe, the one that's searing the pants off me. Huntington Avenue has had to be repaved. All night long automobiles tore past at what must have been sixty miles an hour. The vibration of the motors and the sound of the tires on the new pavement was so loud and so unremitting that I couldn't even get to sleep. It is worse than in 1941 when I tried to kill myself (June 1948, age 53, p. 1409).

No energy after striving to live through the Huntington Avenue traffic noise somehow to write in here. I have no conception as to where this will all end up. I'd rather be dead than anything in the world, certainly than be half-demented from noise I can't escape (July 1948, age 53, p. 1409).
I'm drunk now. The left eye is too much for the old man with whitening eyebrows and the small (they used to be large) brown eyes and the weak, sick-appearing mouth and the big, aggressive nose. I wish I were dead (1956, age 61, p. 1562).

I'm a fool and a fool and a fool, and I could shed tears that are long and pendant gray rain exuding from the heart of a sentimental idiot. I'm sad. I'm no good. I'm only as good (drunk me) as those who love me—love me for myself. Who is myself? A "pile of shit" as Pearl says. More than that—I think. I am honesty and no false estimation. Into this world; into and out of it. A shithead with good intentions—me. I want to be good, to be helpful, to be a person devoted to helping others. Am I? Who knows? I am solitary, poopish, frightened Artie. That's me (1956, age 61, p. 1563).

These mornings are long in passing. It's as if they are the tide going out on a shallow beach. And the years, to one who does not wish them, creep like a tortoise. I suppose that, does one hoard and count the years, the mornings, they pass like driven spume. It is nineteen years since I tried to kill myself, and even then it was as if I had persisted a thousand years. Yet here I am, a thousand cycles added, still in function, however piddling (December 1960, age 65, p. 1584).

I am a man. I am an animal. I am no more, no less, despite my mind, than animal. If I am no more than animal, then as animal dies and amounts only to manure for other forms of life, so do I. If such is the case, what difference I die a natural death or perish by my own desperate hand? . . . Fear (at least with me) is like waves on an incoming tide: Each wave rises, lunges forward, sucks back, to be followed by another, each advancing up the beach as the tide rises. . . . I'd rather die than be uprooted and set down somewhere else, my roots torn and broken and strained. Perhaps (this also I think but do not know) I may find what's ahead so unbearable as to make the final course a matter of hara-kiri [sic] courage (March 1961, age 65, p. 1587–1588).

I am striving with all the inner-directed force I possess to keep my spirits up, be busy, joke with those around me. . . . I may tell myself that all this furor of change may lead me to suicide, but it should be no part of mine to moan and groan and make the days miserable for those around me. If the worst is as I contemplate, I can exit surely. At least that! (January 1962, age 66, p. 1589).
I don't, writing this, mean to be melodramatic, though God knows I feel so. I think I'll get my pistol out of the bathroom where it is kept, wrap it in plastic, put it under the bed in a cubby there where, too desperate, I can grasp and use it. Life becomes less propitious by the week with the next japes of fate closer, and what I write in here constantly more personal and less worthwhile, the former intensity of curiosity no longer uncontainable and artisanship flagging, myself terribly tired, my allotted historical task all but completed (February 1962, age 66, p. 1590).
However silly I am, big tears roll down my far-too-seeing eyes. Here goes America with its confidence and its pride; here comes America and its abdication to credit and purblind destruction of its shaped past. . . . This is where one of my generation should die, be dead. From here on the sanctity of the individual goes by the board. I would be better off not here (September 1962, age 67, p. 1592).

The Prudential Tower is 28 stories into the sky, soon will be goosing God. It keeps creeping up to the sky. The wrecking of buildings continues. I feel nervous constantly as to how loud and how disturbing traffic will be with all of the protecting structures between my bedroom and Huntington Avenue razed. Will this, I wonder, be the end of my resistance, hence of life? I still have no intention of moving. I'd rather kill myself than have to undergo moving and resettlement. I've lived much too long anyway (November 1962, age 67, p. 1592).

Jumping out of my skin with nervousness from the nearer and nearer demolition, motors racing, walls falling (the ball is being used), the building shaking and creaking. . . . With every building demolished, new electric lights and signs are let free to shine into my sitting room where it is so bright I have to shield my eyes with something to raise the window opened at night. As soon as the buildings opposite my bedroom are down, God knows what shafts of light will shine in on my walls past the curtain I tie out at night to get air. I feel a Medieval baron in his besieged keep, forces and weapons constricting ever tighter around his security. It may be I'll survive this, but then again I may not, now that D-day is here, to survive within the limits of my disposable defenses. My truest weapons are designed by ingenuity. They are indeed my final weapons. Until tested, who can know their temper? (March 1963, age 67, p. 1596).

Later in 1963, Inman took 15 sleeping pills and was hospitalized. He found the hospital noises soothing, "not like the angry noise of trucks going up hill near where I was" (p. 1596).

Here are further snippets from his diary in November and early December 1963. 1598–1599:

"I feel a harried ninety years old with gathering pressures closing in about. I have lived too long. I have written too much" (p. 1598).

December 3: "I feel like the tag end of a rough time" (p. 1598).

December 4: "This has truly been, is a session in hell. Eight migraines yesterday, and one more at six this morning, with violent headaches and nausea" (p. 1598).

On December 5, he scrawled,

This is being horrible beyond the credible. Twelve divisions of migraines. Idetic [sic] images until I am harried and frightened into desperation. Can't see more than is adequate to get around. Everything overgrown with hands and the imaginary element of substance visible (p. 1598).

The next day, December 6, 1963, at age 68, he shot himself.

As for treatment during his life, Inman had five different osteopathic physicians and any number of all-around helpers. He seemed determined to control those about him through his medical and pseudomedical symptoms. He was a great somatizer. He eschewed psychotherapy. He was deathly afraid of it. For him, everything was in the bones or the bowels; nothing was in the brain. He thought Freud a great sexually oriented charlatan. He "always denigrated and constantly misunderstood Freud" (Aaron, p. 1537), but he never read him. He attributed to Freud the idea that "we all are, fundamentally, screwing, fucking animals with everything else, even survival, subsidiary" (1963, p. 1537).

When Inman was a young man, his mother arranged for him to see Dr. Boris Sidis, a Boston psychiatrist who had studied with William James. Inman was terrified of the experience. He hated Sidis and passionately resisted the very notion of psychotherapy. He wrote in his diary that in that one session when he was alone with Sidis "a stream of concentrated malevolent will power [was] directed against me. . . . [he was] a human snake" (1918, Age 23, p. 150).

In the published diary, Professor Aaron appended a retrospective medical report on Arthur Inman by Dr. David F. Musto. It runs to 16 printed pages. After listing 23 real and imagined medical illnesses that Inman complained of, Dr. Musto concludes,

A review of Arthur Inman's medical history from the start of his invalidism leaves little doubt that his life—leaving out his singular personality—was cruelly complicated by medical maltreatment and by excessive, chronic ingestion of bromides, alcohol, and other powerful chemicals. These attempts to cure had almost without exception a destructive effect on his emotional stability, judgment, and physical health. And yet, his illness had a positive aspect. . . . The secondary gain was so great and solved so many of his emotional problems that he had little incentive to change his style of life. He persisted in his goal to write a response to the times in which he lived, and he succeeded. Under the envelope of illness, Arthur Inman had an indomitable will; it is in this interplay between sickness and creativity that his fascination lies (p. 1618).

What would I have done had I been called in on this case? I hope that I would have had the wisdom to call in a consultant, someone with clinical experience greater than my own, and then I would have deferred gratefully to that person's judgment. And that is exactly what I did. I sought the expert consultation of Dr. John T. Maltsberger of Harvard Medical School and McLean Hospital. I could paraphrase his suggestions and even try to count them as my own, but honesty and a sense of deep indebtedness dictate that I simply cite them verbatim:

It seems to me that a patient like this might not reject you if you immediately acknowledged his physical suffering as a manifestation of his psychache and did not mentalize it. One would not right away challenge the idea that the problem was one of joints and guts—after all, that's where he hurt—acknowledging right away that one could not, as a mere psychologist, do much about that. But he was always looking for people to pay attention to him, and what was so appealing about those osteopaths was no doubt the fact that they offered him emotional support. Support is an important component in making emotional suffering endurable, as you have said (Shneidman, 1980). After being kindly interested and not too interpretive at the beginning, I think that you might find that he would see you time and again, especially when he was distressed, to rant and rail about all the people who let him down. He would have loved to teach you about his suffering, I suspect, and soon might have entered into some kind of alliance with you as a comforter. At times when he was really getting closer to suicidal action, the acute things that you outlined in that paper would be highly applicable (J. T. Maltsberger, personal communication, November 23, 1992).

Dr. Maltsberger subsequently added these remarks:

The raging against Jews, blacks, and others would pose two serious problems if this patient proved capable of engagement in psychotherapy. Obviously, the first is the offense he would offer his therapist, especially were the therapist a Jew. If, however, the therapist's curiosity about where the devaluation came from proved stronger than his aversion, some exploration would be possible. A tenable working hypothesis would be that the hate, now displaced onto Jews, Roosevelt, blacks, and whoever else, arose from bitter childhood disappointment in someone from whom the patient had longed to be given much but had received little. The best guess is his father, or father surrogates. A boy's idealizing love for a disappointing father often turns to bitterness and hate. The father takes the patient's unconscious blame for his 'sissy-dom' and blighted masculine self respect.

I would proceed by acknowledging how disappointed he must be to discover that his new therapist is a Jew, a member of a group that he detests. I would go on to suggest that the disappointment he felt must have arisen from many experiences of having his hopes dashed, dashed by, among others, the silent Boris Sidis. Had Sidis just sat there and offered little, perhaps like his father? Onto the ineffectual Sidis I would wager that Inman projected all his viperish hatred for an ineffectual but threatening father. I would tell him that not all psychotherapists were so passive as Sidis had been, and that his present therapist, for one, was interested in his experiences of disappointment. Somebody important in his past must have let him down, and let him down badly. What was the story of that? I would ask.

It is my guess that anyone as lonely as Inman might prove eager to talk about the wrongs he had endured. On the side of the therapist would be Inman's eagerness for attachments, something evident in the way he hired so many people to help and nurse him. Diary writers often write their diaries to someone in the future, an imaginary idealized person who might, at long last, finally understand. Unconsciously disappointed in their capacity to find real empathic understanding in their current relationships, they hope that a benign stranger, at some time in the future, will finally read and grasp their special emotional truths (J. T. Maltsberger, personal communication, December 22, 1992).

There is no substitute for a first-rate consultant.

Of course, on embarking on therapy with Inman, I would have had to control my own countertransference. I would have had to decide whether I wanted to treat Inman at all. If I did, I would have then had a professional and ethical responsibility to be the good therapist and let Inman verbalize whatever feelings he had, even those against me. But I would have had to control my feelings, especially those countertransference hate (Maltsberger & Buie, 1974) and immobilization (Litman, 1964).

Whatever would have happened, I am certain that it would not have been an easy case, and I cannot be sure that if our life paths had crossed (actually, for a while we were both in the Boston area at the same time) our meeting would have changed anything about Inman's case, except that I would now be publicly excoriated (probably as an incompetent Jewish charlatan) in a printed suicide diary.

However, I hope that some therapeutic alliance with Inman would have been possible. Had that occurred, I suspect that he might have been helped. But that notion itself is tautological: If there were a relationship, then some good would follow. We know that Inman could be mercurial; however, we also know that, underneath it all, he was very needful. Maybe he could have forgiven me for what I was and let me try to help him, at least for a while. I hope so.

Had he and I worked together, my own special private satisfaction, unbeknown to him, would have been in the fact that this kind of psychoanalytically derived therapy arose from the special insights and merciful humanity of, continentally speaking, a landsman of my father.

REFERENCES

Aaron, D. (Ed.). (1985). *The Inman diary: A public and private confession (2 vols.)* Cambridge, MA: Harvard University Press.

Allport, G. (1942). *The use of personal documents in psychological science.* New York: Social Science Research Council.

Cavan, R. (1928). *Suicide.* New York: Russell and Russell.

Litman, R. E. (1964). Immobilization response to suicidal behavior. *Archives of General Psychiatry, 11,* 282–285.

Maltsberger, J. T., & Buie, D. H. (1974). Countertransference hate in the treatment of suicidal patients. *Archives of General Psychiatry, 30,* 625–633.

Maris, R. (1981). *Pathways to suicide.* Baltimore: Johns Hopkins University Press.

Pavese, C. (1961). *The burning brand: Diary 1935–1950.* New York: Walker.

Shneidman, E. (1979). Risk writing: A special note about Cesare Pavese and Joseph Conrad. *Journal of the American Academy of Psychoanalysis, 7,* 575–592.

Shneidman, E. (1980). Psychotherapy with suicidal patients. In T. Karasu & L. Bellak (Eds.), *Specialized techniques in individual psychotherapy* (pp. 305–313). New York: Brunner/Mazel.

Shneidman, E. (1982). The suicidal logic of Cesare Pavese. *Journal of the American Academy of Psychoanalysis, 10,* 547–563.

Shneidman, E. (1992). What do suicides have in common? A summary of the psychological approach. In B. Bongar (Ed.), *Suicide: Guidelines for assessment, management and treatment.* New York: Oxford University Press.

Part II

Assessment and Crisis Intervention

By definition, intervention efforts with suicidal people involve the evaluation and management of a crisis situation. Many mental health and public health professionals are called on to serve as life-saving agents. Suicide risk assessment is one of the most challenging tasks they face. Intervention rests on sound assessment. Crisis intervention, whether performed by crisis-line staff or by mental health professionals, provides an immediate and informed response to a suicidal person through the use of a systematic process of crisis definition and problem resolution. Part II outlines what has been learned about assessment and crisis intervention with suicidal people. It consists of three chapters: Chapter 2 presents a clinical model for suicide risk assessment, Chapter 3 addresses the role of crisis centers in treatment, and Chapter 4 presents a systematic model for intervention with highly lethal suicidal people.

A Clinical Model for Suicide
Risk Assessment

Michael J. Kral
Isaac Sakinofsky

Prevention rests on assessment; assessment rests on definition.

Shneidman (1985, p. vi)

Of the common categories of suicidal behaviors, completed suicide is the most difficult to predict; it is the least common. Whereas the lifetime prevalence of attempted suicide in the general population in North America is estimated at 3% (Moscicki et al., 1989; Sakinofsky & Webster, 1994), the lifetime prevalence of completed suicide, at a conservative annual mean rate of 10 per 100,000, is 0.5%. A related and classic problem is the extrapolation of characteristics that denote suicidality in high-risk populations to specific individuals in those populations. Maris, Berman, and Maltsberger (1992) have identified several other salient issues in suicide risk assessment, including membership in a high-risk group, the acuteness of risk/probability of action, the need for risk indicators to be clinically relevant, and the fact that ''what is being predicted or assessed is not one thing, but actually many multidimensional, intersecting, and interacting parameters'' (pp. 642–643). In searching for relevant risk factors, the clinician should be cautious about combining clinical features found among suicide ideators, attempters, and completers, because they appear to be overlapping but different populations. The question of suicide risk is thus becoming more refined: Risk for which suicidal behavior, exactly?

Models of risk assessment have often taken the form of lists of discrete symptoms or patterns, without an integrated perspective or guidelines for implementation. An assessment model should help organize the clinician's thinking about specific questions regarding a particular patient. It should be based, however, on current understanding of these questions. We propose a two-tiered model of suicide risk assessment that comprises both background and subjective risk factors. The background factors are the sociodemographic and related indices that have been found to be correlated with increased risk. These indices are based on different cohorts, populations, and cultures, and many of them change over time (we describe North American trends). Background factors are once removed from the individual being assessed, but in the aggregate they can inform the clinician about a patient's general level of risk. They provide the changing contextual background of risk for a particular individual. The assessment of subjectivity, in contrast, is a focus on the individual case: emotions, thinking, idiosyncratic meanings, general mental state, and experience. We believe that the assessment of subjectivity factors is the key to accurate risk assessment. Before seeing the patient, the therapist needs to prepare for subjective assessment by thinking about two questions: "What am I looking for?" and "What might it look like if I come across it?"

Any assessment model is based, either implicitly or explicitly, on a larger conceptual scheme or theory of the phenomenon of interest, from which questions are derived. Although a number of informative approaches to suicide have been presented in this century, perhaps the most clinically valuable theory has been Shneidman's (1985). The clinical relevance of Shneidman's approach to suicide is its focus on subjectivity, defining suicide as the necessary and sufficient combination of two quite different ingredients: *perturbation* and *lethality*. These two subjective states form the primary clinical template for the model of suicide risk assessment presented herein. As Motto (1989) has noted, the clinician's knowledge ultimately derives from only what he or she sees and hears from the patient, together with collateral information from others, if available. The clinician who is aware of the background factors and subjective states of people who have killed themselves, and provides an atmosphere that facilitates the communication and understanding of the person's subjective state as well as possible at the time, is likely to be in as close to an optimal position as one can be to assess risk. Some background factors for suicide risk will be outlined first, after which relevant subjective/psychological states based on Shneidman's model will be highlighted.

BACKGROUND RISK FACTORS

Knowing that an individual belongs to a particular high-risk group may not be a red flag for imminent risk, but this knowledge can add to the clinician's overall formulation. Much background information can be obtained from significant others as well as from the individual, and therefore others should be interviewed if possible. A single background factor may not be very meaningful, but risk increases as these factors accumulate for any given individual suspected of being or known to be suicidal. Many background factors can also provide the clinician the means for inquiry into perturbation (discussed in the next section), given its manifestation in many of them (e.g., alcohol abuse and recent loss).

General Factors

Being male has long been associated with increased risk for suicide; of all the suicides committed in the United States in a given year, 72% are committed by white males and 20% by white females (Clark & Fawcett, 1992). Native American and white males ages 15–24 and older white males have among the highest rates, and the methods chosen by males (e.g., gunshot or hanging) are typically more lethal than those chosen by females. The suicide rate for Native American youth is generally high, but it varies across communities, with some (e.g., more traditional) communities having low rates (Berlin, 1987). In the United States, males and females kill themselves most often with firearms. The use of firearms in suicide has been increasing over time across the sexes, as well as across all age and ethnic groups (McIntosh, 1991). There is evidence that access to firearms and other popular methods of suicide is directly related to their use in suicide (Brent, Perper, Moritz, Baugher, & Allman, 1993; Carrington & Moyer, 1994 and in press) and that people are unlikely to switch to another method when one that has been in mind becomes unavailable (Clarke & Lester, 1989).

Whereas suicide completers are less likely than attempters to have sought help from a mental health professional, and half will never have done so, they are likely to have seen a general practitioner within a year of death. However, only about 7% of suicide completers are in mental health treatment at the time of their death (Clark & Horton-Deutsch, 1992). Whereas the lifetime risk for suicide is low for the general population, it is alarmingly high for some groups. For example, the lifetime probability of suicidal death is estimated at 15% for persons with a major mood disorder and at 10% for individuals with a schizophrenic disorder (Klerman, 1987; Miles, 1977). The majority of persons who complete suicide can be diagnosed as having a mental disorder, most often a mood disorder that is likely to be comorbid with alcoholism (Klerman, 1987). Lifetime rates of major depression range from 4% to 7% for women and 2% to 5% for men (Mollica, 1989).

People who attempt suicide have been differentiated into single-episode and repeat attempters. Compared with single-episode attempters, repeat attempters show more symptom chronicity, worse coping histories, more frequent histories of substance abuse and suicidal behavior in the family, higher lethality and depression scores, greater likelihood of inpatient admission, less impulsivity, and worse prognosis at 1-year follow-up (e.g., Kurz et al., 1987). Even when suicide attempters resolve the problems that led to their self-harm, they remain at risk for further self-harm. Sakinofsky and Roberts (1990) found that individuals who repeated a suicide attempt in spite of having resolved their problems constituted a minority (16%) of all suicide attempts, and were characterized by histories of episodes of self-harm and aggressiveness that, consistent with knowledge of developmental psychopathology, started at a younger age.

Children and Adolescents

Suicidal behavior in children is an infrequent phenomenon that appears to have increased in prevalence since the 1960s. Hoberman and Garfinkel (1988) found impulsivity, anger, and nervousness to be the pervasive characteristics of the younger children in their study of completed suicide among youth age 19 years or younger. Characteristics of suicidal children between the ages of 6 and 12 include antisocial behavior; conduct disorder; and, in males in particular, comorbidity of antisocial behavior and mood disorder (Sokol & Pfeffer, 1992). Family risk factors have been linked to childhood suicidal behavior, indicating that a thorough assessment of family functioning is in order for any suicidal child.

The suicide rate increases with age for adolescents, particularly for males (Hoberman & Garfinkel, 1988; Shafii, Carrigan, Whittinghill, & Derrick, 1985). Having had an intimate relationship, recent academic decline, physical complaints, chronic illness, and disability are some characteristics of adolescents who complete suicide. Most adolescent suicides occur at home. Common precipitants include an argument; school problems; the breakup of a relationship; and, among females, recent assault or discovery of pregnancy. At least half the adolescents who commit suicide demonstrate evidence of chronic psychiatric disorder, the most common being depression, followed by alcohol abuse. About half will have used alcohol or drugs at the time of death. A substantial minority will have a history of nonlethal self-destructive behavior. Most do not appear to take obvious precautions to avoid discovery; however, the psychological autopsy work of Shafii (1989) suggests that suicide among adolescents is not an ''impulsive act.'' A history of serious ideation, intent, and planning is likely, and most adolescents who commit suicide will have communicated their suicidal ideation to others before their death.

When compared with nonsuicidal depressed adolescent psychiatric patients, suicidal depressed adolescent psychiatric patients appear to experience more stressful events, social losses, overt family conflict, and chronic family disorganization or violence. These adolescents are at higher risk for future suicide attempts. Teens who attempt suicide more than once have more chronic emotional distress with a higher likelihood of personality disorder, more school problems, more life stress, more anger and dysphoria, and more serious suicidal intent than those who attempt suicide once (Brent et al., 1993; Pfeffer et al., 1993; Spirito, Brown, Overholser, & Fritz, 1989).

Clinical judgment is better informed by knowledge of relevant population base rates than by ignoring them. Lifetime prevalence rates for major depression among adolescents have averaged around 7% (Petersen et al., 1993), although in a recent study rates of 31.6% for females and 15.2% for males were found (Lewinsohn, Hops, Roberts, Seeley, & Andrews, 1993). Most studies have found lifetime rates of suicide attempts among American adolescents, including college students, of 4–15%.

The Elderly

The prevalence of depression is currently lower among the elderly than among the young or middle-aged, and most elderly subjects reported being satisfied with their lives (e.g., Butler, 1989). Nevertheless, the elderly white male has the highest suicide rate across the life span, and the rate for elderly black males has increased threefold over the last 25–30 years (Blazer, 1991).

The suicide rate among the elderly exceeds their proportion in the population. Stillion, McDowell, and May (1989) cited cumulative loss, alcohol and drug dependence, loss related to retirement, and social isolation as risk factors specific to the elderly. Involuntary retirement increases risk, and the accumulation of stresses over time poses more risk than do the immediate precipitating factors that are often seen in younger suicides. The elderly are also less likely than younger groups to exhibit nonlethal self-destructive behavior, so the clinician should be aware of the relatively high lethality of the suicidal elder. The strongest predictor of elderly suicide, however, is depression—particularly when it is comorbid with alcohol intoxication (Morgan, 1989). Thus, the assessment of depression in elderly patients is critical.

SUBJECTIVITY

Suicidologists are in general agreement that researchers must go beyond background factors in formulating suicide risk. Berman (1991), for example, argued that a better understanding of suicide will come from the study of individuals' personal meanings and experiences of distress. We propose that the evaluation of subjective experience, the psychological state of the suicidal person, is the key to accurate risk assessment.

The Moving Target

One of the main reasons why clinicians ultimately cannot predict suicide for a given individual is that, like many human states, the suicidal state has a temporal, fluctuating dimension. Given this fact, the professional needs to reassess risk continually during treatment, with the primary goal of keeping the person's levels of perturbation and lethality as low as possible. However, the relationship of current patterns of coping to past coping patterns needs to be assessed as well. In assessing personality coherence, Shneidman (1985) urged, the clinician should look for

> deep consistencies with lifelong coping patterns. We must look to previous episodes of disturbance, to capacity to endure psychological pain, and to the penchant for constriction and dichotomous thinking, for earlier paradigms of egression. . . . Each individual tends to die as he or she has lived, especially as he or she has previously reacted in periods of threat, stress, failure, challenge, shock, and loss. (pp. 148 and 201).

Thus, in assessing suicide risk, the clinician looks for a moving, yet internally consistent, target.

Perturbation

According to Shneidman (1985), the best way to reduce a person's level of suicide risk is to reduce his or her current level of perturbation. For any individual, perturbation—the degree of upset, disturbance, tension, anguish, turmoil, discomfort, dread, hopelessness, or other excessive psychological pain—can reach a point at which it is no longer tolerable. At this unbearable level, unique to each individual, the person becomes motivated to do something about it. There are many ways of reducing perturbation. If suicide is the escape plan, perturbation becomes the trigger for its action (Shneidman, 1985). The clinician must therefore carefully evaluate the level of perturbation being experienced by the person, and must try to help the patient respond to the questions, at varying points in time, "How bad is the hurt? Is it bearable?"

Perturbation is subjective. Trying to understand a person's experience of psychological pain can be a difficult task, particularly if the pain generally is too great for the person to bear, let alone talk about. Attempts at empathy, although critically important, may be deceptively reassuring to the clinician assessing the suicidal individual (Maltsberger & Buie, 1989). The clinician needs to try to determine how unbearable the perturbation can become for the person, and may need to take the person slightly, and very carefully, into this state to find out. Jacobs (1989) suggested that clinicians show suicidal persons that they can connect with them through their emotional pain, noting Havens's advice that the goal is "to be with the patient, in a sense to allow him or her to feel suicidal" (p. 331).

Patients who have decided to kill themselves may not admit to being suicidal during the interview, at least initially, and can present as being in control.

Maltsberger (1986) suggested that the therapist look much more closely than usual at mannerisms, physical appearance, and nonverbal behaviors for clues to continuing, serious underlying agitation (perturbation).

Research findings are clear that a high level of perturbation, particularly anxiety, is a danger sign (Clark & Fawcett, 1992). Acute or short-term (<1 year) risk factors in suicidal patients include a history of panic attacks comorbid with affective disorder, particularly depression (Fawcett et al., 1990); mood cycling during the index episode (Fawcett et al., 1987); and bipolar II depression (depressive attacks associated with a history of briefer episodes of hypomania) (Rihmer, Barsi, Arato, & Demeter, 1990). It also appears that an unbearable state of perturbation is related to completed suicide across the life span (e.g., Mattison, 1988; Pfeffer, 1989; Weisman, 1991).

Hopelessness and helplessness are part of the individual's despair. They exacerbate the psychological pain, or "psychache," by increasing the individual's sense of its ubiquity (Shneidman, 1993). A high level of hopelessness, whether rated on a scale or assessed clinically, is among the best predictors of eventual death by suicide (Beck, Brown, & Steer, 1989). Depressed patients have been found to be more motivated to attempt suicide if their level of hopelessness has been rated as high than if they have been rated as less hopeless and more motivated toward seeking help (Kovacs, Beck, & Weissman, 1975). The individual's plans, outlook, self-prognosis, help rejection, and specific options for the future should therefore be assessed directly whenever possible.

Lethality and Cognitive Constriction

Lethality is ideational and conative. It is the conscious selection of suicide as a "viable" option. According to Shneidman (1985), "no one has ever died of elevated perturbation alone. It is elevated lethality which is dangerous to life" (p. 205). Shneidman (1993) has likewise argued that, theoretically, neither does depression alone lead to death. Lethality, however, does. It is based on the person's considering suicide as a specific (and eventually the only) option in alleviating perturbation. Shneidman has noted the necessity of both "the thought (or insight) that cessation of consciousness is the solution for the unbearable psychache" (1993, p. 148), and "the decision for action" (E. Shneidman, personal communication, June 15, 1993). As numerous theorists have stated, suicide is selected as the prime method of escape from an intolerable state. Perturbation and related risk factors merely render people more vulnerable to accepting the idea of suicide into their current concept of self (Kral, in press)—more vulnerable to lethality.

To assess an individual's risk, the clinician must assess the degree to which the individual considers suicide an escape plan. Litman (1970) has noted that the suicide plan is usually developed over time, rehearsed in the person's head, and more or less formulated before a triggering crisis takes place. The idea of suicide does not likely remain at the conscious level all, or even most, of the time. It becomes a schema for action, a readiness in waiting. The clinician assesses the person's degree of lethality by evaluating the deadliness of the suicide plan, including how, where, and when suicide would occur; the steadfastness of the plan; the degree to which the plan has been developed; the accessibility of means; the presence versus absence of alternative choices; and the degree of intent.

Suicidal intent can be assessed both directly, by asking the patient, and indirectly, by inquiring about method, precautions against discovery, and so on. A high degree of intent is associated with hopelessness and a sense of isolation, with older age and a history of suicide attempts, and with a higher risk for completed suicide. Intent is usually related to the medical seriousness of a suicide attempt. It should be pointed out, however, that researchers have used a variety of measures of intent and that assessing intent is problematic. Recall that people at higher risk for completed suicide may be less likely to talk about suicide during the interview. Uncovering a highly perturbed state might make assessment of lethality easier.

Shneidman (1985) discussed a state of cognitive constriction that, although not limited to suicidal individuals, can, when it occurs together with lethal ideation, become "one of the most dangerous aspects of the suicidal state" (p. 139). Constriction can be defined generally as dichotomous thinking, tunnel vision, or a narrowing of the range of options to two and ultimately one (see Neuringer, 1961). Cognitive constriction is related to the seriousness/lethality of the suicide attempt (Paludszny, Davenport, & Kim, 1991). In risk assessment, the clinician needs to find out (a) whether suicide is an option (the person's lethality) and (b) whether suicide is the only option (the degree of cognitive constriction). These may be the two most important questions in assessing risk. If suicide is considered the only option, risk may be extremely high. The primary intervention, after ensuring the person's safety, is to help the person come up with constructive alternatives to suicide. Shneidman (1985) has recommended this as one of the first goals of treatment.

Lethal ideation can be treated, although not without difficulty. For example, there is evidence that certain cognitions are related to, if not central to, depression in both adults (Hamilton & Abramson, 1983) and adolescents (Garber, Weiss, & Shanley, 1993). Researchers are finding that cognitive–behavioral interventions directed at these dysfunctional thoughts can be effective in the treatment of suicide attempters (e.g., Lerner & Clum, 1990; Linehan, Armstrong, Suarez, Allmon, & Heard, 1991; Salkovskis, Atha, & Storer, 1990) and that suicidal intent diminishes over the course of treatment (Schotte, Cools, & Payvar, 1990). Treatment of perturbation will reduce lethality, and it now appears that treatment of lethal ideation and cognitive constriction can reduce perturbation. Because these states feed off each other, both should be viewed as targets for treatment.

ADMISSION VERSUS AMBULATORY CARE

Suicidal patients present to the mental health professional as either having attempted suicide or with suicidal ideation. A mental status examination looking for psychiatric illness should be performed in every case, and assessment of suicidal ideation is an integral part of this. A psychosocial assessment is equally mandatory. Both evaluations are most likely to be successful when conducted within the context of an empathic, semistructured interview and corroborated by collateral information from accompanying persons or significant others contacted by telephone.

When the physical damage done during a suicide attempt necessitates hospitalization, admission is handled by the emergency room physician in consultation with medicine and/or surgery. The mental health professional is usually called in once the person has been admitted. A person with relatively good premorbid functioning who has a disorder of recent onset combined with high suicidality should probably be admitted, unless there are compelling reasons not to do so. However, in the case of the person who has attempted suicide but is not deemed in need of a medical admission and in the case of the suicide ideator with or without hospitalizable psychiatric illness, how does the mental health clinician proceed?

On the basis of the patient's shared subjectivity during an empathic interview (although this is not always possible), the clinician will have formed an impression of the patient's levels of perturbation, lethality, and cognitive constriction. If these levels are high, the patient should be considered at imminent risk of suicide and admitted. This person should be persuaded (with the help of friends or family, if need be) to enter the hospital voluntarily. If this approach fails, the patient should be admitted involuntarily on certification, ideally with the concurrence of the significant other(s). The laws of the particular jurisdiction apply. Assessment of the home environment aids decision making in doubtful cases. If the primary interpersonal contacts are inimical, the highly suicidal patient had better be admitted for temporary protection. If social support is strong, with the treatment staff's, family's, and patient's knowledge and agreement, the patient may be managed on an ambulatory basis if (a) the patient's levels of perturbation, lethality, and constriction are relatively low; (b) the patient is seen at least once or twice a week; and (c) good therapeutic contact has been established.

What sort of treatment should follow? Obviously, treatment is selected on the basis of the assessment and should be part of a comprehensive plan in which psychological, biological, and social elements are all considered. Various forms of psychotherapy are useful in all cases, although in psychotic patients, psychotherapy may need to be delayed until biological methods help make the patient more amenable. The use of biological treatments such as antidepressants, neuroleptics, or electroconvulsive therapy depends on the presence of a psychiatric illness shown to be responsive to such methods. In almost all cases of suicidal patients, the social environment and the precipitating factors need professional attention. For example, marital or family dysfunction and work problems may require attention. Significant others should be involved in the treatment process, in any case. Finally, as Shneidman (1985) has noted regarding patient management, professional consultation must be included.

CONCLUSION

We have outlined a model of suicide risk assessment based in part on Shneidman's conceptualization of suicide. Essential to this model are (a) advance awareness of the clinical and current sociodemographic risk factors for suicide as well as of the subjective elements of suicidality, and (b) recognition and exploration of this subjectivity during an empathic interview in which the person is provided an opportunity to express his or her emotional and cognitive states. The model can be applied to both interview and psychological test methods of assessment when the clinician has an idea of what he or she is looking for and what it might look like in the overall pattern of responses. Management and treatment of the suicidal person proceed best after achievement of an understanding of these dimensions in a given individual within the framework of a comprehensive assessment. Understanding of risk in a suicidal person is limited by the person's willingness or ability to self-disclose and by the nature of suicide risk as a moving albeit internally consistent target.

REFERENCES

Beck, A. T., Brown, G., & Steer, R. A. (1989). Prediction of eventual suicide in psychiatric inpatients by clinical ratings of hopelessness. *Journal of Consulting and Clinical Psychology, 57,* 309–310.

Berlin, I. N. (1987). Suicide among American Indian adolescents: An overview. *Suicide and Life-Threatening Behavior, 17,* 218–232.

Berman, A. L. (1991). Child and adolescent suicide: From the nomothetic to the idiographic. In A. A. Leenaars (Ed.), *Life-span perspectives of suicide: Time-lines in the suicide process* (pp. 109–120). New York: Plenum.

Blazer, D. (1991). Suicide risk factors in the elderly: An epidemiological study. *Journal of Geriatric Psychiatry, 24,* 175–190.

Brent, D. A., Johnson, B., Bartle, S., Bridge, J., Rather, C., Matta, J., Connolly, J., & Constantine, D. (1993). Personality disorder, tendency to impulsive violence, and suicidal behavior in adolescents. *Journal of the American Academy of Child and Adolescent Psychiatry, 32,* 69–75.

Brent, D. A., Perper, J., Moritz, G., Baugher, M., & Allman, C. (1993). Suicide in adolescents with no apparent psychopathology. *Journal of the American Academy of Child and Adolescent Psychiatry, 32,* 494–500.

Butler, R. N. (1989). Psychosocial aspects of aging. In H. I. Kaplan & B. J. Sadock (Eds.), *Comprehensive textbook of psychiatry/V* (5th ed., pp. 2014–2019). Baltimore: Williams & Wilkins.

Carrington, P. J., & Moyer, S. (1994). Gun control and suicide in Ontario. *American Journal of Psychiatry, 15,* 606–608.

Carrington, P. J., & Moyer, S. (in press). Gun availability and suicide in Canada: Testing the displacement hypothesis. *Studies on Crime and Crime Prevention.*

Clark, D. C., & Fawcett, J. (1992). Review of empirical risk factors for evaluation of the suicidal patient. In B. Bongar (Ed.), *Suicide: Guidelines for assessment, management, and treatment* (pp. 16–48). New York: Oxford University Press.

Clark, D. C., & Horton-Deutsch, S. L. (1992). Assessment in absentia: The value of the psychological autopsy method for studying antecedents of suicide and predicting future suicides. In R. W. Maris, A. L. Berman, J. T. Maltsberger, & R. I. Yufit (Eds.), *Assessment and prediction of suicide* (pp. 144–182). New York: Guilford Press.

Clarke, R. V., & Lester, D. (1989). *Suicide: Closing the exits.* New York: Springer-Verlag.

Fawcett, J., Scheftner, W., Clark, D., Hedeker, D., Gibbons, R., & Coryell, W. (1987). Clinical predictors of suicide in patients with major affective disorders: A controlled prospective study. *American Journal of Psychiatry, 144,* 35–40.

Fawcett, J., Scheftner, W. A., Fogg, L., Clark, D. C., Young, M. A., Hedeker, D., & Gibbons, R. (1990). Time-related predictors of suicide in major affective disorder. *American Journal of Psychiatry, 147,* 1189–1194.

Garber, J., Weiss, B., & Shanley, N. (1993). Cognitions, depressive symptoms, and development in adolescents. *Journal of Abnormal Psychology, 102,* 47–57.

Hamilton, E. W., & Abramson, L. Y. (1983). Cognitive patterns and major depressive disorder: A longitudinal study in a hospital setting. *Journal of Abnormal Psychology, 92,* 173–184.

Hoberman, H. M., & Garfinkel, B. D. (1988). Completed suicide in children and adolescents. *Journal of the American Academy of Child and Adolescent Psychiatry, 27,* 689–695.

Jacobs, D. (1989). Psychotherapy with suicidal patients: The empathic method. In D. Jacobs & H. N. Brown (Eds.), *Suicide: Understanding and responding* (pp. 329–342). Madison, CT: International Universities Press.

Klerman, G. L. (1987). Clinical epidemiology of suicide. *Journal of Clinical Psychiatry, 48*(Suppl.), 33–38.

Kovacs, M., Beck, A. T., & Weisman, A. (1975). The use of suicidal motives in the psychotherapy of attempted suicides. *American Journal of Psychotherapy, 29,* 363–368.

Kral, M. J. (in press). Suicide as social logic. *Suicide and Life-Threatening Behavior.*

Kurz, A., Moller, H. J., Baindl, G., Burk, F., Torhorst, A., Wachtler, C., & Lauter, H. (1987). Classification of parasuicide by cluster analysis: Types of suicidal behaviour, therapeutic and prognostic implications. *British Journal of Psychiatry, 150,* 520–525.

Lerner, M. S., & Clum, G. A. (1990). Treatment of suicidal ideators: A problem-solving approach. *Behavior Therapy, 21,* 403–411.

Lewinsohn, P. M., Hops, H., Roberts, R. E., Seeley, J. R., & Andrews, J. A. (1993). Adolescent psychopathology: I. Prevalence and incidence of depression and other DSM-III-R disorders in high school students. *Journal of Abnormal Psychology, 102,* 133–144.

Linehan, M. M., Armstrong, H. E., Suarez, A., Allmon, D., & Heard, H. L. (1991). Cognitive-behavioral treatment of chronically parasuicidal borderline patients. *Archives of General Psychiatry, 48,* 1060–1064.

Litman, R. E. (1970). Suicide as acting out. In E. S. Shneidman, N. L. Farberow, & R. E. Litman (Eds.), *The psychology of suicide* (pp. 293–304). New York: Science House.

Maltsberger, J. T. (1986). *Suicide risk: The formulation of clinical judgment.* New York: New York University Press.

Maltsberger, J. T., & Buie, D. H. (1989). Common errors in the management of suicidal patients. In D. Jacobs & H. N. Brown (Eds.), *Suicide: Understanding and responding* (pp. 285–294). Madison, CT: International Universities Press.

Maris, R. W., Berman, A. L., & Maltsberger, J. T. (1992). Summary and conclusions: What have we learned about suicide assessment and prediction? In R. W. Maris, A. L. Berman, J. T. Maltsberger, & R. I. Yufit (Eds.), *Assessment and prediction of suicide* (pp. 640–672). New York: Guilford Press.

Mattison, R. E. (1988). Suicide and other consequences of childhood and adolescent anxiety disorders. *Journal of Clinical Psychiatry, 49*(Suppl.), 9–11.

McIntosh, J. L. (1991). Epidemiology of suicide in the United States. In A. A. Leenaars (Ed.), *Life-span perspectives of suicide: Time-lines in the suicide process* (pp. 55–69). New York: Plenum.

Miles, C. P. (1977). Conditions predisposing to suicide: A review. *Journal of Nervous and Mental Disease, 164,* 231–245.

Mollica, R. F. (1989). Mood disorders: Epidemiology. In H. I. Kaplan & B. J. Sadock (Eds.), *Comprehensive textbook of psychiatry/V* (5th ed., pp. 859–867). Baltimore: Williams & Wilkins.

Morgan, A. C. (1989). Special issues of assessment and treatment of suicide risk in the elderly. In D. Jacobs & H. N. Brown (Eds.), *Suicide: Understanding and responding* (pp. 239–255). Madison, CT: International Universities Press.

Moscicki, E. K., O'Carroll, P. W., Rae, D. S., Roy, A. G., Locke, B. Z., & Regier, P. A. (1989). Suicidal ideation and attempts: The Epidemiologic Catchment Area. Report of the Secretary's Task Force on Youth Suicide, Vol. 4 (pp. 115–128). Washington, D.C.: U.S. Department of Health and Human Services.

Motto, J. A. (1989). Problems in suicide risk assessment. In D. Jacobs & H. N. Brown (Eds.), *Suicide: Understanding and responding* (pp. 129–142). Madison, CT: International Universities Press.

Neuringer, C. (1961). Dichotomous evaluations in suicidal individuals. *Journal of Consulting Psychology, 25,* 445–449.

Paludszny, M., Davenport, C., & Kim, W. J. (1991). Suicide attempts and ideation: Adolescents evaluated on a pediatric ward. *Adolescence, 26,* 209–215.

Petersen, A. C., Compas, B. E., Brooks-Gunn, J., Stemmler, M., Ey, S., & Grant, K. E. (1993). Depression in adolescence. *American Psychologist, 48,* 155–168.

Pfeffer, C. R. (1989). Life stress and family risk factors for youth fatal and nonfatal suicidal behavior. In C. R. Pfeffer (Ed.), *Suicide among youth: Perspectives on risk and prevention* (pp. 143–164). Washington, D.C.: American Psychiatric Press.

Pfeffer, C. R., Klerman, G. L., Hurt, S. W., Kakuma, T., Peskin, J. R., & Siefker, C. A. (1993). Suicidal children grow up: Rates and psychosocial risk factors for suicide attempts during follow-up. *Journal of the American Academy of Child and Adolescent Psychiatry, 32,* 106–113.

Rihmer, Z., Barsi, J., Arato, M., & Demeter, E. (1990). Suicide in subtypes of primary major depression. *Journal of Affective Disorders, 18,* 221–225.

Sakinofsky, I., & Roberts, R. S. (1990). Why parasuicides repeat despite problem resolution. *British Journal of Psychiatry, 156,* 399–405.

Sakinofsky, I., & Webster, G. (1994). Prevalence of suicidal ideation and attempts in the community: The Ontario Health Survey. Paper presented at the Fifth European Symposium on Suicide and Suicidal Behavior, Cork, Ireland.

Salkovskis, P. M., Atha, C., & Storer, D. (1990). Cognitive-behavioural problem solving in the treatments of patients who repeatedly attempt suicide: A controlled trial. *British Journal of Psychiatry, 157,* 871–876.

Schotte, D. E., Cools, J., & Payvar, S. (1990). Problem-solving deficits in suicidal patients: Trait vulnerability or state phenomenon? *Journal of Consulting and Clinical Psychology, 58,* 562–564.

Shafii, M. (1989). Completed suicide in children and adolescents. In C. R. Pfeffer (Ed.), *Suicide among youth: Perspectives on risk and prevention* (pp. 1–20). Washington, DC: American Psychiatric Press.

Shafii, M., Carrigan, S., Whittinghill, J. R., & Derrick, A. M. (1985). Psychological autopsy of completed suicide in children and adolescents. *American Journal of Psychiatry, 142,* 1061–1064.

Shneidman, E. (1985). *Definition of suicide.* New York: Wiley.

Shneidman, E. S. (1993). Suicide as psychache. *Journal of Nervous and Mental Disease, 181,* 145–147.

Sokol, M. S., & Pfeffer, C. R. (1992). Suicidal behavior of children. In B. Bongar (Ed.), *Suicide: Guidelines for assessment, management, and treatment* (pp. 69-83). New York: Oxford University Press.

Spirito, A., Brown, L., Overholser, J., & Fritz, G. (1989). Attempted suicide in adolescence: A review and critique of the literature. *Clinical Psychology Review, 9,* 335–363.

Stillion, J. M., McDowell, E. E., & May, J. H. (1989). *Suicide across the life span: Premature exits.* Washington, DC: Hemisphere.

Weisman, A. D. (1991). Vulnerability and suicidality in the aged. *Journal of Geriatric Psychiatry, 24,* 191–201.

Chapter 3

Crisis Centers and Their Role in Treatment: Suicide Prevention Versus Health Promotion

C. James Frankish

Suicide is a major health problem in Canada (National Task Force on Suicide in Canada, 1987). In Canada and the other industrialized nations, it remains among the 10 leading causes of death (Centers for Disease Control, 1985). Since the 1960s, there has been a massive effort to reduce suicide mortality in North America through the establishment of suicide prevention centers (Litman, 1966; Seely, 1992). In spite of virtually a total lack of evidence concerning the efficacy of suicide prevention services, such centers have proliferated to the extent that nearly every metropolitan area in North America now has at least one. Overall suicide rates have increased slightly throughout this time.

The author acknowledges the support of the Canadian Association of Suicide Prevention, the Institute of Health Promotion Research at the University of British Columbia, and the Vancouver Suicide Prevention and Crisis Intervention Centre.

EVIDENCE REGARDING THE EFFECTIVENESS OF
SUICIDE PREVENTION CENTERS

Several problems exist in attempting to establish the effectiveness of suicide prevention centers. First, there are multifactorial influences on suicide rates. Second, there are gender differences in rates of calling versus suicide rates (Miller et al., 1984). Third, there is evidence that many attempters never contact preventive services. (Barraclough & Shea, 1970). Finally, there is also the problem of the low base rates of both calling a crisis center and attempting suicide. Schwartz and Reifler (1988) gave a strong example of the low base rate problem in their examination of college student suicide when they concluded that it was virtually impossible to identify differences in rates or to assess directly the influence of environmental or preventive factors on suicide rates.

The first evidence of the potential effectiveness of suicide prevention centers came from the Samaritan group in Britain in the 1950s and 1960s (Varah, 1977). There was initial evidence that the growth of the Samaritans was associated with decreased suicide rates (Bagley, 1968). Other researchers, however, questioned the contribution of crisis interventions to the declining suicide rates (Kreitman, 1976; Sainsbury, Baert, & Jenkins, 1979). There was no evidence of a relationship between the existence of a suicide center in a given area and the suicide rate for the area. Overall, there appeared to be little support for prevention center–suicide rate relationships in various geographic areas (Weiner, 1969).

Numerous researchers have conducted qualitative reviews of suicide rate–crisis center relationships (Auerbach & Killmann, 1977; Clum, Patsiokas, & Luscomb, 1979; Eddy, Wolpert, & Rosenberg, 1987; Salminen & Glad, 1989; Singh & Brown, 1973). These reviewers have examined, first, whether crisis centers reach suicidal or high-risk individuals and, second, whether these centers have a positive impact on reducing the suicide rate in a given geographic location. Quantitative analyses of the effectiveness of suicide prevention centers have also been conducted. Medoff (1986), for example, found that an additional suicide prevention center reduced a state's suicide rate for white males ages 15–64 years by 3.7 suicides/100,000. In a classic study, Miller, Coombs, Leeper and Barton (1984) analyzed the effects of suicide prevention facilities on suicide rates in the United States and found an association between the existence of such a facility in a county and a reduction in the number of suicides among young, white females in the county. The finding was replicated in a different set of counties for a different time span. The authors noted the significance of this result, given that young, white females constituted the major clients of these centers.

Dew and Bromet (1987) suggested that the evidence is mixed concerning whether suicide prevention centers have attracted individuals at risk for suicide and have lowered suicide rates in the communities they serve. Overall, their results indicated that centers did attract a high-risk population, that center clients were more likely to commit suicide than were members of the general population, and that individuals who committed suicide were more likely to have been mental health clients than were members of the general population. However, they also found that the existing studies provided no evidence of center effects on community suicide rates. Eastwood and Brill (1976) also concluded that evidence for the effectiveness of suicide prevention centers is difficult to obtain and evaluate.

Lester (1991) recently reexamined the question of whether suicide prevention centers prevent suicide. He reported that suicide prevention centers were more likely to be set up in states with high suicide rates. He also found that states with more suicide prevention centers and with more suicide prevention centers per capita experienced less of an increase in their suicide rates, suggesting that suicide prevention centers do have a beneficial impact in the United States.

Taken together, the results with respect to the impact of the existence of a crisis center on the suicide rate of an area indicate a very mixed picture. There is some evidence of a positive impact on the suicide rates within specific age groups. However, there is also strong evidence of the numerous confounding variables that plague any analysis of such a relationship. Clearly, the data do not meet Hill's (1965) criteria for proving a causal relationship, and they do not provide definitive support for the argument that a crisis center reduces the prevalence of suicide in a given community.

THE ROLE OF THE SUICIDE PREVENTION CENTER

The question remains, however, as to the appropriate role for community-based crisis intervention and suicide prevention centers (Delworth, 1972). Morgan (1992) correctly noted that, at its most basic level, suicide prevention must include (a) risk assessment that focuses both on sociodemographic and personal characteristics and (b) a matching of those characteristics to well-established risk factors and an accompanying gradient of increased risk. Assessment of suicide risk involves assessment of lethality and intentionality. The ability to conduct such an assessment and to make appropriate judgment and intervention lies at the heart of telephone counseling. Farberow, Heilig, and Parad (1989) suggested the following useful guidelines for suicide counseling:

Directly explore suicidal thoughts,
Assess suicide risk,
Attempt to diffuse the potential for lethality,
Encourage social connection,
Implement behavioral contracting,
Seek consultative support,
Make appropriate referrals,
Take suicidal gestures seriously, and
Remember the healing power of therapeutic availability.

Each of these guidelines bears on the policies and procedures that should be adopted by a suicide prevention center.

Regarding suicidal clients, therefore, the potential roles of a suicide prevention center are multiple and may include crisis intervention and suicide prevention with suicides in progress, empathic communication with at-risk individuals, and nonemergency follow-up of moderate-risk callers. In-house programs may also include face-to-face counseling when appropriate resources and support are available.

Crisis centers also bear a great responsibility to their volunteers. This responsibility lies in providing appropriate screening of volunteers, providing comprehensive training, and creating an environment that facilitates and enhances the volunteer experience. The provision of such an environment reduces the rate of attrition among volunteers and leads to improved coverage of counseling shifts and a more positive attitude to callers.

Suicide prevention centers also have a role to play in the community. The community role involves school-based suicide awareness programs, training of peer counselors, and possible postvention activities; outreach training and support in the form of community education; advocacy for health public policy; liaison with other agencies; and possible provision of distress management training to health care personnel who must deal with crisis and/or suicide-related issues.

Suicide prevention programs may benefit from an examination of other health-related prevention programs. Price, Cowen, Lorion, and Ramos-McKay (1989) made several important points in reporting on the efforts of an American Psychological Association task force to identify model prevention programs for high-risk groups throughout the life span. First, many so-called prevention programs are not, in fact, preventive in nature. Second, prevention programs *can* be effective. Third, effective programs share a number of common features. Fourth, programs for adults and the elderly are underrepresented. Fifth, rigorous evaluations of preventive programs are much needed. (Powers, 1990, recommended specific evaluation procedures and experimental designs for improving the current quality of evaluations of crisis interventions.) According to Price et al., 1989, the following are features of effective prevention programs:

1   They are targeted.
2   They are shaped by an understanding of the risks and problems encountered by the target group.
3   They are designed to alter the life trajectory of clients.
4   Their aim is to set individuals on a new developmental course (by opening up new opportunities, changing life circumstances, and providing support).
5   They provide people with new coping skills or with social support in times of crisis or stress.

6 They strengthen natural support systems in the community.
7 They collect rigorous data on their effectiveness.

FUTURE DIRECTIONS: SUICIDE PREVENTION AS HEALTH PROMOTION

Over the past four decades, researchers have struggled with demonstrating the effectiveness of suicide prevention programs or interventions. The question has always been, Does crisis intervention or counseling reduce suicide rates? This is a crucial question, but it is not the only issue that must be addressed.

A new field of health promotion has recently grown out of the disciplines of public health education and the social and behavioral sciences. Health promotion has been defined as "the process of enabling people to increase control over, and to improve their health" (World Health Organization, 1986, p. 28). The science of health promotion provides an alternative focus for those interested in the role of crisis centers in health, and an equally important set of questions to be addressed.

The Precede–Proceed Model of Health Promotion

Green and Kreuter's (1991) Precede–Proceed model of health promotion has been widely applied in disease prevention and health promotion programs and tested in research and evaluation projects, with more than 300 published applications. It also provided the framework for the construction of Canada's Health Promotion Survey (Health and Welfare Canada, 1988). The Precede–Procede model may be used for planning and evaluating suicide prevention programs.

The multiple levels of variables in the model are displayed in Figure 1. The Precede (upper) portion of the model is read from right to left. Precede deals with issues related to suicide prevention program planning and reads from social diagnosis (Phase 1) to administrative and policy diagnosis (Phase 5). The Proceed (lower) portion of the model is read from left to right. Proceed deals with issues related to the implementation (Phase 6) through long-term or outcome evaluation (Phase 9). The levels of the Precede–Proceed model include the planning process itself; the implementation of intervention strategies and policies; the role of educational, organizational, and political factors; the process of change in these factors; predisposing, enabling, or reinforcing behavioral or environmental suicide risk factors; and outcomes measured in terms of the risk factors themselves or in terms of health or quality of life. The model is thus comprehensive enough to encompass the full range of activities and outcomes that suicide prevention often attempts to address.

Precede

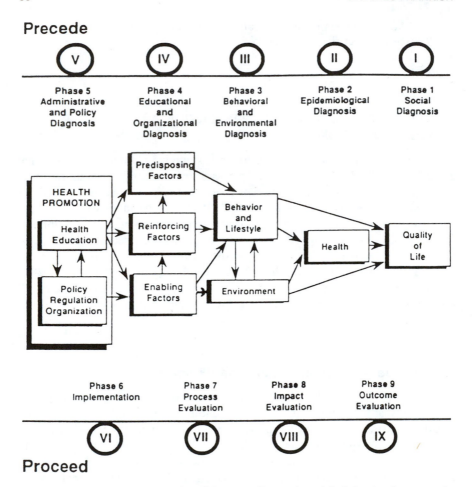

Figure 1   Green and Kreuter's (1991) Precede–Proceed model of the development of a health promotion program may be applied to the development of a suicide prevention program.

Precede: Suicide Prevention Program Planning   The first phase of the Precede–Proceed model focuses on the question of social diagnosis. Clearly, the prevention of suicide and the diminution of distress during crisis are important quality of life issues for the client, for the caregiver, and for society as a whole.

The second phase is the epidemiological diagnosis, in which researchers or community leaders examine the availability data on the prevalence and distribution of mortality, morbidity, and other health outcomes from suicide. They must also examine their contribution to the issues raised in the social diagnosis and the risk factors associated with suicide. The long-term objectives for the community suicide prevention program being planned should flow from this analysis.

The third phase is the behavioral and environmental diagnosis, in which the controllable or preventable risk factors related to suicide are assessed to identify which of them should be given priority in the suicide prevention program. The third phase examines relationships among life-style, behavior, environment, and health. Like the epidemiological diagnosis, this analysis is more efficient if the community has previously analyzed the epidemiological data available on suicide and related conditions in the community. If the planning process skips one of these phases or fails to prioritize the multiple problems or goals identified within a phase, the subsequent phase of planning often will be made more complex and inefficient as a result of lack of focus and specificity.

The fourth phase of planning the suicide prevention program is the educational and organizational diagnosis. Here the factors that predispose, enable, and reinforce the behavioral risk factors for suicide and the factors that enable environmental changes to reduce suicide risk behavior or improve health outcomes are identified. Predisposing factors include knowledge, attitudes, and beliefs that may predispose a person to attempt suicide and, equally important, may predispose a person to phone a crisis center. Reinforcing factors include the attitudes and behavior of family members, peers, and health personnel that may reinforce suicidal behaviors and, again, those that may reinforce phoning a crisis center. Enabling factors include environmental factors, such as the availability and accessibility of crisis counseling. They also include referrals, rules (i.e., criteria for being an appropriate client), and skills (i.e., the ability to display the behavior necessary to contact a crisis center).

The analysis of administrative and educational factors would completely overwhelm the planning process if it were attempted in relation to every possible risk factor for suicide, without some priorities having been set in the previous phases of the planning process. Objectives should be set on the basis of the predisposing, enabling, and reinforcing factors deemed most important and changeable. These objectives are short-term in character and are the main targets of evaluation in the first years of a suicide prevention program.

The fifth phase in this idealized suicide prevention planning process is the administrative and policy diagnosis. In this phase, the resources required to set into motion the process of change in the predisposing, enabling, and reinforcing factors for suicide are compared with the resources available. Barriers to change in suicide rates other than crisis center resources also need to be identified at this stage. The gap between required and available resources for suicide prevention identifies the areas for administrative and policy action. Administrative actions may include rebudgeting, reassignment of personnel, tighter enforcement of existing regulations, or reorganization of a crisis center, for example. Policy actions might include changing organizational objectives or mandates and adding new regulations or incentives to constrain or encourage the behavior of those who control resources (e.g., school personnel) or those whose risk factors can be more reasonably controlled by their own actions.

Proceed: Suicide Prevention Program Evaluation Phases 6–9 of the Precede–Proceed model address program evaluation. They range from implementation questions to outcome evaluation. The distinction among process, impact, and outcome evaluation is crucial.

Process evaluation accepts that tracking the process of change is as important as identifying the results associated with change. The process of change in community- or caller-related behavior and norms is both social and psychological, necessitating support of different kinds at different stages of the change process. The critical product from a process evaluation is a clear, descriptive picture of the quality of the suicide prevention program elements that are being implemented and of what is taking place as the program proceeds.

Impact evaluation focuses on the short-term effect of the suicide prevention program. It sets aside the question of the program's impact on suicide-related morbidity and mortality in the area. Given their nature and their limited resources, most suicide prevention programs are able to test their effectiveness only in relation to short-term, impact variables (i.e., changes in predisposing, enabling, and reinforcing factors) and, at best, some behavioral and environmental changes. The important point is that changes in these variables can have a positive impact on health and quality of life without involving a change in the suicide rate.

Finally, *outcome* or *long-term evaluation* looks at the penultimate question of the impact of the suicide prevention center on the area's suicide rate. Two points must be made with respect to the long-term evaluation of a suicide prevention intervention. First, a change in the suicide rate is neither a necessary nor a sufficient condition for establishing indicators of change or criteria for success. That said, it is possible that the use of a thorough planning process, as depicted in the Precede–Proceed model, and the acquisition, through process and impact evaluation techniques, of a thorough understanding of the predisposing, reinforcing, and enabling factors for both attempting suicide and calling a crisis center may lead one closer to the goal of reducing suicide rates.

Assumptions of Health Promotion

In addition to the methodological and conceptual issues and evaluation questions raised in the Precede–Proceed model, health promotion practice is based on a number of theoretical underpinnings of the concept of health promotion. Three such notions are the theories of participation, of local (decentralized) self-determination or control over the determinants of health, and of self-monitoring as the best method of surveillance and evaluation of local programs. All three of these core themes of health promotion point toward local, rather than national, control over the priorities assigned to various health concerns, including suicide prevention. They suggest that individuals should be empowered to participate in decisions regarding their health and the distribution of health services in their community.

Two pressures bear against a movement toward the clientele's greater participation and empowerment in suicide prevention. The first is the notion that suicidal persons need to be taken care of and cannot cope with empowerment. The second is the decline of human and material resources in communities in recent decades that has led to alienation; dehumanized, centralized services; and the disempowerment of local groups and individuals to cope with the problems of their communities. This process of disempowerment has fed the growing rates of depression and suicide in community samples.

To counter these forces, crisis centers may act as agents of social and community change. They may promote an environment in which community groups, schools, and individuals feel empowered to participate in suicide prevention. In addition, the three themes of health promotion can only hope to provide antidotes to the three poisons of community disempowerment if suicide prevention centers are supported by appropriate reallocations of resources.

CONCLUSION

This discussion has focused on the development and evaluation of telephone-based crisis centers devoted primarily to suicide prevention. The evidence regarding the effectiveness of suicide prevention programs in reducing suicide rates is mixed. There is some evidence that suicide counseling has a positive impact on behaviors related to suicide in specific groups. The evidence for a direct causal relationship between exposure to crisis counseling and a reduced suicide rate remains in question, however. The identification of specific components of evaluation of crisis-line interventions suggests possible predisposing and reinforcing factors that may be examined. Further classification of suicide prevention interventions and discussion of suicide counseling issues, the role of crisis centers in suicide prevention, and standards of quality for crisis centers also suggest a set of possible factors or indicators that could be examined in a process or impact evaluation.

Suicide prevention programs have clearly had a positive impact on the lives of countless callers and volunteers. However, many programs have a long way to go to measure up to the recommended standards for prevention programs. The Precede–Proceed model of health promotion program planning and evaluation provides a tested conceptual framework for furthering the work of suicide prevention. The philosophy of health promotion argues for greater community participation in health promotion.

REFERENCES

Auerbach, S., & Killmann, P. (1977). Crisis intervention: A review of outcome research. *Psychological Bulletin, 84,* 1189–1217.

Bagley, C. (1968). The evaluation of a suicide prevention scheme by an ecological method. *Social Science and Medicine, 2,* 1–4.

Barraclough, B., & Shea, M. (1970). Suicide and Samaritan clients. *Lancet, 24,* 868–870.

Centers for Disease Control. (1985). *Suicide surveillance, 1970–1980.* Atlanta, GA: Author.

Clum, G., Patsiokas, A., & Luscomb, R. (1979). Empirically based comprehensive treatment program for parasuicide. *Journal of Counseling and Clinical Psychology, 47,* 937–945.

Delworth, U. (1972). *Crisis center hotline: A guidebook to beginning and operating.* Springfield, IL: Charles C Thomas.

Dew, M., & Bromet, E. (1987). A quantitative literature review of the effectiveness of suicide prevention centers. *Journal of Consulting and Clinical Psychology, 55,* 239–244.

Eastwood, M., & Brill, L. (1976). Suicide and prevention centres. *Canadian Psychiatric Association Journal, 21,* 571.

Eddy, D., Wolpert, R., & Rosenberg, M. (1987). Estimating the effectiveness of intervention to prevent suicides. *Medical Care, 25*(12, Suppl.), s57–s65.

Farberow, N., Heilig, S., & Parad, H. (1989). The suicide prevention center: Concepts and clinical functions. In H. Parad & L. Parad (Eds.), *Crisis intervention: The practitioner's handbook for brief therapy.* Milwaukee, WI: Family Service America.

Green, L., & Kreuter, M. (1991). *Health promotion planning: An educational and environmental approach.* Mountain View, CA: Mayfield.

Health and Welfare Canada. (1988). *Canada's Health Promotion Survey: Technical report.* Ottawa: Health Services and Promotion Branch, Ministry of Supply and Services Canada.

Hill, A. (1965). *President's Address. The environment and disease: Association or causation? Proceedings of the Royal Society of Medicine, 58,* 295–300.

Kreitman, N. (1976). *Parasuicide.* New York: Wiley.

Lester, D. (1991). Do suicide prevention centres prevent suicide? *Homeostasis in Health and Disease, 33*(4), 190–194.

Litman, R. (1966). The prevention of suicide. In J. Masserman (Ed.), *Current psychiatric therapies.* Orlando, FL: Grune & Stratton.

Medoff, M. (1986). An evaluation of the effectiveness of suicide prevention centres. *Journal of Behavioral Economics, 15,* 43–55.

Miller, H., Coombs, D., Leeper, J., & Barton, S. (1984). An analysis of the effects of suicide prevention facilities on suicide rates in the United States. *American Journal of Public Health, 74,* 340–343.

Morgan, H. G. (1992). Suicide prevention: Hazards on the fast lane to community care. *British Journal of Psychiatry, 160,* 149–153.

National Task Force on Suicide in Canada. (1987). *Suicide in Canada.* Ottawa, Ontario, Canada: Ministry of Health and Welfare.

Powers, G. (1990). Design and procedures for evaluating crisis intervention. In A. Roberts (Ed.), *Crisis intervention handbook: Assessment, treatment, and research.* Belmont, CA: Wadsworth.

Price, R., Cowen, E., Lorion, P., & Ramos-McKay, J. (1989). The search for effective prevention programs: What we learned along the way. *American Journal of Orthopsychiatry, 59,* 49–58.

Sainsbury, P., Baert, J., & Jenkins, J. (1979). Suicide trends in Europe. In *Proceedings of the 10th International Congress for Suicide Prevention and Crisis Intervention* (pp. 365–366).

Salminen, S., & Glad, T. (1989). Why do people phone the helping telephone? *Psykologia, 24,* 367–371.

Schwartz, A., & Reifler, C. (1988). College student suicide in the United States: Incidence data and prospects for demonstrating the efficacy of preventative programs. *Journal of American College Health, 37,* 53–59.

Seely, M. (1992). Hotlines—our heritage and challenges. *Crisis, 13*(1), 14–15.

Singh, A., & Brown, J. (1973). Suicide prevention—review and evaluation. *Canadian Psychiatric Association Journal, 18,* 117–121.

Varah, C. (1977). Why and how I started the Samaritans. *The Samaritan,* 2–3.

Weiner, I. (1969). The effectiveness of a suicide prevention program. *Mental Hygiene, 53,* 357–363.

World Health Organization. (1986). The Ottawa charter for health promotion. *Health Promotion, 1,* 3–5.

Chapter 4

Crisis Intervention with Highly Lethal Suicidal People

Antoon A. Leenaars

Crisis intervention is a systematic process of problem resolution that occurs in a relationship. Within the context of the relationship, the interventionist attempts quickly to focus on and address a presenting problem, whether the patient is presenting suicidal or other traumatic experiences.

Crisis intervention is not magic. It is systematic, model-guided intervention. Crisis work of any kind requires a structure that allows one to intervene constructively and professionally.

True suicidal crises involve highly suicidal people, those who would be assessed as high on lethality, as distinguished from those with moderate or low lethality. In understanding suicidal people, knowledge of the concepts of lethality and perturbation is essential (Shneidman, 1973, 1980, 1985). *Lethality* refers to the probability of a person's killing him- or herself, as assessed quantitatively from low to moderate to high. *Perturbation* refers to the person's subjective distress (disturbed, agitated, sane-insane, discomposed) and can also be rated

I thank Edwin Shneidman not only for his kind permission to use his information and ideas, but also for his education. Direct quotes are taken from discussions and/or publications of Dr. Edwin Shneidman with his kind permission. Equally, the editorial direction of John T. Maltsberger and Robert Neimeyer was invaluable.

from low, to moderate, to high. Both lethality and perturbation must be evaluated in crisis intervention with suicidal people. It is lethality, not perturbation, that kills. All sorts of people are highly perturbed but are not suicidal. Perturbation is often relatively easy to assess; lethality is not. When intervening with highly lethal people, one must stay alert to both concepts. In practice, the two may be difficult to differentiate, because lethal states are likely associated with high perturbation (although the converse is not necessarily true).

The purpose of crisis intervention is to afford immediate avenues of response to individuals poised between living and dying, and it is not to be confused with the usual psychotherapies appropriate for less lethal individuals. Of course, a suicidal act (deed, occurrence, threat, attempt) of whatever lethality is always genuine in its own light and merits serious consideration. Thus, in crisis intervention, there is almost no place for hostility, anger, a sardonic attitude, pejorative comments, daring the person, pseudodemocratic indifference, or other aversive behavior on the part of the interventionist.

Crisis intervention with highly suicidal people differs from other human relationships (Hoff, 1984, Leenaars, 1991; MacKinnon & Michels, 1971; Parad, 1965). The goal is simple: to keep the person alive. The procedures are often not simple, however. Working with a suicidal person demands a different kind of involvement than usual psychotherapy. The activity required can be likened to that of a cardiologist in an emergency unit. It is more assertive than what transpires in a routine office visit. The focus is to sustain life. In crisis intervention, the professional actively works to increase the patient's psychological sense of possible choices and feeling of emotional attachment (Leenaars, 1993).

Case Study Having been referred by their family physician, Peter and Rita, a married couple, both arrived at my office looking disheveled and depressed. Rita, unlike Peter, also was agitated. She could not be still, and her speech was racing. She was distraught. Peter, on the other hand, was quieter, withdrawn, but deeply distressed. I learned that Rita had just returned from a trip to San Francisco with her lover, David. Peter wanted me to make Rita stop seeing David.

Because the focus in crisis intervention is not personality change, but problem resolution, I shall say little about Peter and Rita except the following: Peter came from a dysfunctional family; his only brother had killed himself 2 years earlier. Rita also came from a dysfunctional family; her father was an alcoholic, and her mother had a major affective disorder. Rita had been on antidepressants since she was 16; she was now 36 (Peter was 40). Peter and Rita had two children in late adolescence, both of whom were experiencing social and academic problems. I later learned both often had been physically abused by Rita.

The intake focused on the marriage. As is commonly the case, each person had a different perception of the problem with the marriage. Rita described Peter as controlling, dominating, and rigid. Peter was beside himself over Rita's infidelity. Both denied any suicidal thoughts or plans. An appointment was made for them to return in 2 days.

Peter arrived for the second appointment by himself. Rita had gone to David and had not returned the previous night. Peter was extremely perturbed, agitated, and very angry. He saw the situation as hopeless. Upon inquiry (see Kral & Sakinofsky, 1994; Leenaars, 1992; Maris, Berman, Maltsberger, & Yufit, 1992), it became clear that he was moderately suicidal. He refused a referral either to a psychiatrist for medication or to his general practitioner, who had first referred him. He refused hospitalization. He had earlier refused a referral for psychiatric help or hospitalization from the general practitioner, reluctantly accepting a referral only to a psychologist for marital counseling. As in other such cases, I did not insist on hospitalization; when a therapeutic relationship is developing, the alliance can be destroyed by involuntary commitment. The therapeutic relationship may be essential in keeping the person alive; however, each case needs to be evaluated individually. Yet Peter was willing to return the next day, a plan probably not optimal but the only one to which he would agree. I felt that he would be safe until our next meeting. Thus a crisis intervention plan was initiated.

The next day, Peter returned with Rita. She reported that Peter had been emotionally abusive during the last night, demanding sex. She announced she was going to leave him, whereupon Peter became quite upset. Both were seen individually. In my meeting with him, Peter continued to refuse additional assistance and left the room.

Alone with me, Rita declared she was in love with David and that they intended to live together. Although she had met David only a month earlier, she saw no problem in this plan and, when I questioned it, said, "It's none of your business." Nevertheless, she was worried about Peter. Although he had earlier denied the availability of a weapon, I now learned he had a collection of guns. With the assistance of the police, Rita had removed the guns from the home the night before.

Suggestions that Rita needed help were dismissed; she insisted, "I'm okay." I never saw her again. She promptly moved out of the house and left Peter and the children in tears.

That night, the police were called back to Peter's house. He had gone to the car and attempted to kill himself; however, before he had gone to the car, he had telephoned a friend and informed him of his suicidal plan (indicating his striking ambivalence). The friend called the police. Peter was taken to the emergency unit of a local hospital, but again he refused admission and signed himself out. He assured the hospital that he would see me the next day and left with his friend.

Peter arrived the next day at my office, less agitated, with his friend. He was much more verbal and open than before. In light of the ongoing developments, we continued with a modification of our crisis plan, the basis of which is outlined in the next section. It is important to emphasize that crisis intervention with highly suicidal people is best not attempted in isolation; we therefore included Peter's friend, his family, his general practitioner, and others in the evolving plan.

Peter's case is not unusual for crisis interventionists. He was suicidal, but he responded to intervention positively. No further suicide attempts occurred. He continues to be seen, 2 years later, in psychotherapy. Indeed, good crisis intervention with suicidal people should lead to long-term psychotherapy. Interventionists who do not offer good follow-up care with their highly suicidal patients leave themselves open to questions about their mode of care in the event of a later suicide (Bongar, 1991; Bongar & Greaney, 1994).

THE MODEL

Here are some organizing questions for intervention with Peter:

What is Peter's problem?
What is he feeling?
What does he want?
What is he going to do?
Why is he in my office?
What does he want from me?

These questions and permutations and combinations of them must be asked by a therapist, a crisis-line volunteer, and any interventionist in a high-risk suicidal situation. Therefore, a model, a planned conceptual construction of interaction, is essential. Such a model provides a framework for intervention. For example, by asking questions such as the preceding ones, the therapist approaches the situation rationally and simultaneously reduces his or her own anxiety. Without a model, one is slippery in approach.

Although there are other models, here are the five steps of mine:

1 Establish rapport.
2 Explore.
3 Focus.
4 Develop options and a plan of action.
5 Terminate.

This model is not unique; it is a common framework found in intervention.

No single response can be isolated to be life-saving in all suicide crises. But a clear understanding of suicide has allowed the development of certain general guidelines for crisis intervention and therapy, on the basis of which a response is chosen that is appropriate for the unique individual. In considering responses, the interventionist should never mimic the suicidal person's all too narrow perception. One's thinking, planning, and action do not need to be constricted.

Establish Rapport

Crisis intervention begins in the first encounter. The patient talks, and the interventionist listens. An active, nonjudgmental rapport must be developed. Rapport is the ability to relate mutually in a human encounter. A capacity for good object relations is of crucial importance in establishing rappport. Good object relationship has been defined by Tarachow (1963) as a "strong interest in, affection for another person, a willingness to give up something for another person, a willingness to assume responsibility for another person. It is quite an achievement to have a real interest in someone else" (p. 103). In a sense, for rapport to be established, love must predominate over hate. If an interventionist has difficulty expressing attachment, he or she should not be doing crisis intervention (or therapy). In my view (Leenaars, 1988, 1993), the key to working with suicidal people is the relationship. This was certainly true with Peter, and, fortunately, rapport was quickly established. He looked forward to the visits. No rapport ever developed with Rita, a circumstance that is extremely problematic for an interventionist.

Responding to an intensely suicidal person is a special task. It requires a special relationship marked by genuine caring and nonjudgmental response. It is not just traditional therapy; it demands a different kind of involvement. The goal is different, namely, to keep the person alive. This goal is achieved by lowering the level of lethality. The way to decrease lethality in an individual is to decrease dramatically the felt perturbation—a process in which the relationship is the key. The interventionist defuses the person's constricted focus on suicide and creates social interest around the person. The person's temporarily unbearable problems or injustices are made just better enough that he or she can stop to think and reconsider and discern alternatives to suicide.

The psychotherapist can focus on any number of emotions (distressing feelings of pitiful forlornness, deprivation, distress, grief, and especially hopelessness and helplessness). He or she works to improve the external and internal situations related to these emotions and other aspects of the suicidal state, to achieve a just noticeable difference (JND). This can be accomplished initially through ventilation, interpretation, instruction, and realistic manipulation in the outside world. This requires an increased amount of interaction and rapport during the period of heightened lethality. The therapist needs to work diligently, always giving the suicidal person realistic transfusions of hope until the intensity of the pain subsides enough to reduce the lethality to a tolerable, life-permitting level.

Explore

A crisis is defined by a perception, that is, the way an individual construes his or her circumstance. A "B" grade on an examination is acceptable to many, but to others it may occasion unbearable pain. After reading thousands of suicide notes, I am struck by how divergent crises are, but the patient's perception is critical in the total suicidal scenario (Leenaars, 1988). Peter and Rita, obviously, had very different views of their marital crisis. Rita saw Peter as all of the problem; Peter saw Rita's affair with David and the subsequent separation as painfully problematic. The two children, who I saw later, also gave the contretemps a different reading.

The belief that a crisis is defined by a person's perception does not mean that the therapist accepts the person's view of the problem without question. Given the person's view, suicide has adjustive value. It abolishes pain. For example, Rita's announcement that she was leaving made the situation unbearable for Peter. Because there was no possibility that Rita would return to the marriage, had he and I accepted the proposition that preserving the marriage was the only solution, Peter would be dead now. One must translate the patient's perception into a wider adaptive view. One widens the patient's blinders. One does not talk only about the low grade or the lost spouse. One explores a wider array. Despair over a low grade, for example, can be translated into a need for perfection. With Peter, we reached beyond the agony of his immediate abandonment.

As one explores, one redefines the trauma as painful but tolerable to the individual. One develops the person's adaptive potential. The interventionist who accepts the perspective "I can't live with this" is tacitly colluding with the person's decision to die, and the patient cannot survive. Yet, the interventionist cannot simply provide naive reassurance, saying, "You can too!" A better response is something like, "When you say I can't live with *this,* what is the *this*?" The interventionist then redefines (reframes) the problem in terms of, say, a need for perfection, or another limiting, intolerable value (view).

One may be tempted in crisis intervention to take away the person's responsibility. A rule of thumb for all stages of crisis intervention, including the early stages, is to never to take away the person's responsibility. Statements like "Don't worry—I won't let you hurt yourself" or "I will help you and you won't have to kill yourself" are inappropriate and, indeed, may be deadly. Yet, the therapist needs initially to assume some responsibility by fostering life-sustaining action, not thought alone. The therapist assists in the development of some constructive behavior; the person's state of mind makes it imperative.

Two further points are relevant to the exploration phase of the model:

First, the suicidal person's pain relates to the frustration or blocking of important psychological needs, that is, needs deemed to be important by the person (often attachment, as in the case of Peter). It is the therapist's function to help the individual in relation to those thwarted needs. Even a little bit of improvement can save a life. The person needs some indication that his or her life has meaning, an affirmation of his or her self-esteem. A small amount of exploration often gives a perturbed individual enough hope and comfort to divert the suicidal course. In general, the goal is to increase the person's psychological comfort. Questions such as "What is going on?", "Where do you hurt?", and "What would you like to have happen?" can be asked.

Second, the suicidal individual is ambivalent. The person feels a need to die and yet yearns for intervention, rescue, and life. For example, minutes before his attempt, Peter called a friend. Rescue often implies improvement or change in one of the major details in the person's world, such as the wish to have an A+, to be loved, and so on. In general, the therapist should work with the life-directed aspects of the ambivalence, without, of course, being too timorous to touch on the death-oriented element in the patient.

Focus

It is imperative for the crisis interventionist to understand how the suicidal person defines the trauma—what it is that cannot be endured. A crisis is a perception, not a thing in itself. Suicidal patients often cannot concentrate; they are too perturbed. It is therefore useful to bear in mind the question, "What is it that we are going to focus on?" Although the interventionist assists, the suicidal person should do the focusing. Questions to facilitate focusing are "What is the problem?", "What were you hoping to accomplish?", "What would be most helpful?", and "We've talked about a lot, what do you want to discuss?" The focusing allows not only the patient but also the interventionist to focus so that clarity can emerge.

One does not exacerbate the crisis by focusing on it. The patient is already angry and hostile (and also hopeless and helpless). This was certainly the case with Peter. At first, he could talk only about Rita; he was hurt, angry, agitated, and hopeless. He said, "Without Rita I'm nothing," adding that he now understood the words in his brother's suicide note: "No one loves me. Mom hates me. I'm all alone. I have no reason to live."

With help, Peter quickly focused on these feelings, addressing his need for attachment. (The dynamics with his mother were explored much later.) Ventilation, lightening of angry feelings, adequacy of expression, and need for contacts have a critical place in crisis intervention, contributing to focusing on the trauma.

Experience has shown that it is neither useful nor wise to respond to an individual in an acute suicidal crisis with punishment, moral persuasion, or confrontation. The most effective way to help is to assuage the anguish of the trauma, thereby reducing the perturbation. It is the elevated perturbation that fuels the elevated lethality; therefore, one tries to reduce the anguish, tension, and pain. The rule is: Reduce the level of perturbation, and the level of lethality will come down with it.

Develop Options and Constructive Action

The purpose of crisis intervention is to assist the patient with problem resolution, not personality change.

A suicidal act is an individual's attempt to stop unbearable anguish and pain. The anguish and pain usually relate manifestly to only one thing but latently to much more. The person wants prompt relief. To save the person's life, the therapist has to do something! This may include letting others know that the person is in trouble, breaking what could be a fatal secret; proffering help; and always showing interest and deep concern. I do not agree with those individuals who argue for a no-rescue stance in this field. One should have at least a provisional rescue approach with moderately lethal individuals and should always have an action plan with highly lethal individuals. This was essential with Peter, given the not unusual constriction in his options (e.g., hospitalization).

When developing options and constructive action, the therapist should bear in mind three things. First, a key to intermediate and long-range effectiveness with the suicidal person is to increase the options of actions available, to increase awareness of adjustment processes, to widen the blinders, and to increase the number of people available to help. Second, when the patient is no longer highly suicidal, the usual methods of psychotherapy can be used. The professional does not leave the patient with his or her weakened, not adequately developed ego. The person needs therapeutic assistance. Finally, given all that, the therapist should remember that work in suicide prevention is risky and dangerous, and there are casualties. In the case of Peter, the first two actions were implemented. His family and friend were involved; for example, his father uncharacteristically helped, although he was overwhelmed with guilt about his other son. Peter entered therapy, and so did his children. He and the children are still being seen 2 years later.

A primary goal in developing options is to reduce the trauma—the real-life pressure—that is driving up the patient's sense of perturbation. The aim is to decrease the stress to a level just below the traumatic degree (a JND). The therapist assists the person in making the pain bearable, but this is not done by denying, repressing, or deflecting it, because ultimately it is this pain that will serve as the energy for change. The person needs to face the trauma, whether interpersonal or otherwise.

Suicidal patients are all-or-nothing thinkers. A common premise is that something is either black or white. Something is either A or not A. To presume that suicidal individuals either want to kill themselves or do not want to kill themselves is to take an erroneously limited point of view, even if they generate only such permutations and combinations. Peter wanted to be dead or to have

Rita back (with "back" meaning before her affair with David). However, it is not necessary to work within a view of the world as A or not A. To follow this all-or-nothing logic is to foster a limited and harsh view of life. Thus, the therapist's task is to increase the options, to reframe the individual's thoughts, and to widen the range of thoughts and fantasies. All of this is critical to keeping the highly lethal individual alive.

The main point with a suicidal person is to increase that individual's psychological sense of possible choices *and* his or her sense of being emotionally supported. After they have been determined to be on the side of life, relatives, friends and colleagues should be included in discussions of the treatment process as options for providing direct assistance (as in the case of Peter). The suicidal person needs other objects (people) with whom to identify and on whom to depend. Others can assist in establishing or reestablishing positive relationships, and all this will help to build self-esteem and self-support. Being so perturbed, Peter could not give up even a negative part of his identity and could not search out objects on his own. He was simply in too much pain and too pessimistic to do so. Yet, support was there. As Peter eventually stated, "I'm not alone."

The highly suicidal person wants out. It follows that, when possible, the means of exit should be blocked. A practical application of this view is to "get the gun" in a suicidal situation in which it is known that the individual intends to shoot him- or herself and has a weapon. The explosive situation needs to be defused until the person no longer has the need for a suicidal weapon (see Berman, 1990). Clearly, consultation is needed in some cases. Maltsberger offers guidance on such cases:

> I would consult as much to avoid charges of negligence as to deal with my own anxiety. I think that any time I get into a difficult case, where I am concerned that somebody is imminently suicidal . . . I would want to be careful. It is enormously helpful to ask a colleague to help to monitor one's own judgment when in a tense, anxiety-provoking situation. (cited by Berman, 1990, p. 118)

When a suicidal person has access to a lethal weapon, the therapist may even want to speak to a lawyer. In Peter's case, the guns had already been removed, although the fact that he had such means needed to be monitored. What would have happened, for example, if the police had returned the weapons? Peter had a permit for the guns and could easily have had them returned.

As already discussed, the focus in crisis intervention with highly lethal people is not on why suicide has been chosen as the method of solving the problems. This issue is better addressed in more usual psychotherapy, once the lethality is lower. Instead, the focus is on solving the problem(s), so that the pain is mollified. The problems are discussed and addressed in terms of what can be done about them. The person needs to see some hope, although at the same time I agree with those (e.g., Smith, 1991) who point out how critical the hopelessness is to the therapeutic intervention. The therapist may talk about practical items—job, rent, sickness, food, or whatever makes the person hopeless. The individual needs immediate partial reduction of the urgently felt suicidal impulse or wish. To address these impulses, the therapist must address the unmet needs. This is done not only in the consultation room, but also in the real world.

The interventionist should always guard against buying into the suicidal person's overpowering emotions and constricted logic. It is vital to counter the person's cognitive constriction by attempting to widen the mental blinders the person is wearing and to increase the number of options, certainly beyond the two options of either having some magical resolution or being dead, such as Peter's either having Rita or being dead.

A case example, following a prototypical example (Shneidman, 1981), illustrates how the therapist can widen the number of options for the suicidal patient.

A middle aged businessman, forlorn, rather traumatized, was referred for psychotherapy. He was recently separated, although the 'event' that brought him to the therapist was the loss of his job. He was a bank manager working for the same bank for 18 years. He was suicidal with a clear suicidal plan. He demanded of the therapist that the therapist somehow, magically, obtain his job back. Losing his job resulted in overpowering emotions and constricted logic and perception. He simply could not "bear to live." At that point, it seemed that *only* suicide was an alternative for him.

Initially, the therapist did several things. For example, the therapist attempted to begin to "widen his blinders" and said something like, "Now let's see . . . you could look for another job."

"I couldn't do that."

(It is precisely the "can't" and "won't" and "have to" and "never" and "always" and "only" issues that are addressed with highly lethal individuals.)

"You could hire a consulting firm to help you look for a job."

"I couldn't do that."

"You could enlist the help of your business friends." (The patient was well respected and perceived to be quite competent.)

"I couldn't do that.'"

"We can look for alternatives."

"I couldn't do that."

"We could call your wife."

"I couldn't do that."

"We could contact your family."

"I couldn't do that."

"You can always commit suicide, but there is obviously no need to do that today."

No response.

"Now let's look at our ideas and rank them in order of your preference, keeping in mind that not one of them is perfect."

The very making of the list within the context of a nonthreatening and nonjudgmental relation had a calming influence on him, a JND. Within a few minutes he was less lethal. His emotions were less overpowering and his logic and perception were less constricted. What was important was that suicide was no longer ranked first. The patient and his therapist were then simply searching for a broader action plan.

The point is not how the issue was eventually resolved. Let it suffice to say that the contact with his estranged wife was ranked first and this subsequently led to family therapy. What is important is that it is possible to lower his lethality by reducing his perturbation. One could widen his range of realistic options from only the choice between suicide and one other choice.

The question for the suicidal patient is, "What is that you are going to do?" The answer needs to be active, not passive. If the answer is passive, the therapist must go back to Steps 1, 2, and 3 of the model. Active contact; letting others know about the situation; encouraging the person to talk to others; getting loved ones involved, interested, and responsive; and creating action around the person are examples of active intervention.

The following are some further guidelines that were derived from discussions with Edwin Shneidman (personal communication, June 29–30, 1991; for details, see Shneidman, 1981, 1985).

1 Monitorship.   Maintain daily monitoring of the patient's lethality.

2 Consultation.   There is almost no instance in a therapist's professional life when consultation with a peer is as important as when he or she is dealing with a highly suicidal patient. The items to be discussed might include the therapist's treatment of the case; the therapist's own feelings of frustration, helplessness, or even anger; countertransference reactions; and the advisability of hospitalization for the patient.

3 Hospitalization.   Hospitalization is always a complicating event in the treatment of a suicidal patient, but it should not be eschewed on these grounds. Obviously, the quality of care—from doctors, nurses, and others—is a crucial consideration.

4 Confidentiality.   Carefully modify the usual canons of confidentiality. Admittedly, this is a touchy and complicated point, but the therapist should not ally him- or herself with death. Statements the patient makes during the therapy session relating to overt suicidal (or homicidal) plans obviously cannot be treated as a secret between two collusive partners.

Finally, one must limit one's caseload in crisis intervention to only a very few highly lethal individuals. It is impossible to deal effectively with many highly lethal individuals without risking burnout or emotional withdrawal from the demands of such patients.

Termination

Before terminating the treatment, the therapist summarizes, rehearses, and develops the patient's planning skills; identifies resources; makes referrals; identifies emergency procedures; and establishes follow-up, to identify but a few essential steps before ending contact with a patient in crisis.

Crisis intervention does not completely fix a situation. Once the lethality is lowered and the difficulties more bearable, the patient should be guided toward more usual therapy—psychoanalytic, cognitive, existential, behavioral, whatever. In a professional psychotherapeutic exchange, the focus is on feelings, emotional content, and unconscious meanings, rather than immediate difficulties. The emphasis is on the latent significance of what is being said, rather than on manifest difficulties. Peter's case raised many latent issues, including the meaning of his brother's suicide note. However, these endeavours usually are addressed after the lethality is lowered, although it is sometimes possible to embark on these efforts in one's earliest interventions (see, e.g., Leenaars, Maltsberger, & Neimeyer, 1994; Maltsberger, 1991).

Regardless of the type of intervention chosen, termination can be difficult. The therapist should always affirm the person (i.e., provide ego strengthening) in the process. The therapist concludes by asking, "Have you gotten what you wanted?" If the answer is no, one goes back to Step 2. Finally, the therapist must leave the door open, even if referring the individual for treatment elsewhere. The person may again be in need for crisis intervention.

A NOTE ON TRANSFERENCE AND COUNTERTRANSFERENCE IN CRISIS INTERVENTION

Although the issues of transference and countertransference are critical, and every crisis worker must be fully aware of these concerns, they are so broad that space allows only a brief note (see Eyman, 1991; Freud, 1910/1957; Heimann, 1950; Maltsberger & Buie, 1974).

Transference is the reactivation in a therapeutic situation of the patient's previous experience, recollections, and unconscious wishes regarding (often early) significant people (objects) in his or her life. Such processes in object relations must be identified in treatment, even in crisis intervention.

Suicidal people, for example, could feel angry, injured, or rejected in the following situations:

- after premature termination or discharge;

- when waiting (even 1 hr or 1 day) for help;
- when treatment time is short and they feel cut off;
- if referred to others;
- if dealt with too directively;
- if given inadequate rapport, interest, etc.;
- if the therapist forgets important details;
- when confronted about an issue too early;
- when presented with simplistic use of a written suicide contract; or
- when contacted by persons other than the crisis interventionist.

Countertransference comprises all the therapist's unconscious reactions to the patient and the patient's transference. These reactions originate in the therapist's own conflicts or real objective interactions (object relations). They may not necessarily be negative; indeed, they can be most constructive in developing an understanding of the patient (and oneself). However, negative countertransference can be not only problematic, but also suicidogenic. The following reactions in the therapist may arise, if confrontation with the suicidal patient provokes feelings of guilt, incompetence, anxiety, fear, or anger in the therapist and these feelings are not worked through:

- Underestimation of the seriousness of the suicidal action;
- Absence of discussion of suicide thoughts, attempts, etc;
- Allowing him- or herself to be lulled into a false sense of security by the patient's promise not to repeat a suicide attempt (such as in the use of a simplistic written suicide contract);
- Disregard the cry-for-help aspect of the suicide attempt and exclusive concentration on its manipulative character;
- Exaggeration of the patient's provocative, infantile, and aggressive sides;
- Denial of his or her importance to the patient;
- Failure to persuade the patient to undergo further treatment;
- Feeling of lacking the resources the patient requires;
- Displaying exaggerated hopelessness in response to the patient's troubled social situation and abuse of drugs or alcohol;
- Being pleased when the patient claims to have all problems solved after only a brief contact, without reflecting closely on the plausibility of this statement; or
- Feeling upset when the patient shows insufficient progress after a brief course of assistance, despite the therapist's initial profound commitment.

Obviously, issues of transference and countertransference are complex and the interventionist who is experiencing them can benefit from contact with a supervisor or consultation with a colleague, as well as from consideration of the broader literature on these reactions.

CONCLUSION

Ultimately, the crisis interventionist must understand that there is no universal formulation regarding how to respond to a highly lethal person. One can speak of understanding, but never with precision. When the subject matter is suicide intervention, professionals can be no more accurate or scientific than the available ways of responding, the subject matter, permit. Yet, understandably, the yearning for universal suicidological laws persists. A sweeping psychological statement with a ring of truth becomes a dictum. I believe that the search for singular universal response to suicide is a chimera, our own negative countertransference. The search for a singular universal response is a foolish and unrealistic fancy. There is no one method for intervention. There is no cookbook!

I wish to add several concluding ideas: Therapists should feel free to use all measures with highly lethal individuals. These measures include support, behavioral techniques, psychodynamic interpretation, hospitalization, medication, etc. . . . and especially the involvement of others, not only others to whom the patient is attached, but also other sources of support—teachers, priests, elders, the Chief, doctors, social workers, anyone who can help, directly or indirectly, to mollify the pain. The model presented herein provides guidance in this task.

I do not believe, in principle, in the solely individual private practice of suicide intervention with highly lethal individuals. Suicide intervention is optimally practiced in cooperation with a number of colleagues, representing various disciplines, and even individuals outside the helping professions (such as family and community members). The treatment of a suicidal person should reflect the learning and response of individuals with different points of view. Peter is alive today not only because of his therapist, but also because of the many people who helped make his life hopeful and more bearable (although not perfect).

In summary, intervention in the trenches, as for the cardiologist, is not as clean as described. Crisis workers constantly must adjust, widening their formulations and actions to meet the needs of those they try to assist.

REFERENCES

Berman, A. L. (Ed.). (1990). *Suicide prevention. Case consultation.* New York: Springer Publishing Company.

Bongar, B. (1991). *The suicidal patient: Clinical and legal standards of care.* Washington, DC: American Psychological Association.

Bongar, B., & Greaney, S. A. (1994). Essential legal issues when working with the suicidal patient. *Death Studies, 18,* 529–548.

Eyman, J. R. (1991). Countertransference when counseling suicidal school-aged youth. In A. A. Leenaars & S. Wenckstern (Eds.), *Suicide prevention in schools* (pp. 147–158). Washington, DC: Hemisphere.

Freud, S. (1957). The future prospects of psycho-analytic therapy. In J. Strachey (Ed. & Trans.), *The standard edition of the complete psychological works of Sigmund Freud* (Vol. 2, pp. 139–151). London: Hogarth Press. (Original work published in 1910)

Heimann, P. (1950). On countertransference. *International Journal of Psycho-Analysis, 14,* 81–84.

Hoff, L. A. (1984). *People in crisis.* Reading, MA: Addison-Wesley.

Kral, M., & Sakinofsky, I. (1994). Clinical model for suicide risk assessment. *Death Studies, 18,* 311–326.

Leenaars, A. A. (1988). *Suicide notes.* New York: Human Sciences Press.

Leenaars, A. A. (1991). Suicide notes and their implications for intervention. *Crisis, 12,* 1–20.

Leenaars, A. A. (1991). Suicide notes, communication and ideation. In R. W. Maris, A. L. Berman, J. T. Maltsberger, & R. I. Yufit (Eds.), *Assessment and prediction of suicide* (pp. 337–361). New York: Guilford Press.

Leenaars, A. A. (1993). Unconscious processes. In A. A. Leenaars (Ed.), *Suicidology: Essays in honor of Edwin S. Schneidman* (pp. 125–147). Northvale, NJ: Jason Aronson.

Leenaars, A. A., Maltsberger, J. T., & Neimeyer, R. A. (Eds.). (1994). *Treatment of suicidal people.* London: Taylor & Francis.

MacKinnon, R. A., & Michels, R. (1971). *The psychiatric interview in clinical practice.* Philadelphia: W. B. Saunders.

Maltsberger, J. T. (1991). The prevention of suicide in adults. In A. A. Leenaars, (Ed.), *Life span perspectives of suicide* (pp. 295–309). New York: Plenum.

Maltsberger, J. T., & Buie, D. (1974). Countertransference noted in the treatment of suicidal patients. *Archives of General Psychiatry, 30,* 625–633.

Maris, R. W., Berman, A. L., Maltsberger, J. T., & Yufit, R. I. (Eds.). (1992). *Assessment and prediction of suicide.* New York: Guilford Press.

Parad, H. (1965). *Crisis intervention.* New York: Family Service Association of America.

Shneidman, E. S. (1973). Suicide. In *Encyclopedia Britannica* (Vol. 21, pp. 383–385). Chicago: William Benton.

Shneidman, E. S. (1980). *Voices of death.* New York: Harper & Row.

Shneidman, E. S. (1981). Psychotherapy with suicidal patients. *Suicide and Life-Threatening Behavior, 11,* 341–348.

Shneidman, E. S. (1985). *Definition of suicide.* New York: Wiley.

Smith, K. (1991). Therapeutic care of the suicidal student. In A. A. Leenaars & S. Wenckstern (Eds.), *Suicide prevention in schools* (pp. 135–146). Washington, DC: Hemisphere.

Tarachow, S. (1963). *An introduction to psychotherapy.* New York: International Universities Press.

Part III

Therapeutic Approaches

Once a patient is no longer in an acute suicidal crisis, a diversity of psychotherapeutic approaches can be used, depending on the patient's unique requirements. The suicidal person is, as Arthur Inman's case shows, in deep pain. As a rule, suicidal people need psychotherapy to make their unbearable pain more bearable and to prompt them toward long-term solutions to their problems. In choosing among the range of specialized treatment formats and approaches now available, the clinician must give special consideration to an array of patient factors: age, sex, health status, cultural issues, and more. Part III outlines state-of-the-art psychotherapeutic techniques for suicidal patients. An overview of psychodynamic and cognitive–behavioral psychotherapy is presented in Chapter 5; the unique role of family therapy in the treatment of suicidal people is discussed in Chapter 6; two high-risk groups—adolescents and the elderly—are discussed in Chapters 7 and 8; a conceptual model of gender issues in the treatment of suicidal people is presented in Chapter 9; and Chapter 10 considers treatment of the suicidal terminally ill, perhaps the most controversial and elusive group requiring treatment today.

Chapter 5

Psychotherapy for Suicidal Clients

David Lester

In many discussions of counseling for suicidal clients, the level of analysis does not proceed much beyond the training given to nonprofessional crisis counselors working at suicide prevention centers, training that focuses on active listening (person-centered therapy), assessment of resources, and formulation of a plan for action. Rudestam (1985–86) observed that a crisis-oriented approach is rarely useful for chronically suicidal clients, whose level of functioning has been quite poor throughout most of their life. Such clients need long-term psychotherapy.

Textbooks on systems of psychotherapy, based on well-established theories of human behavior that provide a rationale for therapeutic techniques, typically ignore the problem of suicide, however. Because of this omission, I recently reviewed the scholarly literatures on the major systems of psychotherapy, searching for cases in which they had been applied to suicidal clients (Lester, 1991). Whereas some psychotherapists, such as psychoanalysts and cognitive therapists, have occasionally reported applications of their systems to suicidal clients, others, such as Gestalt therapists, have rarely provided such examples.

Psychotherapists who work with suicidal clients need to consider several issues. The first is whether all of the systems of psychotherapy may be used safely with suicidal clients. Some, such as person-centered therapy, seem safe enough to use with any client, including the suicidal individual. But what about the more confrontive and emotional therapies, such as Gestalt therapy and primal therapy?

A second important question is whether the major therapeutic issue is the client's suicidal preoccupation or the problems (e.g., depression and social isolation) underlying it, a question that relates to whether the suicidal preoccupation is acute or chronic. If the suicidality is chronic, it makes sense for the psychotherapist to focus on the client's underlying psychological problems. There has been a great deal of research on suicidal behavior in the last 40 years, and some of this research has implications for therapeutic strategies that may be used specifically with suicidal clients. In addition, individual therapists have formulated their own conceptualizations of the genesis of suicidal preoccupation, some of which are empirically based (e.g., Leenaars, 1991) and some of which are clinically based (e.g., Richman & Eyman, 1990), and have suggested goals and techniques for psychotherapy based on these conceptualizations.

The third issue psychotherapists should consider is whether particular systems of psychotherapy are suitable for particular types of clients. This leads to the problem of devising a taxonomy of suicidal clients that has relevance for psychotherapy (rather than, say, research). For example, Fremouw, de Perczel, and Ellis (1990) listed six types of suicidal clients (those who are depressed and hopeless, those with communication and control problems, psychotic clients, alcoholic clients, individuals with organic brain dysfunction, and rational clients), but they kept close to traditional psychiatric categories and failed to show that classification of suicidal clients into these six types was useful for psychotherapists.

PSYCHOANALYSIS

Freud's View of Suicidal Behavior

Brief mentions of suicidal behavior can be found throughout Freud's writings, and Litman (1967) documented and synthesized these dispersed thoughts. From an analytic perspective, the clinical features of suicidal behavior include guilt over death wishes toward others, identification with a suicidal parent, refusal to accept loss of gratification, suicide as an act of revenge, suicide as an escape from humiliation, suicide as a communication, and the connection between death and sexuality.

The essential feature of suicidal behavior is that the person loses a loved object and energy is withdrawn from this lost loved object, relocated in the ego, and used to re-create the loved one as a permanent feature of the self, in an identification of the ego with the lost object. Litman (1967) called this process *ego-splitting*. Even before becoming suicidal, the person has probably already introjected some of the desires of the loved one. Children introject desires of their parents, and adults introject the desires of their lovers. In this way, it is as if part of our mind is symbolic of our loved one. If this person is lost to us, for example, by death or divorce, we still possess those introjected desires, and thus the symbolization of the lost loved one remains as part of our mind.

This process can lead to suicide if we also harbor hostile wishes toward the lost object, for now we can turn this anger toward the part of our mind that symbolizes the lost object.

More generally, however, one major influence of psychoanalytic theory on the analysis of suicide is the asking of the question, What is the real reason for this suicide? Although researchers often cite the obvious precipitating event for suicidal preoccupation, such as the breakup of a close relationship, financial problems, or legal problems, the vast majority of people who experience such traumas do not kill themselves. These precipitating events are neither necessary nor sufficient to account for suicide. This had led psychoanalysts to probe for the unconscious motives behind the suicidal act.

For example, the suicide of Sylvia Plath, an American poet, in 1963 was ostensibly precipitated by her husband's adulterous affair. However, Oedipal conflicts appear to have been involved in the suicidal act. In her poem *Daddy* (Plath, 1966), Plath casts her father as a Nazi guard for the concentration camp in which a Jewish Sylvia is interned and as a devil who bites her heart in two. She expresses both affection and anger toward her deceased father, describes her marriage as an attempt to find a father substitute, and casts her suicide as a reunion with Daddy.

The Goals of Psychoanalysis

There are many possible goals in psychoanalysis with the suicidal client, but one possible goal is to make conscious to the client what is unconscious. If clients can become conscious of their unconscious desires, then they will not necessarily satisfy them directly, but at least they will be able to make more appropriate choices in the future. Psychoanalysis does not attempt to change the client's choice, but rather to make it an informed choice.

To make a client conscious of unconscious desires is not easy. The process may make the client anxious, perhaps to the point of panic. Thus, increasing the client's awareness must be done slowly and carefully. Psychoanalysis proceeds cautiously, with three to five meetings a week for 3–7 years or longer.

The techniques of psychoanalysis include free association, in which the client permits his or her mind to wander freely from memory to memory and informs the psychoanalyst of the chain of associations. The psychoanalyst listens to what the client says and observes how the client behaves toward him or her. In particular, the psychoanalyst behaves with total neutrality toward the client, so that when the client attributes thoughts and desires to the psychoanalyst that he or she does not possess, the psychoanalyst can observe this transference. Some psychoanalysts say that the psychoanalysis is finished when the client fully understands and has resolved this transference and can relate to people as they really are. Finally, the psychoanalyst interprets the client's behavior to him or her. The psychoanalyst tries to get the client slowly to become aware of the unconscious desires behind his or her behavior.

Because most of the client's unconscious desires derive from childhood wishes, and most of the client's superego wishes (primarily involving conscience and ego ideals) derive from demands that the client's parents made on him or her, psychoanalysts place much importance on the client's childhood. In psychoanalysis, much time is spent discussing the early years and the client's parents and siblings. The slow tempo and historical orientation of psychoanalysis make it unsuitable for crisis intervention with acutely suicidal clients.

Discussion

The psychoanalytic perspective on suicide has generated a good deal of research, much of which is supportive of the theory. For example, in a review of the research on the experience of loss in suicidal people and the relationships between suicide and depression and between suicide and anger, I found that the psychoanalytic perspective had been useful in furthering our understanding of suicidal behavior (Lester, 1988).

Because psychoanalysis is a slow process, it is difficult to document the use of its techniques for dealing with suicidal people. The goal of psychoanalysis is a thorough exploration of the contents of the conscious and unconscious mind, and this has to proceed slowly for both suicidal and nonsuicidal clients. The usefulness of the perspective for suicidal clients can be illustrated in the analysis of particular cases of suicide, such as that of Sylvia Plath, mentioned earlier, in which a psychoanalytic perspective reveals the real motives underlying the superficial precipitating causes for the suicide.

COGNITIVE THERAPY

The cognitive therapies are based on the notion that negative emotions and disturbing behaviors are a consequence of irrational thinking. The symptoms result not from the unpleasant events that we experience, but from our thoughts about those events. It is not the fact that we were fired from our jobs or that our spouse divorced us that makes us anxious or plunges us into despair. Rather, it is what we say to ourselves after these traumatic events that leads us to anxiety and despair.

The first systematic statement of these views was outlined by Ellis (1962, 1973) in his rational–emotive therapy. As an example, let us say that the client experiences rejection by a woman. This is the *activating experience*. In the unhealthy sequence, *irrational beliefs* are activated by this experience. "Isn't it awful that she rejected me? I am worthless. No desirable woman will ever accept me. I should have done a better job of getting her to accept me. I deserve to be punished for my ineptness." Particular emotional states result from these irrational beliefs. The client may feel anxiety, depression, worthlessness, or hostility. This emotional state is the *consequence*.

In the healthy sequence, the activating experience is followed by a *rational belief*. "Isn't it unfortunate [or annoying or a pity] that she rejected me?" The consequence of the rational belief is an emotional state of regret, disappointment, or annoyance.

Cognitive psychotherapy involves teaching the client that his or her emotional states result not from the activating experiences, but from the irrational, absolutistic, and demanding beliefs they activate. The client must be taught to dispute his or her irrational beliefs. "Why is it awful? How am I worthless? Where is the evidence that no one will ever love me? Why should I have done a better job? By what law do I deserve to be punished?" Once clients can substitute rational for irrational beliefs, they will be much happier and make appropriate choices.

Beck's (1976) cognitive–behavioral therapy is a more recent version of cognitive therapy. The goal of cognitive–behavioral therapy is to modify faulty patterns of thinking both directly and indirectly. It focuses on the client's cognitions (thoughts and attitudes) and the assumptions and premises that underly them.

Clients are taught to recognize their idiosyncratic cognitions. The term *idiosyncratic* is used because the cognitions reflect a faulty appraisal of some aspect of the world. A person may have a distorted perception or may misinterpret what he or she perceives. Despite the fact that the cognitions are faulty, they seem to the client to be plausible, and they occur involuntarily and automatically. Often, they lead to unpleasant emotions.

Clients are taught first to distance themselves from their cognitions. They then learn to examine their cognitions objectively, evaluate them critically, and distinguish between their evaluations and reality. Finally, clients are taught to correct their cognitive distortions. To do this, it helps if clients can specify the particular kind of fallacious thinking they practice. For example, the client who tends to overgeneralize makes unjustified generalizations on the basis of one incident, as when a single failure leads the client to believe that he or she will never succeed at anything.

Therapy provides a safe situation in which to test cognitions. The client is helped to confront them and examine them. The client transfers this learning process to real-life situations by directly modifying the thoughts and by rehearsing the reality-oriented thoughts.

Thought Patterns in Suicidal Individuals

Research has appeared in recent years that has identified specific patterns of thought commonly found in suicidal individuals. Awareness of these patterns can help the cognitive therapist who is working with suicidal clients.

For example, Neuringer (1988) has shown that suicidal people are prone to dichotomous thinking and tend to have rigid patterns of thought that work against their identifying solutions to the problems they face. Hughes and Neimeyer (1990) have elaborated on Neuringer's work, noting that suicidal people have polarized and extreme views of themselves, life, and death and have closed themselves off to examining alternative solutions to suicide. In addition, a growing body of research indicates that suicidal people are extremely pessimistic and hopeless about the future (Beck, 1970; Lester, 1992). Even when compared with depressed clients in general, suicidal people have a higher level of hopelessness, which may be caused in part by irrational thinking, as proposed in Ellis's theory (Revere, 1985).

Trexler (1973) has noted that therapists may find it useful to focus cognitive therapy on these distortions. However, the decision to commit suicide is often an impulsive decision. It is important to point out to clients that impulsive decisions are often bad decisions. It may be helpful to tell suicidal clients that individuals who survive a suicide attempt are almost invariably grateful, as well as to point out that a rash decision made at a time of emotional upheaval would be an error they could not correct. Thus, they should give the decision careful and prolonged consideration.

Several cases of cognitive therapy with suicidal clients have been published. Cautela (1970), Ellis (1989), Burns and Persons (1982), and Emery, Hollon, and Bedrosian (1981) reported cases in which they helped suicidal clients using cognitive therapy techniques. In addition, some researchers who are exploring suicidal individuals' cognitive distortions and deficiencies have devised therapeutic strategies to remedy them (Clum & Lerner, 1990; Linehan, Armstrong, Suarez, Allmon, & Heard, 1991).

Therapist Anxiety

Therapists who work with suicidal clients often feel great anxiety over the possibility that the client might commit suicide. If a client does commit suicide, the therapist may blame him- or herself and feel guilt for failing to help the client. Trexler (1973) pointed out that these feelings are often the result of irrational thinking that needs to be challenged. Although therapists are responsible for their words and actions with clients, clients are ultimately responsible for their decisions and actions. Furthermore, the therapist's input into the client's life is but one small part of the total picture, and the therapist obviously has no control over the other inputs.

Discussion

Cognitive therapy is one of the few therapies for which current research on suicide is providing new insights and guidelines. Researchers are actively exploring the thinking patterns of the suicidal individual, and their discoveries will suggest possible dysfunctional thinking patterns for cognitive therapists to look for in their suicidal clients (Hughes & Neimeyer, 1990; Neuringer, 1988). This area promises to develop considerably in the next few years.

TRANSACTIONAL ANALYSIS

Transactional analysis is a simplified, holistic conception of psychoanalysis, and transactional analysts have frequently written about suicidal behavior. They believe, in general, that the genesis of suicidal behavior lies in the early years of life when the child picks up "Don't exist" injunctions from the parents and incorporates them into the script of the self (Woollams, Brown, & Huige, 1977).

Transactional analysis proposes three ego states: the *child ego state,* which resembles the state of mind the individual had as a child; the *adult ego state,* a mature, information-processing state of mind; and the *parent ego state,* which is a state of mind based on the individual's identification with his or her parents or parent substitutes. Orten (1974) noted that it is the suicidal client's child ego state that is feeling despair and hopelessness and suggested that the counselor attempt to get the client's adult ego state in control at times of suicidal preoccupation. Nurturing responses from the counselor's parent ego state will not accomplish this. Messages that convey "Somebody loves you," "Promise me you won't kill yourself," or "I won't let you do it" simply reinforce the executive role of the client's child ego stage.

Asking questions designed to elicit information is the most effective method of getting the client's adult ego state to take control. The questions should be nonthreatening, that is, unrelated at first to the problems causing the suicidal preoccupation (e.g., ascertaining the client's current life situation—job, marriage, living arrangements, etc.). Prematurely rushing into consideration of the client's problems strengthens the child ego state's position. Upon being firmly established in the adult ego state, the client may immediately feel relief, because in this ego state he or she sees the world differently and feels more capable of dealing with it.

The counselor then decides whether it would be useful to begin discussing the problems confronting the client or to postpone such a discussion to the next visit. If the counselor begins an exploration of the personal problems, he or she must be alert for signs that the child ego state is taking control again. If this happens, the counselor should recontact the adult ego state by moving away from the topics that have elicited the child ego state.

BEHAVIOR THERAPY

Behavior therapists have described how their techniques can be applied to suicidal clients. Stuart (1967) reported treatment of a suicidal client who was receiving inadequate reinforcement, and Jansson (1984) described a suicidal client with poor social skills. Bostock and Williams (1974) and O'Farrell, Goodenough, and Cutter (1981) have also reported treatment of suicidal clients with behavioral therapy.

Rosenthal (1986) outlined steps for treating clients who are suicidal within the context of a learned-helplessness syndrome. First, clients sign a written contract to call the therapist if they feel suicidal. This shows clients that their behavior has had an effect on at least one person, the therapist. There is some debate, however, as to the usefulness of such contracts and the extent to which they should be used with suicidal clients.

Second, it helps if the therapist intervenes in the clients' environment. For example, perhaps the therapist can talk to a suicidal teenager's parents. This shows clients that the therapist is on their side and that they do not have to tackle their problems alone. It demonstrates that the situation, although undesirable, is not catastrophic and can be approached rationally.

Third, Rosenthal (1986) suggested having clients keep a log of self-defeating thoughts and feelings. Unlike cognitive therapists, Rosenthal did not advocate challenging these thoughts and changing them. He believed that simply tabulating the thoughts lessens their frequency and impact.

Fourth, the therapist can work on anger. Rosenthal believed that anger and suicide are closely related. Shy and timid people need to be taught assertiveness skills and how to express anger in socially acceptable ways. Aggressive clients need to be given homework assignments in which they practice more empathic ways of expressing their feelings.

Finally, Rosenthal (1986) suggested that the therapist hold out hope that solutions are possible. For example, a teenager ignored by her parents can be told that the therapist will talk to them or can be taught ways of dealing with them. A physically abused wife can be told that tomorrow the therapist will take her to court to get a police protection order and then to a women's shelter.

OTHER SYSTEMS OF PSYCHOTHERAPY

In addition to psychoanalysis, cognitive therapy, transactional analysis, and behavior therapy, other systems of psychotherapy may be useful for suicidal clients. I have discussed the applicability of these systems for the treatment of suicidal clients elsewhere (Lester, 1991) and in this section briefly outline a few of them.

Primal therapy. Primal therapy is a derivative of psychoanalysis, and the extreme emotions aroused during primal therapy might be thought to be too stressful for suicidal individuals. However, Janov (1974) has reported using primal therapy with suicidal clients with no adverse effects.

Gestalt therapy. Gestalt therapy (Perls, Hefferline, & Goodman, 1951), a more confrontive style of therapy than many other systems, might also be thought to be too stressful for suicidal clients. There is also perhaps a danger in having suicidal clients dwell too intensely and too experientially on the here and now of their feelings. However, some Gestalt therapists have worked through the current feelings of suicidal clients. Many psychotherapists may not feel comfortable with encouraging such reencounters; of course, the psychotherapist must be very experienced in using such techniques so that he or she can monitor the client's psychological state carefully during the experiences and calm the client when necessary. In addition, when closing the therapy session with the suicidal client, the therapist should take greater care than usual to ensure that the client has achieved a temporary resolution of the conflicts and feelings just experienced.

Reality therapy. Adherents of reality therapy (Wubbolding, 1989), which focuses largely on what the client is doing, also find that suicidal clients pose no particular problem and can be helped by its standard techniques.

Person-centered therapy. Person-centered therapy (Rogers, 1959) has long been the basis for the crisis counseling of suicidal clients. The usefulness of this therapy in suicide crisis counseling has now been widely acknowledged. Person-centered therapy differs from other therapies in maintaining that simply listening empathically to clients is sufficient for therapy; most psychotherapists would not accept this, however.

Existential therapy. Existential psychotherapy (Yalom, 1980) and Jungian analysis (Stein, 1982) seem to fit together, with existential therapists seeing the search for meaning for one's life as a powerful force in human behavior and Jungian analysts believing that the meaning is there if the individual can perceive it. Although neither system of psychotherapy proposes techniques specifically for the suicidal client, both systems seem relevant for the long-term treatment of suicidal clients.

DISCUSSION

The usefulness of systematically considering the major forms of psychotherapy for their applicability to the treatment of suicidal clients is that the theorists of each system take a rather narrow and extreme position about the rationale for, purpose of, and techniques of their system of psychotherapy, exploring their perspective to the full, and this permits examination of the power of the system acting in isolation. For example, what can psychoanalysis or person-centered therapy achieve if either is used exclusively with a suicidal client? It also reveals where the system of therapy fails, for example, what issues it overlooks and for which types of suicidal clients it may not be appropriate.

The practicing psychotherapist, in contrast, is able to use whatever theory and techniques best fit the client, both in the long term and in each moment of therapy. Thus, despite their orientation, psychotherapists often need to be eclectic in their approach, drawing on whatever system of psychotherapy seems appropriate in the moment. For example, if the client experiences an acute suicidal crisis, the psychotherapist can use the short-term strategies suggested by transactional analysts and behavior therapists or can use a standard crisis-counseling approach. After the suicidal crisis has subsided, the psychotherapist can then switch to more long-term strategies, such as modifying dysfunctional patterns of thinking or undertaking a psychoanalytic exploration of the client's conflicts. Suicidal clients may thus be able to make use of all of the techniques discussed herein to leave the abyss of despair.

REFERENCES

Beck, A. T. (1970). The core problem in depression. *Science and Psychoanalysis, 17,* 47–55.

Beck, A. T. (1976). *Cognitive therapy and emotional disorders.* New York: International Universities Press.

Bostock, T., & Williams, C. L. (1974). Attempted suicide as an operant behavior. *Archives of General Psychiatry, 31,* 482–486.

Burns, D., & Persons, J. (1982). Hope and hopelessness. In L. E. Abt & I. R. Stuart (Eds.), *The newer therapies* (pp. 33–57). New York: Van Nostrand Reinhold.

Cautela, J. R. (1970, September). *The modification of behaviors that influence the probability of suicide in elders.* Paper presented at the 78th Annual Convention of the American Psychological Association, Miami, FL.

Clum, G. A., & Lerner, M. (1990). A problem solving approach to treating individuals at risk for suicide. In D. Lester (Ed.), *Current concepts of suicide* (pp. 194–202). Philadelphia: Charles Press.

Ellis, A. (1962). *Reason and emotion in psychotherapy.* Secaucus, NJ: Lyle Stuart.

Ellis, A. (1973). *Humanistic psychotherapy.* New York: Julian.

Ellis, A. (1989). Using rational–emotive therapy (RET) as crisis intervention. *Individual Psychology, 45,* 75–81.

Emery, G., Hollon, S. D., & Bedrosian, R. C. (1981). *New directions in cognitive therapy.* New York: Guilford Press.

Fremouw, W. J., de Perczel, M., & Ellis, T. E. (1990). *Suicide risk.* New York: Pergamon.

Hughes, S. L., & Neimeyer, R. A. (1990). A cognitive model of suicidal behavior. In D. Lester (Ed.), *Current concepts of suicide* (pp. 1–28). Philadelphia: Charles Press.

Janov, A. (1974). Further implications of "level of consciousness." *Journal of Primal Therapy, 1,* 193–212.

Jansson, L. (1984). Social skills training for unipolar depression. *Scandinavian Journal of Behavior Therapy, 13,* 237–241.

Leenaars, A. A. (1991). Suicide notes and their implications for intervention. *Crisis, 12,* 1–20.

Lester, D. (1988). *Suicide from a psychological perspective.* Springfield, IL: Charles C Thomas.

Lester, D. (1991). *Psychotherapy for suicide clients.* Springfield, IL: Charles C Thomas.

Lester, D. (1992). *Why people kill themselves.* Springfield, IL: Charles C Thomas.

Linehan, M. M., Armstrong, H. E., Suarez, A., Allmon, D., & Heard, H. L. (1991). Cognitive–behavioral treatment of chronically parasuicidal borderline patients. *Archives of General Psychiatry, 48,* 1060–1064.

Litman, R. E. (1967). Sigmund Freud on suicide. In E. S. Shneidman (Ed.), *Essay in self-destruction* (pp. 324–344). New York: Science House.

Neuringer, C. (1988). The thinking processes in suicidal women. In D. Lester (Ed.), *Why women kill themselves* (pp. 43–52). Springfield, IL: Charles C Thomas.

O'Farrell, T. J., Goodenough, D. S., & Cutter, H. S. G. (1981). Behavioral contracting for repeated suicide attempts. *Behavior Modification, 5,* 255–272.

Orten, J. D. (1974). A transactional approach to suicide prevention. *Clinical Social Work Journal, 2,* 57–63.

Perls, F. S., Hefferline, R. F., & Goodman, P. (1951). *Gestalt therapy.* New York: Julian.

Plath, S. (1966). *Ariel.* New York: Harper & Row.

Revere, V. L. (1985). Treatment of suicidal patients. *Independent Practitioner, 5,* 17–18.

Richman, J., & Eyman, J. R. (1990). Psychotherapy of suicide. In D. Lester (Ed.), *Current concepts of suicide* (pp. 139–158). Philadelphia: Charles Press.

Rogers, C. R. (1959). A theory of therapy, personality, and interpersonal relationships, as developed in the client-centered framework. In S. Koch (Ed.), *Psychology: A study of a science* (Vol. 3, pp. 184–256). New York: McGraw-Hill.

Rosenthal, H. (1986). The learned helplessness syndrome. *Emotional First Aid, 3*(2), 5–8.

Rudestam, K. E. (1985–1986). Suicide and the selfless patient. *Psychotherapy and the Patient, 2,* 83–95.

Stein, M. (1982). *Jungian analysis.* La Salle, IL: Open Court.

Stuart, R. B. (1967). Casework treatment of depression viewed as an interpersonal disturbance. *Social Work, 12,* 27–36.

Trexler, L. (1973). The suicidal person and the restoration of hope. *Rational Living, 8*(2), 19–23.

Woollams, S., Brown, M., & Huige, K. (1977). What transactional analysts want their clients to know. In G. Barnes (Ed.), *Transactional analysis after Eric Berne* (pp. 487–525). New York: Harper's College Press.

Wubbolding, R. E. (1989). Professional issues: Four stages of decision making in suicidal client recovery. *Journal of Reality Therapy, 8*(2), 57–61.

Yalom, I. D. (1980). *Existential psychotherapy.* New York: Basic Books.

Chapter 6

Family Therapy for Suicidal People

Peter McLean
Steven Taylor

The death of an individual by suicide is forever perplexing to the individual's acquaintances, friends, and family members, who are haunted by questions such as "Why didn't I know?" and "What should I have done?" Suicide rates among adolescents and young adults tripled from 1950 to 1980 (O'Carroll, Mercy, Hersey, Boudreau, & Odell-Butler, 1992), and there is reason to believe these rates will continue to climb, given recent evidence of a growing incidence of psychopathology in the general population (Lewinsohn, Hops, Roberts, Seeley, & Andrews, 1993; Lewinsohn, Rohde, Seeley, & Fischer, 1993). Most contemporary formulations of suicide (e.g., Blumenthal, 1990) propose that suicidal behavior arises when precipitants (risk factors) interact with predisposing factors (vulnerabilities).

Major risk factors for suicide attempts and completions include hopelessness and depression, substance abuse, personality disorder, previous suicidal behavior, and poor coping skills (Blumenthal, 1990; Brent et al., 1990; Garland & Zigler, 1993). Factors such as social support and a sense of direction in life appear to inhibit the development of suicide ideation and suicide behavior.

We recently examined the coroner's files on 250 cases of youth suicide in British Columbia in the years 1987–1991 and found that in more than 80% of cases there was at least one precipitating event that would have been noticeable to family members and friends (e.g., family disruption, job failure, interpersonal loss, or academic failure). Similarly, Patterson and Stoolmiller (1991) found evidence to suggest that peer rejection and academic failure contributed to depression, and hence suicide risk, in three samples of adolescent boys. These findings suggest that suicide warning signs may not be difficult to detect by parents and that the event that precipitates suicide may be common knowledge in the family with an at-risk child. Although such events often do not lead to suicide, they are sufficient reasons for parents to be alert for signs of depression and hopelessness. Thus the family is a powerful influence on suicide risk, not only because of the enormous number of opportunities it provides, over time, to increase or erode a family member's hopefulness and self-esteem, but also because of its ability to recognize and respond to signs of suicide risk. Of course, a significant number of people kill themselves in the absence of apparent warning signs, but such cases represent a relatively small minority of total cases (Leenaars, 1988; Richman, 1986).

In this article, we present a cognitive–behavioral family therapy approach to the identification and management of suicide risk. Cognitive–behavioral family therapy (Beck, 1988; Bornstein & Bornstein, 1986; Freeman, Epstein, & Simon, 1987) is based on the assumption that a person's cognitions (e.g., expectations, beliefs, and attitudes) are powerful determinants of how the person feels and how he or she responds to others' behaviors. Distressed families are characterized by poor communication (Beck, 1988; Bornstein & Bornstein, 1986; Freeman et al., 1987), and so their members often misinterpret one another's intentions and behaviors.

Cognitive–behavioral family therapy further assumes that family interactions and other behaviors are a function of their perceived consequences. That is, individuals perform behaviors depending on whether they expect to be rewarded or punished for them. Interactions among distressed families—including those with a suicidal member—are characterized by a high rate of reciprocal punishment among members (Beck, 1988; Bornstein & Bornstein, 1986; Freeman et al., 1987). This is partly a product of poor communication (i.e., mistakenly attributing malicious intent to other members) and partly due to the fact that in distressed families the members are infrequently reinforced for rewarding one another.

Hopelessness—the expectation that nothing can be done to resolve life's difficulties—is a particularly important cognitive factor, because there is a good deal of evidence to suggest that hopelessness contributes to depression and suicidal behavior (see Beck & Weishaar, 1990, for a review).

The goals of cognitive–behavioral family therapy for the suicidal individual are

1 An alleviation of the individual's hopelessness by correcting maladaptive cognitions,

2 Improved communication among family members,

3 An increase in mutually rewarding behaviors among family members, and

4 A decrease in punishing behaviors among family members.

In the following section, we explain and illustrate the principles used to attain these goals.

PRINCIPLES OF COGNITIVE–BEHAVIORAL FAMILY THERAPY

Focus on Behavior

From the outset of therapy, the therapist conveys the message that all family members are responsible for their actions. The therapist also encourages family members to focus on what they do or fail to do to one another, rather than on why they do or don't do something or on what they intend to do. This strategy encourages clear communication and discourages the family from making accusations about one another's motives (i.e., mind reading) and making commitments that cannot be verified (e.g., "I'll try"). In this approach, family members are also encouraged to influence one another's behaviors (including emotional reactions) by first changing their own behaviors and thoughts. As a result, family distress is reframed in terms of problem behaviors that are addressed by methods of problem solving. This strategy, like many of the methods in cognitive–behavioral family therapy, tends to lessen family conflict and promote collaborative problem solving and mutual support.

Specificity

Cognitive–behavioral family therapy attempts to operationally define expectations, commitments, and requests. The goal of this specificity is to improve communication and accountability among family members. Members of conflicted or distressed families tend to apply overgeneralized labels to one another, which are commonly used as a means of assigning blame (e.g., "You're *always* late" and "Why can't you *ever* be responsible?"). This form of communication escalates family conflict and can lead family members to feel hopeless about the possibility of getting along with one another. To reduce this destructive form of labeling, the therapist asks family members to specify what they mean in behavioral terms (e.g., "How would you know if he was being responsible?" and "What do you mean when you say things are hopeless?"). Family members are encouraged to represent themselves by communicating their thoughts and feelings directly and clearly. This helps lower the tension and conflict among the family members, which in turn lessens the likelihood that suicide will be chosen by the individual who is threatening it as the form of escape from an aversive family environment.

Reciprocity

Familywide behavioral contracts are often the engine of change in improving the relationships among the individuals in a family with a suicidal member. Behavioral contracts specify contingencies for behaviors or interactions among family members (e.g., "If you do X, then I will do Y" or "If you do X, then you will receive Z"). Explained within a social bargaining context, a contract is usually readily accepted by all members because its reciprocal nature allows each member to expect that he or she will benefit as well as sacrifice. Such behavioral contracts are typically developed under the supervision of the therapist and include four to seven specific requests for change on the part of one family member, who in turn will make requests of the other members. Once requests for change are negotiated and agreed to, they are reviewed in each therapy session and changed or updated as needed. The use of such contracts helps to counter the sense of hopelessness and helplessness that characterizes people who are depressed and suicidal. Contracting also increases family support and morale.

Goal Directedness

By definition, people who are depressed and suicidal lack constructive goals. In cognitive–behavioral family therapy, the suicidal member is asked to defer the question of suicide until the course of therapy has been completed, whereupon it will be reviewed privately with the therapist. The suicidal family member is asked to inform the therapist, however, if he or she is unable to avoid suicidal preoccupation. Problems are translated into goal statements. Several studies have shown that depression and suicidal behavior are ameliorated by successful goal attainment, particularly if the goals involve increased social activation and personal activity (Gotlib & Colby, 1987; McLean & Hakstian, 1979, 1990). Thus, the therapist encourages family members to lend direct support to the suicidal member's goal attainment in order to encourage successful performance and, consequently, increased self-esteem. In this way, the family is encouraged to function like a self-help group, a strategy advocated by many family therapists who treat suicidal people (e.g., Richman, 1986). Goals cover a variety of areas. The patient is encouraged to attempt easy goals initially and more difficult goals later. With this graduated approach, the individual is likely to experience progress in goal attainment.

Positive Interchanges

Individuals who contemplate suicide typically have feelings of low self-worth and are prone to feel rejected by others. They are often frustrated in interpersonal relations and immersed in painful and unresolved dilemmas for which they see no hope of resolution. Studies of suicide notes (Leenaars, 1988; Leenaars et al., 1992) have revealed the pervasive negativity that characterizes the cognitive and emotional states of suicidal individuals. In cognitive–behavioral family therapy, the therapist attempts to reverse negative interchanges by helping the family replace them with positive means of interpersonal influence. Destructive means of communication (e.g., criticism, sarcasm, yelling, and demeaning comments) are targeted in advance and prohibited. Family members are taught to (a) translate their complaints into positive and specific requests and (b) provide three to five forms of positive recognition (e.g., paying a compliment; expressing approval of appearance, ideas, or behavior; and openly boasting of one another's accomplishments) per person, per day.

Focus on Present and Future

Depressive thinking and conflictual family interchanges largely concern events that happened in the past. Such thoughts and interchanges can have a toxic effect on family morale. Cognitive–behavioral family therapy places emphasis on the present and future. This is because the present and future, unlike the past, can be changed. Discussions about past grievances do not undo past injustices or resolve current difficulties. Instead, they represent a high risk for family conflict and demoralization. In therapy it is acknowledged that discussions about the past can lead to improved understanding of current difficulties. However, due to the risks involved, discussions of aversive past events are deferred until there are clear improvements in the functioning and mood on the part of at least the identified patient.

Cognitive Interventions

Cognitive–behavioral family therapy, like conventional cognitive–behavioral therapy (e.g., Beck, Rush, Shaw, & Emery, 1979), attempts to identify and restructure maladaptive cognitions. The therapist trains the family members to identify and challenge their dysfunctional beliefs.

To illustrate, 16-year-old Anne made her first suicide attempt after being rejected twice by potential boyfriends. She felt helpless and depressed and believed that the prospect of finding a boyfriend was a hopeless pursuit. During therapy, Anne was able to identify many of her dysfunctional beliefs (e.g., "I'll never find anyone" and "I can never be happy unless I find a boyfriend") and was encouraged to challenge these beliefs (e.g., "Who says I'll *never* find a boyfriend? Do I have a crystal ball?'' and ''I can always find happiness in other ways; I don't *need* a boyfriend in order to feel happy'').

A second important cognitive intervention is problem solving, which has been shown to be an important method for overcoming hopelessness and suicidal behavior (Salkovskis, Atha, & Storer, 1990). To continue with Anne's case, she and her family were instructed in methods of collaborative problem solving to help her improve her range of social activities (which would improve her chances of finding a suitable boyfriend) and also cultivate other sources of happiness. These goals were achieved by working through the following steps:

   1   Identifying the problem (i.e., forming a precise description of the problem),
   2   Taking a large problem (e.g., finding a boyfriend) and breaking it down into several subgoals,
   3   Evaluating possible solutions,
   4   Implementing selected solutions, and
   5   Evaluating the solutions implemented and doing any necessary fine-tuning.

An extended discussion of problem-solving methods has been provided by D'Zurilla (1986).

These principles and strategies are applicable to most cases of family therapy for suicidal individuals. Modification of therapy methods or the inclusion of other methods may be necessary, depending on whether the suicidal member is a parent or one of the children. In the following sections, we describe these presentations and illustrate the interventions that are commonly used.

FAMILY THERAPY FOR YOUTH AT RISK FOR SUICIDE

Cognitive–behavioral family therapy for suicidal youths aims to

   • Monitor suicide risk,
   • Identify and restructure maladaptive thoughts and behaviors, and
   • Facilitate social support.

Occasionally, crisis management or hospitalization may be required to ensure the safety of the suicidal person. As soon as possible, the therapist draws the family back to the main issues, namely, developing an environment for open communication and supportive problem solving. We typically meet individually with the suicidal member and the main players of the family (i.e., parents and key siblings) in advance of family therapy in order to orient the parties to therapy; listen to their concerns; and enlist the family's support, understanding, and tolerance for a time-limited trial of family therapy. During the individual meeting with the suicidal family member, the therapist establishes a contract with the individual to postpone consideration of suicide for a period of time.

Education

An important element of treatment is to educate the family about the nature and causes of depression and suicide and strategies to avoid. For example, 17-year-old Nancy had been depressed since her second serious romantic relationship ended against her will, a little more than a year before therapy began. She was in conflict with both parents, who saw her as listless and argumentative. They routinely admonished her to "better yourself," "snap out of it," "go back on medication," and "find some nice friends." Family therapy helped Nancy's parents reduce their counterproductive criticism, understand the reasons for her behavior, generate alternative solutions to these concerns (several of which were acceptable to Nancy), and give her support for her efforts to change.

Establishing Open Communication to Facilitate Problem Solving

Family therapy recognizes that psychopathology is not simply within the identified patient and may represent dysfunctional reactions of other family members. An important step in therapy is to assess the patient's perceptions of his or her problems and goals in a nonjudgmental atmosphere. This process usually takes the major proportion of the first session and is reviewed every few sessions thereafter. The family is usually unaware of the nature and magnitude of the suicidal youth's worries and preoccupations. The therapist gently prods first the suicidal youth and then other family members to discover the subject matter of failed expectations and current problems. Consider, for example, the hypothetical case of a client we shall call Alex. The therapist's questioning would proceed as follows:

"Alex, what do you think has gone wrong for you?"
"How are you different from your friends?"
"What makes you feel better and worse?"
"Have you noticed other things that are problems for Alex?" (to Alex's mother)
"Alex, do you agree?"
"Alex, if things were going much better for you, what are some of the things you'd be doing that you aren't now?"

Of course, many of Alex's concerns may stem from outside the family, such as peer rejection or scholastic performance. These issues are still relevant to family therapy because the family needs to understand them in order to establish a supportive atmosphere of collaborative problem solving. Throughout this discovery process, the therapist would ask Alex for evidence for his various conclusions and help him question dysfunctional beliefs and replace them with more adaptive ones. Training in problem solving is particularly emphasized because it is well established that suicidal adolescents have deficits in social problem-solving ability (e.g., Marx, Williams, & Claridge, 1992; Sadowski & Kelly, 1993), as indicated by difficulties in generating alternatives to problems, making decisions, and implementing solutions. To some extent, the routine problems of suicidal adolescents can be predicted from their stage of development. Grotberg, Feindler, and Stutman (1991) identified the following situations as common stressors for adolescents and as possible precipitating events for suicide in depressed adolescents:

1   Being confused about goals or direction in life;
2   Being prevented from participating in rule making;
3   Being unable to express or manage anger;
4   Fighting or arguing with siblings;
5   Being compared with siblings or friends;
6   Being labeled as messy, selfish, inconsiderate, or lazy;
7   Being teased or talked about by friends;
8   Being made to feel inadequate or treated like a baby;
9   Being humiliated or embarrassed in front of friends.

To facilitate problem solving, the family therapist ensures that any criticisms made by family members are translated into positive, specific requests; for example, if Alex's sister states, "Alex is too inconsiderate," the therapist would ask, "What would you like him to do instead?" The therapist also should be prepared to be the patient's advocate as necessary and to support his or her efforts at self-disclosure.

Tactics of Interpersonal Influence

Regardless of the reason for the youth's suicidal thinking, it is safe to assume that the family members are less than effective in dealing with this problem. This is easily evident in conflicted families but may not be clear in seemingly well-adjusted families that have a suicidal member. The development of strategies of interpersonal influence can greatly help family members assist one another in times of crisis.

For example, Allan, then a 15-year-old boy in a loving family, was serious, conscientious, and sensitive and had excessively high standards for himself. He had always been an A student. Recently, Allan had become pressured by academic expectations, and he quit his job delivering newspapers in order to devote more time to his studies. As a result of his devotion to work, he neglected his friends and felt increasingly isolated. He made a suicide attempt after learning he received a C and a B instead of all As on his final report card. During therapy, his parents learned to help Allan talk about his fears by rewarding his self-disclosures. They also learned to help Allan lower his excessively high standards. This was done by demonstrating that although it is desirable to get good grades, it is not a disaster if he doesn't succeed. The parents reinforced this message by describing their own scholastic goals as children and pointing out that the attainment of these goals were "wants" rather than musts. Ironically, when Allan began to make fewer demands on himself, he was less anxious at school and his grades began to improve.

Behavioral Contracts

An important vehicle of therapeutic change is the use of reciprocal agreements, or behavioral contracts, to negotiate change among family members. The family therapist begins by asking each party (smaller children are excluded for practical reasons) to state in positive and specific terms two to four things they would like other members to do for them over the next week to improve the quality of their life. All parties are encouraged to be selfish and think of their own best interests when generating their requests. The therapist assists by keeping track of requests, ensuring that they are neither vague nor negative (e.g., "Stop screaming all the time" becomes "I would appreciate it if you would speak quietly in the morning before leaving for work") and vetting those that seem inappropriate or too difficult. Family members are then asked if they would agree to do what the other party asks of them in return for receiving what they asked for. The outcome of this assignment is assessed during the following session. Adjustments are often necessary. However, the primary motivation for each individual is the expectation of negotiated control over some aspects of the other's behavior.

To illustrate, Elaine is 18 years old, lives at home, and feels managed by her parents. She is ridiculed, often in public, by her 15-year-old brother, Evan. Elaine has requested that her parents "speak nicely to me, let me decide where I'll apply for jobs, be polite to my friends, and be accepting of what I wear." Elaine asked Evan to "stay out of my room without permission and to avoid making comments about my weight." In turn, her parents (acting together as one party, in this case) requested that Elaine "let us know roughly where she is going and when she'll be home, be up by 8:00 A.M. on weekdays, clean the kitchen three evenings a week, and go to exercise class twice a week." Evan asked his sister to "give me a ride to work on Saturdays and to take clear phone messages for me."

To promote accountability, the therapist asks all parties to keep a simple record of how often they received their requests from others. These records are reviewed at the next meeting. Noncompliance is discussed if it occurs. It may be due to an unclear understanding of what was being requested, or there may have been a reasonable excuse. All parties are reminded that they are, in effect, judged by others as a result of what they do, rather than what they intended to do. This process allows family members to clarify what they expect of one another and to influence one another in a process that is cooperative, equitable, and accountable.

FAMILY THERAPY FOR A SUICIDAL PARENT

Compared with suicidal adolescents, a suicidal parent typically has a less acute onset of depression and is easier to engage in treatment. The depressed parent is most often the mother, because depression occurs two to three times more often in females than males (American Psychiatric Association, 1987). This difference has not been attributed to biological factors. Instead, women appear to be at greater risk for depression because they carry a greater burden than men do in their social roles, and are economically less advantaged (McGrath, Keita, Strickland, & Russo, 1990).

The combination of unipolar depression and suicidal behavior in either gender is viewed as a reaction to a crisis or a response to an unrewarding life-style. In either case, the ratio of positive to negative events is low, and the future appears bleak to the person (Bandura, 1986; Lewinsohn, 1975). Like suicidal adolescents, the suicidal parent and family will benefit from education about suicide; open communication that clarifies expectations; behavioral contracting; and cognitive restructuring to correct pessimistic beliefs about the self, world, and future. In addition, the depressed and suicidal parent needs a plan to increase the amount of time he or she spends on goal-directed and rewarding activities.

Through cognitive–behavioral family therapy, the suicidal parent can both acquire more effective and positive means of influencing family members and receive more support and positive family recognition. The first step for the therapist is to address the parent's suicidal intent and to get him or her to agree to postpone contemplation of suicide until therapy has had a chance to take effect (10–12 weeks), whereupon it will be reviewed with the therapist. Because in the case of a depressed parent the spouse's role in the resolution of the depression is normally more important than the children's, family therapy sessions (i.e., parents and children age approximately 12 years and older) are alternated with sessions attended only by the parents. Treatment is then assembled in the following steps.

Identification of Problems and Treatment Goals

From the outset of therapy, the suicidal behavior is reframed as maladaptive problem solving. Problems refer to barriers to goals, conflicts with others, and unresolved issues. The suicidal parent is simply asked what he or she thinks has caused this depression and contemplation of suicide. The spouse and children are asked for their opinions. The suicidal parent should not be pathologized in family treatment. Instead, suicide contemplation is viewed as an understandable but maladaptive reaction to adverse life circumstances, which the family must help resolve. Problems are identified jointly by all family members and then are operationalized and transformed into positive requests for change within the behavioral exchange format.

To illustrate, Joan was a 43-year-old mother of three children. She had always been nonassertive, was somewhat isolated from the community, and became depressed after learning that her husband had an affair with a coworker. The children learned of the affair and sided with the mother. Joan's husband, Norm, was regretful of his actions and ended the affair. Therapy involved the development and implementation of behavioral contracts to lessen family tension, to increase Joan's sense of control over her life, and to decrease her isolation. Joan requested that Norm spend more time with the family, help with household chores more often, and limit his alcohol consumption. In turn, Norm asked Joan to develop some community interests and to lose weight. Both parties honored their commitments. There was a marked reduction of family tension, and Joan became more hopeful about her future with Norm.

Development of Behavioral and Cognitive Foci

People who are depressed and suicidal tend to be mood driven. That is, their performance depends on their mood. For example, Bill said, "I'd do the things you ask if I felt better." He was told by the therapist that in order to feel better, he first had to increase his level of enjoyable and rewarding activities. Depression, hopelessness, and suicide intent are framed for patients as the products of inadequate goal attainment. Problem solving and other strategies for goal attainment can mobilize hope and alleviate depression. Bill was encouraged to tolerate his depressive symptoms temporarily while attempting to increase his participation in constructive and rewarding activities. He also was encouraged to question his pessimistic predictions about goal attainment and to identify and challenge other negative beliefs. These strategies shifted Bill's focus away from depression-inducing ruminative thoughts and toward adaptive problem solving and behavior.

Graduated Attainment of Goals

Clinical depression, which characterizes most suicidal adults, is usually accompanied by indecision and behavioral inertia. Because depressed and suicidal patients are typically demoralized, we attempt to limit the chance that the pursuit of a goal will deepen their despair by breaking goals down into graduated steps of increasing difficulty. This is illustrated by the case of Bert, a 53-year-old man who had sustained a work-related spinal injury and was on disability. Bert experienced chronic back pain and became depressed after his compensation claim, now in its third year, was delayed yet again. He was withdrawn and preoccupied with his pain. During therapy, his wife and teenage son requested that Bert become more active socially. Because he was shy, Bert found it difficult to socialize, and he initially failed to comply with his family's request, despite agreeing to do so. Accordingly, the task was broken down into smaller and easier steps. Bert first called several former friends under the pretense of borrowing tools, then arranged to do something with them once he saw them, and eventually had them over to his house for dinner one evening.

Social Recognition of Gains

Family members often take one another for granted. Because self-esteem is influenced by the reactions of others, it is critical that the suicidal parent receives a reasonable, consistent, and accurate volume of positive recognition by other family members. The therapist will likely have to prompt this activity, because family members are often unaccustomed to complimenting one another and may be relatively unskilled in this regard.

In helping family members overcome depression and suicidal ideation, the therapist may find it useful to prompt activities that are incompatible with depression. This can be done during supervision of the development of bilateral behavioral contracts among family members. Depression-incompatible activities that may be prompted include

- Maintaining a high rate of social activity,
- Setting personal goals,
- Pursuing interests outside the family (e.g., recreation, job, music),
- Developing problem-solving skills,
- Receiving positive recognition, and
- Practicing assertive behavior rather than acting passively or aggressively.

CONCLUSION

The prevalence of attempted suicide is high and is increasing across several age groups (Centers for Disease Control, 1991; O'Carroll et al., 1992). Social-learning factors, such as family interaction patterns, play an important role in precipitating and preventing suicide. Thus, family therapy is an important approach to managing the suicidal patient. In cognitive–behavioral family therapy, techniques derived from social–cognitive theory are used to help families develop better methods of interpersonal influence and to correct dysfunctional thinking. Depression and suicidal behavior are viewed within an interpersonal context in terms of both cause and resolution. Family therapy is directed at overcoming problems such as distorted expectations (e.g., hopelessness), maladaptive problem solving, and interpersonal conflicts. This type of treatment is practical and goal oriented. In contrast to other forms of family therapy, the therapist plays an active, directive, and educative role. The emphasis on action typically appeals to families in crisis and, at least in our experience, appears to be a potent intervention.

The treatment strategies described in this article were derived from the works of cognitive–behavioral theorists (e.g., Beck, 1988; Beck et al., 1979; Bornstein & Bornstein, 1986; Lewinsohn, 1975) and from our clinical experience. An important further step is the empirical evaluation of the efficacy of cognitive–behavioral family therapy for suicidal people. There is much evidence for the efficacy of cognitive–behavioral therapy when treatment is conducted either with just the identified patient (McLean & Carr, 1989) or with the entire family (Hahlweg & Markman, 1988). Further research is needed to evaluate the efficacy of these treatments when they are applied specifically to families with suicidal members.

REFERENCES

American Psychiatric Association. (1987). *Diagnostic and statistical manual of mental disorders* (3rd ed., rev.). Washington, DC: Author.

Bandura, A. (1986). *Social foundations of thought and action.* Englewood Cliffs, NJ: Prentice Hall.

Beck, A. T. (1988). *Love is never enough.* New York: Harper & Row.

Beck, A. T., Rush, A. J., Shaw, B. F., & Emery, G. (1979). *Cognitive therapy of depression.* New York: Guilford Press.

Beck, A. T., & Weishaar, M. E. (1990). Suicide risk assessment and prediction. *Crisis, 11,* 22–30.

Blumenthal, S. J. (1990). An overview and synopsis of risk factors, assessment, and treatment of suicide patients. In S. J. Blumenthal & D. J. Kupfer (Eds.), *Suicide over the life cycle: Risk factors, assessment, and treatment of suicidal patients* (pp. 685–733). Washington, DC: American Psychiatric Press.

Bornstein, P. H., & Bornstein, M. T. (1986). *Marital therapy: A behavioral-communications approach.* New York: Pergamon.

Brent, D. A., Perper, J. A., Goldstein, C. E., Kolko, D. J., Allan, M. J., Allman, C. J., & Zelenak, J. P. (1990). Risk factors for adolescent suicide. *Archives of General Psychiatry, 45,* 581–588.

Centers for Disease Control. (1991). *Attempted suicide among high school students— United States, 1990. Morbidity and Mortality Weekly Report, 40,* 633–635.

D'Zurilla, T. (1986). *Problem-solving therapy: A social competence approach to clinical intervention.* New York: Springer Publishing Company.

Freeman, A., Epstein, N., & Simon, K. (1987). *Depression in the family.* New York: Haworth.

Garland, A., & Zigler, E. (1993). Adolescent suicide prevention. *American Psychologist, 48,* 169–182.

Gotlib, I. H., & Colby, C. A. (1987). *Treatment of depression: An interpersonal systems approach*. New York: Pergamon.

Grotberg, E. H., Feindler, C. B., & Stutman, S. S. (1991). Using anger management for prevention of child abuse. In P. A. Keller & S. R. Heyman (Eds.), *Innovations in clinical practice: A source book* (Vol. 10, pp. 5–21). Sarasota, FL: Professional Resource Exchange.

Hahlweg, K., & Markman, H. J. (1988). Effectiveness of behavioral marital therapy: Empirical status of behavioral techniques in preventing and alleviating marital distress. *Journal of Consulting and Clinical Psychology, 56,* 440–447.

Leenaars, A. A. (1988). *Suicide notes*. New York: Human Sciences Press.

Leenaars, A. A., Lester, D., Wenchestern, S., McMullin, C., Rudzinski, D., & Brevard, A. (1992). Comparison of suicide notes and parasuicide notes. *Death Studies, 16,* 331–342.

Lewinsohn, P. M. (1975). The behavioral study and treatment of depression. In M. Hersen, R. M. Eisler, & P. M. Miller (Eds.), *Progress in behavior modification* (Vol. 1, pp. 19–64). San Diego, CA: Academic Press.

Lewinsohn, P. M., Hops, H., Roberts, E., Seeley, J. R., & Andrews, J. A. (1993). Adolescent psychopathology: 1. Prevalence and incidence of depression and other DSM-III-R disorders in high school students. *Journal of Abnormal Psychology, 102,* 133–144.

Lewinsohn, P. M., Rohde, P., Seeley, J. R., & Fischer, S. A. (1993). Age-cohort changes in the lifetime occurrence of depression and other mental disorders. *Journal of Abnormal Psychology, 102,* 110–120.

Marx, E. M., Williams, J. M., & Claridge, G. C. (1992). Depression and social problem solving. *Journal of Abnormal Psychology, 101,* 78–86.

McGrath, E., Keita, G. P., Strickland, B. R., & Russo, N. F. (1990). *Women and depression: Risk factors and treatment issues*. Washington, DC: American Psychological Association.

McLean, P. D., & Carr, S. (1989). The psychological treatment of unipolar depression: Progress and limitations. *Canadian Journal of Behavioural Science, 21,* 452–469.

McLean, P. D., & Hakstian, A. R. (1979). Clinical depression: Comparative efficacy of outpatient treatments. *Journal of Consulting and Clinical Psychology, 47,* 818–836.

McLean, P. D., & Hakstian, A. R. (1990). Relative endurance of unipolar depression treatment effects: Longitudinal follow-up. *Journal of Consulting and Clinical Psychology, 58,* 482–488.

O'Carroll, P. W., Mercy, J. A., Hersey, J. C., Boudreau, C., & Odell-Butler, M. (1992). *Youth suicide prevention programs: A resource guide*. Altanta, GA: Centers for Disease Control, U.S. Department of Health and Human Services.

Patterson, G. R., & Stoolmiller, M. (1991). Replications of a dual failure model for boy's depressed mood. *Journal of Consulting and Clinical Psychology, 54,* 491–498.

Richman, J. (1986). *Family therapy for suicidal people*. New York: Springer Publishing Company.

Sadowski, C., & Kelly, M. (1993). Social problem solving in suicidal adolescents. *Journal of Consulting and Clinical Psychology, 61,* 121–127.

Salkovskis, P. M., Atha, C., & Storer, D. (1990). Cognitive–behavioral problem solving in the treatment of patients who repeatedly attempt suicide: A controlled trial. *British Journal of Psychiatry, 157,* 871–876.

Chapter 7

Treatment of the Suicidal Adolescent

Alan L. Berman
David A. Jobes

The help needed by the adolescent identified to be at risk for suicide or suicidal behavior may be conceptualized as having two foci. The first is the crisis model, wherein interventions are designed to prevent death or injury by restoring a presuicidal equilibrium. The therapist helps restore equilibrium mostly by providing the resources and supports, both internal and external, necessary to allow a normal healing process to occur (in a hurry). It is presumed that these resources and supports are, perhaps only temporarily, unavailable as a result of the constriction of thought and dysregulation of emotion that overwhelm the adolescent during the period of crisis.

The help that the suicidal adolescent needs must then transcend the resolution of the immediate crisis and deal with the underlying vulnerability that gave rise to the present crisis and has the potential to cause future crises. The adolescent is thus offered a variety of longer term therapeutic interventions designed to reduce psychopathology and teach adaptive skills. The hope is that together crisis intervention and longer term psychotherapy will end the chronicity of psychopathology that may make threats of suicide a life-long behavior.

THE SUICIDAL CRISIS

The acute suicidal crisis is produced by a unique synergy of individual, socioenvironmental, and temporal variables. Under conditions of time-limited stress and the impact of trauma or loss, the suicide-vulnerable teen responds with constricted perception/cognition and limited resources. Unable to find a way out of the situation of perceived threat, the teen may experience helplessness and panic and make predictions of dire consequences. The sense of hopelessness betrayed by these predictions, in the absence of alternative coping strategies, makes the idea of a suicidal escape or plea for help acceptable, even compelling.

The intent of the suicidal action depends on the adolescent's goal. For example, when the suicidal threat is an immediate and impulsive response to a crisis in the family (as is typically the case for girls who ingest pills, the most common type of adolescent suicide attempter), the intent may be antidotal to the felt loss of connection and may communicate pain; rage; or an appeal for love, caring, and attachment. Alternatively, when the action is the consequence of planning and premeditation during a long period in which needs have gone unmet (or are perceived to be unmeetable), surcease, death, or disconnection may be sought.

The clinician's immediate task is to assess the adolescent's potential for self-destructive behavior while concurrently acting to protect the adolescent from that possibility. These tasks must be accomplished under conditions of often incongruent expectations and goals. Adolescents are notoriously reluctant to seek help, particularly from mental health professionals. Like children, adolescents are mostly brought or sent to therapy by adults. As with all irrational beliefs, those that make the adolescent resistant to entering treatment are held to steadfastly. These beliefs are verbalized in comments such as "Shrinks need therapy more than I do," "No-one can really understand," and "Everyone will find out." Underlying these statements are real concerns about being seen as crazy (rather than being joined against a crazy system) and not being able to trust a transference object, within the context of the teenager's need to affirm an as yet too-fragile sense of autonomy. Because the initiator of treatment may be the very person from whom distrust was learned and distance is sought, therapy with the adolescent often begins in an atmosphere of suspicion, conflict, combativeness, and intense affect.

On the other hand, both the adolescent and his or her parents may be highly ambivalent about allowing an outsider to shift the fragile homeostasis of family dynamics. Once the immediate danger of a suicidal crisis is over, the family may prefer quick restoration of its pathological but familiar equilibrium over having to deal with new (unknown) roles, endure exposure (and consequent public humiliation and embarrassment), and admit failure. Denial of problems is reinforced by the cessation of observable crisis, making entry into voluntary treatment easily avoided. Because of this, adolescents who are treated in the hospital emergency room and released to follow-up outpatient care after a suicide attempt often do not comply with that referral. Yet if there is no structural change in the family dynamics that gave rise to the suicidal behavior, repeated suicidal behaviors may follow.

For the average clinician, the suicidal adolescent brings unaccustomed problems to the office. Among them are family enmeshment and possible parental psychopathology that may lie outside the reach of clinical intervention. Because many clinicians have little, if any, formal training in clinical suicidology, the prospect of working with a demanding/dependent patient (who typically consumes more than his or her fair share of the clinician's time and energy) can be daunting. The white noise of the threat of malpractice litigation, should treatment prove ineffective in preventing a suicidal death, can be a further source of worry to the clinician.

We have outlined elsewhere a number of steps for increasing the adolescent's compliance with treatment, establishing a working therapeutic alliance, and minimizing negative countertransference reactions to potentially suicidal adolescent patients (Berman & Jobes, 1991). Attention to these macrotherapeutic issues underlies the potential success of any crisis or longer term intervention, regardless of its theoretical foundation. The experienced therapist knows that the most important element in psychotherapy is the stability and quality of the clinician–patient relationship. Collaborative and trustworthy alliances often are notably absent in the presenting histories of suicidal adolescents. Beginning work with an individual intent on not being alive or one who is habitually self-assaultive does not connote collaboration toward a desired goal of health. When the adolescent enters the therapeutic dyad with hopelessness, rage, or ambivalence about staying alive, or perhaps a regressive dependency, the therapist has much work to do simply in order to begin.

ASSESSMENT OF RISK

Effective intervention and treatment must begin with a thorough assessment of risk and of the conditions, both situation specific and chronic, that have given rise to suicide risk. Ongoing assessment of risk through all phases of work with the suicidal adolescent is an imperative, because risk may wax and wane with the vicissitudes of the youth's character or psychopathology, family dynamics, or the stresses of everyday life.

We have described strategies for assessing the risk of suicidal behaviors in detail elsewhere (Berman & Jobes, 1991). Briefly, the clinician must familiarize him- or herself with current empirical findings regarding risk factors that discriminate adolescents who have been suicidal (e.g., have completed suicide or made serious suicide attempts) from those who have not. The following are common themes among these findings.

1 A negative personal history. Early life events may have caused a narcissistic injury that makes the adolescent particularly sensitive and vulnerable to loss or the threat of loss. In addition, parental psychopathology, negligence, or negative modeling may have produced significant skill deficits, particularly interpersonal and social, making coping in adolescence difficult.

2 Psychopathology and significant negative personality attributes. Mental disorders found most common to more lethal suicidal behaviors include mood disorders, substance abuse disorders, and conduct disorders. Comorbidity of psychopathologies, such as borderline personality disorder and depression, is especially conducive to self-aggressive behaviors. Signs of affect dysregulation, such as rage, impulsivity, and an intolerance of aloneness; and cognitive constriction, such as hopelessness, are potential precursors of lethal acts.

3 Breakdown of typical defenses. Evidence of acute behavioral change, such as withdrawal or agitation, increased irrationality or other disturbances of thinking, heightened substance use, and heightened anxiety or symptoms of anxiety (e.g., changes in sleep patterns) may point to an increased inability to control troubling affective states.

4 Social/interpersonal isolation and alienation. Removal from typical attachments may result in increased cognitive constriction and a lack of protection from internal urges. Particular attention must be paid to signs of antagonism toward authorities, identification with alienated identities, social withdrawal, or help-rejecting behaviors.

5 Self-deprecatory ideation, dysphoria, and hopelessness. Negative views of the self, others, and the future may turn into ideations of self-abuse and attack. When not buffered by pleasure or a meaningful sense of the self, these ideations may lead to a constricted view of life (tunnel vision) in which an attitude of ''Life sucks'' may be countered only by the sense that it should be ended.

6 Stress. Under conditions of heightened or anticipated stress (unacceptable loss, rejection, humiliation, or punishment), anxiety is aroused and available coping strategies are challenged. Suicidal adolescents may lack effective coping skills under these conditions and have been shown to use more explosive, aggressive, or withdrawal strategies than their nonsuicidal peers do.

THE TREATMENT PLAN

The starting point of any intervention effort is the assessment of lethality and intentionality. *Lethality* refers to the immediate threat of significant self-harm behavior, or the medical–biological danger to the self. When a self-harm behavior has already occurred, the logistics of rescue must be addressed (e.g., the location of the adolescent, what has occurred, and the availability of significant others). Assessment of potential lethality is aided by the use of published scales (Smith, Conroy, & Ehler, 1984); the lethality of an attempt already made may be determined through consultation with a poison control center and may require the initiation of emergency medical intervention for prompt medical treatment and further triage once stabilization is achieved.

Intentionality is the psychological aim or purpose of the self-harm behavior. It is crucial to the success of further treatment efforts to establish whether the adolescent's behavior was (or is, in the case of an individual who is threatening to commit suicide) meant as an operant in his or her interpersonal world (e.g., to make connections happen, to express unverbalized emotion, or to change another's behavior) or whether the adolescent truly wished (or wishes) to die. To understand suicidal intent fully, the clinician must consider the bottom line: What does it mean for this patient to be suicidal with me right now?

In cases in which danger of significant harm is not imminent, the need for psychotherapeutic treatment is no less indicated. Similarly, in cases in which no action has yet occurred, the potential for action must still be addressed. This means the clinician must be alert to red flags—communications from the adolescent in the form of verbalizations, writings, drawings, and the like that indicate that suicide is on the mind. These warnings then need to be put into a context of understanding that ideation does not lead to self-harm behavior without the presence of further indices of risk, such as diagnosable mental disorders that compromise rational thought or emotional regulation; other signs of poor impulse control or the use of acting out as a coping strategy; intolerable stress; a lack of protective factors, such as working alliances with caring others; and the availability and accessibility of means to harm (e.g., a gun in the home).

Treatment Site

The need for emergency medical care, the presence of significant psychopathology, and the assessment of imminent and unabated risk of suicidal behavior are primary indicators for consideration of inpatient treatment. Once the adolescent is stabilized, or in cases in which resources are sufficient, the adolescent is best treated as an outpatient. Outpatient treatment is less likely to reinforce regression and dependency. In addition, the stigma of hospitalization is avoided while the coping demands of the everyday social milieu can be met with the support of outpatient psychotherapy.

Overview of Treatment Modalities

Individual psychotherapy is the treatment of choice with the suicidal adolescent; however, family therapy is often the more appropriate treatment when family conflict or psychopathology is central to the adolescent's struggle toward autonomy. The primary goals of family therapy with suicidal adolescents are to modify pathological interactions among family members, increase the family's support for the adolescent's attempt at self-care, and increase the family's tolerance for separation. In addition, the family as a unit can learn to increase problem-solving skills, accept change, and understand the adolescent's suicidal behavior from a systems perspective. When a family refuses a recommendation for family therapy, the therapist should be wary of scapegoating of this adolescent as a central dynamic in the family's life.

In institutional settings, homogeneous group psychotherapy may be offered. With its emphasis on verbal expression and ventilation of affect, communication and listening skill development, peer support, and role modeling, particularly on issues related to family and peer relationships, group work can be particularly effective.

Pharmacotherapy should be considered carefully in light of any underlying diagnosed mental disorder, particularly when symptoms (e.g., insomnia) interfere with cognitive functioning and impulse control. There is no such thing as an antisuicide pill, but the potential for beneficial effects makes medication a standard treatment where indicated. Proper compliance with the administration of medications, of course, must be carefully monitored by a treatment ally (e.g., parent) and dosages controlled by the prescribing physician. If the therapist is not a physician, he or she should make sure the lines of communication with the psychopharmacologist remain open.

Individual Psychotherapy

As noted earlier, the mainstay of the treatment plan with the suicidal adolescent is individual psychotherapy, because of the close attention, ongoing assessment, and individualized focus it affords. In general, the length of treatment depends on the severity of psychopathology and the patient's response to intervention. Most effective, at least in the short run, are treatments in which the therapist is active, assertive, explanatory, and responsive. We have found that adolescents are particularly responsive to cognitive–behavioral interventions focused on enhancing instrumental skills. There remains, however, considerable room for interpretation and psychodynamic therapies (Jobes, in press).

Crisis Intervention Strategies

Reduce lethality   The initial goal of any therapeutic plan is to protect the adolescent from self-harm behavior. Sometimes this requires placing the individual in a protected environment, such as a hospital. More often, this requires taking an empathic, interactive problem-solving approach that offers the adolescent support and caring warmth while actively reducing sources of stress and distress. Once stabilized, the adolescent is better able to process information and use now-available cognitive resources to deal with the predisposing risk for another suicidal crisis.

To reduce immediate lethality, the clinician together with significant others must make every effort to remove available and accessible means of self-harm, particularly any gun kept in the home or pills in the medicine chest. At the very least, one must ensure some delay between the thought or plan of suicidal action and its implementation. Parents or significant others must be involved in these efforts.

Consider negotiated agreements   Time-limited and renewable agreements between the adolescent and the therapist should be negotiated to provide a structuring tool for maintaining safety and delineating mutual treatment responsibilities. Treatment negotiation can also be used as a valuable diagnostic tool to determine the adolescent's ability to delay self-destructive behavior, comply with therapeutic instructions and work in a collaborative manner. The clinician should be aware, however, that negotiated agreements are static and easily broken. Thus, no-suicide contracts do not guarantee what can be expected of a suicidal character, except for a very short period of time; they also have no predictive validity.

Provide support   The adolescent patient should not be left alone until it is clear the crisis has abated. A trusted family member or friends should be given explicit instructions to stay with the patient and remain in communication with the therapist. The therapist similarly aligns with the patient's need to know he or she is not alone, by being both available and accessible and by providing surrogate contacts (colleagues, crisis centers, etc.) when this is not possible.

Treat anxiety and insomnia   Acute anxiety and chronic insomnia are treated aggressively so that they do not potentiate the adolescent's acting out or irrational thinking. Medication, removal of the adolescent from known sources of stress, and anxiety management techniques should be considered to reduce the intrusiveness of these symptoms.

Replace the client's tunnel vision with a broader perspective   The immediacy of the suicidal crisis constricts the patient's attention to the here and now. One of the important goals of crisis intervention is figuratively to remove the patient's blinders, replacing tunnel vision with a broader perspective. This is accomplished in four ways.

First, to encourage a future orientation, both therapist and client can work toward establishing small, measurable steps toward a long-term goal, helping the adolescent gain distance from the crisis while simultaneously seeing change (and his or her part in effecting it) as a gradual stepwise process.

Second, the therapist can attempt to decrease the client's egocentricity and isolation by increasing linkages to others. This begins with the contactability of the therapist and 24-hr telephone services and extends to potential attachments to both individuals and networks of support. Possible support networks that exist naturally in the adolescent's environment are cultural, interest-based, or, where relevant, religious groups. In some settings, peer counseling models are available and can be used as well.

Third, to increase stabilization, efforts at structuring treatment or pretraining for therapy can help the adolescent establish reasonable expectancies and footholds of security in place of unrealistic demands and confusion. Factual descriptions of diagnoses, symptoms, and dynamics and realistic appraisals of their treatability and changeability might be given. In addition, specific descriptions of what the adolescent can expect from his or her suicidality (e.g., its episodic nature) and therapy (when and how often sessions will be held, the nature and limits of confidentiality, etc.) help prepare the adolescent to form a trusting alliance.

Finally, the crux of crisis intervention is establishing a problem-solving strategy involving relatively standardized procedures for problem exploration and definition, generation of alternative solutions, hypothesis testing, and resolution or redefinition of the problem. Inherent in this approach is a functional assessment of the motive(s) for suicidal behavior so that non-self-harmful strategies may be identified to accomplish what usually are reasonable goals. Central to the efficacy of crisis intervention is the establishment of a collaborative alliance, built on reasonable rapport and communication between the patient and therapist. We have presented a model for this work elsewhere (Jobes & Berman, in press).

Beyond Crisis Intervention

The immediate goals of intervention with the suicidal adolescent are to develop a working relationship, to protect the adolescent from self-harm, and to decrease the level of perturbation and lethality. In a treatment plan that extends beyond immediacy, the work of psychotherapy now proceeds to focus on the underlying conditions that made the adolescent vulnerable to suicide in the first place. Typically, this focus includes reducing the effects of psychopathology and maladaptive cognitions and behaviors, increasing self-esteem and self-worth, enhancing instrumental skills, and improving object relations. Ideally, this work also gets to the core psychodynamic conflict(s), with sufficient opportunity to work these through in the transference relationship.

Also, ideally, it is helpful for the therapist to have sufficient eclecticism in orientation and style to incorporate (perhaps even to integrate) both behavioral and psychodynamic techniques into the therapeutic armamentarium. For example, increasing the patient's attachment to a sense of future time (a temporal linkage) can be accomplished through a variety of maneuvers ranging from interpretation (which establishes temporal connectedness from the present to the past) to cognitive rehearsal (of problem-solving alternatives) and the use of homework assignments (as links between the current and the next future session).

Cognitive therapy has gained repute as an effective treatment for individuals with an underlying affective disorder, especially when depressive symptoms make introspection difficult. In addition, by learning to alter their irrational beliefs, patients increase their potential to gain from insight-oriented treatments. Beck's model of treatment is both highly structured and collaborative, relying on a "collaborative empiricism" (Beck, Hollon, Young, Bedrosian, & Budenz, 1985) to identify, test, analyze, and target for change the invalid underlying assumptions that are responsible for the patient's negative mood.

Linehan (1993) has refined cognitive–behavioral strategies into a dialectical behavior therapy for the treatment of suicidal young women. Drawing from social–behavioral theory, Linehan postulates that suicidal actions are due to aversive affective states caused by negative environmental events, self-generated dysfunctional behavior patterns, and deficiencies in both tolerance for distress and resources for reducing distress. Her treatment protocol is designed to modify these deficits and teach affect regulation, self and behavior management, interpersonal problem-solving skills, and competency in developing and maintaining social supports.

Shure and Spivack (1978) have developed models for interpersonal problem-solving skill training that include didactic exercises, modeling, and behavioral rehearsal and may be adapted for use with suicidal adolescents, who are notably deficient in social reasoning skills.

Depression management (Lewinsohn, Antonuccio, Steinmetz, & Teri, 1984), anger management (Feindler & Ecton, 1986), self-control training (Rehm, 1987), social skills training (Lindsay, 1987), and the modification of loneliness (Young, 1982) are just a few of the many, primarily cognitive and behavioral, approaches that have been reported to be effective with some of the underlying and predisposing problems of the suicidal adolescent. Given the tools these approaches provide, the adolescent increasingly can master, or at least cope with, that which has been overwhelming enough to make him or her feel hopeless about the future. With the consistent, stable, and active involvement of an empathic caregiver who serves as collaborator, teacher, and cheerleader, the long-term gains from therapy can be a significant contributor to the adolescent's learning (or relearning) to set positive expectancies and produce reinforcing outcomes—a corrective emotional experience.

Termination Notes

Because attachment issues, and therefore separation and individuation issues, are primary in the genesis of suicidality, termination is a crucial phase of the treatment process. The specter of termination raises the patient's separation anxiety and, often, the use of denial to defend against the impending loss. Therapists are often surprised by self-destructive acts during this phase of treatment.

We have argued (Berman & Jobes, 1991) that termination should be a process of weaning, a graduated series of steps involving decreased direct contact with the therapist and leading to the adolescent's decision to end treatment. Leaving therapy is analogous to leaving home. As appropriate, follow-up sessions and telephone and mail contact should be extended over the long term. In this way, the adolescent's status and risk can be continuously monitored. Issues of loss can be integrated and framed within the context of measurable progress, and "booster shots" of therapy can be scheduled as necessary to smooth out rough edges or in anticipation of significant anniversary dates.

FROM GOOD PRACTICE TO MALPRACTICE

As noted earlier, the suicidal adolescent is not likely to be readily described as the ideal patient. By the time suicidal adolescents enter therapy, usually not of their own volition, they have developed character pathologies or multiproblem presentations that make a positive working relationship difficult to achieve. Often, as well, their parents understandably will expect of the therapist what they themselves have not been able to accomplish and, because it is the therapist's duty, will expect him or her to safeguard their child from harm. Should their child commit suicide, their grief may be externalized as anger and blame, which may take the form of bringing litigation against the therapist in which alleged failures (acts of omission or commission) on the part of the therapist are claimed to be direct and proximate causes of the child's suicide.

The courts may hold against the therapist if it can be demonstrated that the therapist breached the duty to safeguard. The standard of care expected of the therapist requires "reasonable and prudent" behavior, or what knowledgeable peers (experts) state may be expected of professionals with training and experience similar to the therapist's.

We lack space here to do justice to the topic of appropriate risk management to minimize the likelihood of successful malpractice actions in cases of completed suicide. A few guiding principles must suffice. First, there must be proof that the potential ("foreseeability") for suicide was assessed. Evidence should appear in the clinical record that questions were asked and observations made relevant to known risk factors. In this regard, it behooves the therapist to conduct a relevant historical interview, obtain documented histories from prior caregivers, conduct a mental status exam, arrive at a working diagnosis, etc. Judgments based on this information should lead to a statement of risk (none, low, moderate, etc.) and an appropriate treatment plan. The treatment plan should be reasonable for the diagnosis and problems presented and should include appropriate precautions based on the level of assessed risk. Both hospitalization and pharmacological intervention should be considered if appropriate. Finally, the treatment plan should be appropriately and dependably implemented, updated, and revised as needed.

Needless to say, should a negligence complaint be made, the only defense a therapist has is the clinical record, a contemporaneous documentation of observations, judgments, and decisions regarding the assessment and treatment of the patient. Thus it is essential that the issues just listed be reflected in documentation presented by the therapist. The courts do not expect psychotherapists to have either 20:20 foresight or perfect clinical judgment; they do expect reasonable and prudent professional behavior. More extended discussions of these issues, particularly as they pertain to outpatient treatment, are available elsewhere (Bongar, Maris, Berman, & Litman, 1993; Jobes & Berman, 1993).

CONCLUSION

Irrespective of the theoretical foundation on which it is based, therapeutic work with the suicidal adolescent requires attention to the core role attachment plays in both the dynamics of the adolescent's suicidality and the process of successful treatment. Central to accomplishing treatment goals is the establishment of a working alliance with a stable attachment figure who appreciates the adolescent's pain, respects his or her strengths, and reaches the part of the patient's ambivalence that desires life. Using a reasonably considered protocol for treatment that is attentive to the presenting dynamics and skill deficits, the therapist should be able to lend the particular tools that the adolescent needs to reduce the suicidal crisis and lessen predisposing risk for future crises. Of course, this can be accomplished only within a context of dynamic assessment of risk and the conditions that increase risk.

Working with the suicidal adolescent is challenging, demanding, and often frightening—the therapeutic equivalent to mountain climbing or parasailing, perhaps. It is also validating and life-affirming work, the consequences of which are experienced by both patient and therapist.

REFERENCES

Beck, A. T., Hollon, S. D., Young, J. E., Bedrosian, R. C., & Budenz, D. (1985). Treatment of depression with cognitive therapy and amitriptyline. *Archives of General Psychiatry, 42,* 142–148.

Berman, A. L., & Jobes, D. A. (1991). *Adolescent suicide: Assessment and intervention.* Washington, DC: American Psychological Association.

Bongar, B., Maris, R. W., Berman, A. L., & Litman, R. E. (1993). Outpatient standards of care and the suicidal patient. *Suicide and Life-Threatening Behavior, 22,* 453–478.

Feindler, E. L., & Ecton, R. B. (1986). *Adolescent anger control: Cognitive–behavioral techniques.* New York: Pergamon.

Jobes, D. A. (in press). Psychodynamic treatment of adolescent suicide attempters. In J. Zimmerman & G. M. Asnis (Eds.), *Treatment approaches with suicidal adolescents.* New York: Wiley.

Jobes, D. A., & Berman, A. L. (1993). Suicide and malpractice liability: Assessing and revising policies, procedures, and practice in outpatient settings. *Professional Psychology: Research and Practice, 24*, 91–99.

Jobes, D. A., & Berman, A. L. (in press). Crisis assessment and time-limited intervention with suicidal youth. In A. Roberts & B. Liese (Eds.), *Clinical issues, crisis intervention, and time-limited treatment.* New York: Guilford Press.

Lewinsohn, P. M., Antonuccio, D., Steinmetz, J., & Teri, L. (1984). *The coping with depression course: A psychoeducational intervention for unipolar depression.* Eugene, OR: Castalia.

Lindsay, W. R. (1987). Social skills training with adolescents. In J. C. Coleman (Ed.), *Working with troubled adolescents: A handbook* (pp. 107-122). San Diego, CA: Academic Press.

Linehan, M. M. (1993). *Cognitive behavioral treatment of the borderline personality disorder.* New York: Guilford Press.

Rehm, L. (1987). Approaches to the prevention of depression with children: A self-management perspective. In R. F. Munoz (Ed.), *Depression prevention: Research directions* (pp. 79–91). Washington, DC: Hemisphere.

Shure, M. B., & Spivack, G. (1978). *Problem-solving techniques in childrearing.* San Francisco: Jossey-Bass.

Smith, K., Conroy, R. W., & Ehler, B. D. (1984). Lethality of suicide attempt rating scale. *Suicide and Life-threatening Behaviour, 14*, 215–242.

Young, J. E. (1982). Loneliness, depression, and cognitive therapy: Theory and application. In L. A. Peplau & D. Perlman (Eds.), *Loneliness: A sourcebook of current theory, research, and therapy* (pp. 379–405). New York: Wiley.

Chapter 8

Psychotherapy with Older Suicidal Adults

Joseph Richman

Suicide in the elderly is treatable and preventable; nevertheless, it is one of the most neglected areas in the entire field of suicidology. The suicidologist needs to know much more about therapy, the therapist needs to know more about suicide, and both need to know more about gerontology. To this end, the following account presents some general principles that apply to all psychotherapies that may be used with suicidal clients, with an emphasis on the suicidal elderly. Included are assessment, risk management, and reduction of the tensions in the patient and family that fuel the suicidal state through crisis intervention and strategy.

The best therapist for a suicidal person is the one with a broad foundation in theory and practice. This is because suicide has multiple causes, the understanding of which involves a wide spectrum of disciplines. I came to this realization while working on a multidisciplinary psychogeriatric team, one of the highlights of my 45 years as a practicing clinician. The members included a psychiatrist, a psychologist, a nurse, social workers, social work trainees, medical students, and—briefly—a physician assistant.

What follows is a personal testament, based on 27 years of specialization in the treatment of suicidal persons. My experiences have reinforced my belief in the use of social and family resources and in the intrinsic healing forces of people, including those who have been considered hopeless by much of society.

The published literature either ignores psychotherapy for the suicidal elderly or implies they are unsuitable for it. My clinical experiences and those of my colleagues indicate that either attitude is erroneous. The question is not whether, but how, to conduct psychotherapy with the elderly. Do we treat a suicidal 70-year-old man or woman differently from a suicidal 7- or 47-year-old? The answer is, in some ways we do and in some ways we do not.

Some variables in the suicidal state are age specific, such as the effects of life-span developmental tasks and crises. For example, few young people become suicidal in reaction to retirement or entry into a nursing home, and few old people are faced with failure in school or the breaking up of a love affair. However, there are some components of the suicide state, the self-destructive effects of separation and social alienation, that may be found in suicidal people at all stages of the life cycle. Consequently, much of what is said here is relevant to suicidal people of all ages, as well as to the suicidal older person.

Certain general principles of psychotherapy are intrinsic to the treatment of suicidal elderly persons and their families, despite differences among the therapies in theory, training, practice, and personality. Many of these principles are found in the writings of those who have successfully treated elderly patients with a major depression and related conditions. The reason for this is that other than myself, almost no one has written explicitly on psychotherapy with the suicidal elderly.

ASSESSMENT

Assessment of Risk

A comprehensive assessment is a primary requirement in the treatment of the suicidal elderly, culminating in a flexible treatment plan, the initial disposition (e.g., whether to hospitalize, what treatment methods or modalities to use, and what initial target symptoms to select), and preparations for follow-up.

Before any formal assessment can occur, the professional must recognize that a suicidal risk exists that must be addressed. The earlier the recognition of suicidal risk, the quicker the intervention, and the better the outcome. There is a point at which the suicidal process takes on a life of its own, escalating and building up to an almost inevitable conclusion. The professional is frequently not contacted or informed of the problem until it has reached the point at which it is difficult to arrest or reverse. For successful assessment as well as therapy, timing is of the essence.

Several excellent works on the assessment of the suicidal person are available (see Bongar, 1991), and everyone involved in diagnostic work with suicidal people should become familiar with these resources. I also recommend a little-known but stimulating article by Lettieri (1972), who developed separate risk factor scales for male and female and older and younger suicidal clients.

A systematic evaluation using the following formal demographic and clinical signs is an effective beginning for assessment. The greater the number of these indicators, the greater the risk. A striking finding with the suicidal elderly is the increase in the sheer number of danger signs that distinguish them from their younger counterparts. The risk factors fall into four major categories.

Ego-weakening factors   Ego-weakening risk factors include mental and physical illness, both chronic and acute; alcoholism; prolonged stress; and a failure to respond to treatment. They contain a strong biological component, in terms of either their origins or their effects. This is not to say they are only biological, however. Depression, for example, has been implicated as an almost universal component of suicide, especially in the elderly. Research has found many biochemical factors related to depression, including a significant correlation between the level of clinical depression and decreased functioning of the immune system, especially in the elderly (Herbert & Cohen, 1993). Yet, it is obvious that more than biology is at work when one considers that the vast majority of the depressed elderly do not attempt suicide. Furthermore, women are more often diagnosed as having a major depression than are men, but the suicide rate is much higher in men. Biology may be a necessary but not a sufficient explanation.

Social Factors   Social factors, such as living alone and having few friends or family contacts, are another category of risk factors for suicide. People who are isolated but comfortable with being alone are not at risk. The problem is with those who are isolated but need others. For these people, social isolation is a component of alienation. I have found that family dissension is typically behind the isolation.

Another factor is that many elderly individuals are socially isolated even when they are not physically alone. They are increasingly relegated to the periphery in social and family events. A minor but typical example is the statement, when there has been a crisis or event in the family, "Don't tell Grandma [or Grandpa, or whomever]." Group and family therapies are highly recommended for addressing this marginalization.

Psychodynamic Factors   Psychodynamic risk factors most often include stresses and strains related to loss, such as the death of a spouse. Major crises in the elderly also involve retirement, loss of work roles and activities, decreased income, and other events that lower self-esteem. An impending move to a nursing home is another such crisis. Especially vulnerable are those faced with a loss of independence for whom dependence is unacceptable. Any of these factors can precipitate a crisis.

As an example, I recall a 72-year-old engineer who retired and made plans to move to his country of origin. However, his plans led to severe conflicts with his wife, who had no intention to move. The man developed a wide variety of somatic symptoms and complaints. These were handled impersonally through a series of laboratory and magnetic imagery procedures, with no recognition of their possible depressive origin. The man committed suicide. It was his daughter who then came in for therapy.

Other variables include a previous history of suicide attempts in a depressed or otherwise symptomatic patient; a history of suicide in the family; and a variety of character traits such as stubbornness, denial of suicidal impulses, and help rejection (Clark, 1992).

Clinical Signs   Certain well-known verbal and non-verbal, behavioral, and characterological signs enable the educated or knowledgeable individual to detect a person at risk for suicide (Richman, 1993). Although these danger signs may be well known, many nonprofessionals lack the knowledge of how to respond to them or where to obtain help. In addition, there are often dynamic reasons for the family members' failure to respond or to obtain help.

The problem is not the identification of the danger signs but the fact that those involved react with panic and hopelessness or are too involved to take the distance necessary to see the danger. The disturbed communication patterns that are so important in the development of a suicidal act include not responding to or reporting suicidal messages.

For example, a 78-year-old depressed man told his 43-year-old son that he saw no reason for living and wanted to kill himself. "Can you give me one reason why I should live?" he asked. His son neither responded nor told anyone else of this conversation. His father committed suicide the next day.

The nonreporting of suicidal communications occurs at all ages; it can have a ripple effect leading to escalating resentments and tension. Chance (1992) described the great anger she experienced after the suicide of her son, Jim, after being told by her father that Jim had been telling him for a year of his suicidal feelings. The author may not have realized the universality of the phenomenon of the nonreporting of suicidal communications. Professionals need to devote more energy to improving not only the recognition of, but also the response to, such communications.

Assessment of Context

The assessment literature pays too little attention to the *context* in which suicide occurs, especially the family context. I have described the family evaluation process in detail elsewhere (Richman, 1986, 1993.) The primary social and family components to be assessed are described in the following sections. The family is not necessarily characterized by these traits all the time, but they are likely to be present at the time of a suicidal crisis.

Intolerance for Separation   An intolerance for separation is accompanied by an association of necessary change with loss, and an inability to grieve appropriately. The result is family dissension in three situations. First, in younger suicidal people, the suicidal situation may arise in connection with their efforts to separate from the family. With the older suicidal individual, the conflict is more frequently associated with an effort to maintain closeness and avoid separation.

Second, when an elderly family member becomes ill either physically or emotionally, and very often both, old, unresolved family conflicts are often aroused. The result is increased family dissension and alienation, and separations associated with family conflict.

Third, the upsurge of anger and resentment serves a defensive function, especially in the older suicidal person who is responding to the loss of a loved one. The younger members of the family, in my experience, are less able to tolerate death and the mourning process than older individuals, who are more openly grieving, as well as depressed. Anger and old resentments thus serve the additional purpose of a smokescreen to shield younger family members from their pain.

Role and Behavior Disturbance   A variety of disturbances in roles and behavior, such as double binds, sadomasochistic relationships, and intense rage combined with a death wish are often a context for a suicide attempt. Success in activities outside the family may be viewed as a threat, as are new friendships developed by family members. The fear they arouse is the same: the fear of loss.

The family's disapproval of and efforts to prevent new relationships even applies to the older suicidal person. I interviewed a 67-year-old woman whose family said they could not take care of her and she could not live with them but, nevertheless, forbade her to move in with a companion.

Such family reactions occur because any change in one member can be perceived as a potential threat to the entire family system, especially when the members already feel the system is under threat. That is why therapists must pay more attention to understanding and working with the family of a suicidal person.

Closed Family System   Melanie Klein (1935/1975) first developed the concept of splitting people into good and bad. This concept is helpful in understanding family relationships. A closed family system, whereby family members view the outside world as a danger to the integrity of their unit, is a major context for suicide and other major disturbances. The closed family system arises when the family members see the outside world as bad and the family as good. The splitting may continue within the family, with different persons assigned good or bad status. The setting is ripe for the development of favoritism, blaming, scapegoating, and other difficulties in roles and behavior.

Disturbed Intrafamily Communication   Intrafamily communication disturbances include an extreme secretiveness and covert or indirect messages concerning suicidal acts. Virtually every example of a suicide case discussed here included such problems in communication.

Intolerance Yet Compulsion for Crisis   An intolerance for crisis yet a compulsion to repeat old crises and create new ones is why the treatment of suicide is crisis oriented. What can be called a crisis repetition compulsion takes place, with the latest crisis built on earlier crises that are pushing for resolution. The past thus becomes part of the here and now. Consequently, in family meetings with the suicidal elderly, when anger erupts and unfinished business surfaces, there is an opportunity to heal old wounds.

Assessment of Assets

Assessment also includes evaluation of resources and recovery factors. These factors are the personal resources and abilities of the suicidal individual and the availability of social and family supports. Many elderly people's sense of self-worth and conviction that their continued existence is desirable are heavily dependent on the love and support of others. The list of recovery factors includes the suicidal person's actual or potential ability to understand and empathize, to relate, to benefit from experience, and to accept help. When these assets are not overtly present, a family interview is invaluable for determining their potential emergence. A family interview can also give a resistant patient the family's permission, as it were, to engage in individual therapy.

The family is not the only social resource. A major source of support is an interested, available, and caring professional health network. No matter how large his or her caseload, no health worker should become so impersonal that the actuality of the patient is lost.

The suicidal individual's resources and social supports are the basis of success in treatment. The suicidal elderly often know what is the best treatment for them, making use of their vast reservoir of experience. Most psychotherapists do not realize how much potential the suicidal aged possess for overcoming their depressed and despairing state. A thorough evaluation places these positive features in bold relief.

SOME RISKS OF RISK ASSESSMENT

Not picking up the presence of a serious suicide risk when it is present—making a false-negative assessment—is a prevailing problem in the assessment of suicide. I have found that serious danger signs of depression and suicide in the elderly are often disregarded and even laughed at as the foibles of old age. Clearly, the entire health profession needs to respect the wisdom as well as the needs of the elderly.

In addition, staff supervisors and consultants who are experienced in suicidology, gerontology, and family interviewing must be available. The importance of immediate treatment or crisis intervention must also be recognized. A parallel and much neglected requirement is the need for all health professionals to be adequately trained and experienced in recognizing signs of suicidal risk and responding to them appropriately.

A perennial and opposite "problem" is a false-positive evaluation—classifying someone as a high suicide risk who then spoils the statistics by not committing suicide. My response is, "Wonderful!" The failure of someone diagnosed as at high risk for suicide to commit suicide is not necessarily a failure of evaluation. Professionals do not predict a high risk in order to agree with the statistics. On the contrary, the goal of assessment should be to take the steps necessary to make the assessment false. The occurrence of false-positive evaluations may be higher in the elderly because as a group they are subject to more of the vicissitudes and life events statistically associated with suicide.

Another major risk that deserves more attention than it has received is a suicidal reaction to the reporting of the findings of the evaluation for suicide risk to the patient and family. Kobler and Stotland (1964) found that relatives often reacted with hopelessness and helplessness to the information that a family member was suicidal. Suicides have been precipitated because the meaning of the diagnosis of suicide risk and treatment recommendations was not explained to the patient and family. Not only the information, but also the meaning of the information, is part of the assessment process and must be explored.

Some patients and families react with irrational and primitive fears to a positive evaluation of suicide risk, precipitating a destructive act. To them, mental illness is an untreatable condition that means the threatened dissolution of the family system. They respond to diagnosis with terror, helplessness, hopelessness, despair, bringing on a crisis to which they react maladaptively. One result may be a covert and implacable resistance to treatment by the suicidal individual.

Obviously, the assessment of the suicidal person is part of an interaction that has profound repercussions for the person. It is often a deeply felt and anxiety-laden experience. Assessment and therapy shade off into each other, and the response to early or trial treatment interventions is also an aspect of assessment. The person's responses to early interventions help determine the disposition and the treatment plan for which the patient is ultimately most suited.

CRISIS INTERVENTION

Whatever the age of the actively suicidal person, treatment begins with crisis intervention. The components include establishment of rapport, assessment of suicidal risk, early stress reduction, determination of the disposition, development of a treatment plan, and intervention.

In the initial stage, rapport is more important than information gathering, although it is more accurate to say that the two take place concurrently. The most therapeutic attitude is to emphasize the realistic positive, without denying or avoiding conflicts and problems.

Emphasizing the positive means welcoming the turmoil and destructive interactions that frequently occur in the treatment of the suicidal person. The expression of rage, despair, and grief is remarkably difficult for the therapist to tolerate, especially when the elderly person in despair is blamed by the family for the situation. Nevertheless, such expressions provide the greatest opportunity for healing. Zuk's (1990) advice to family therapists applies to treatment of all suicidal persons: The therapist must be able to take the heat or get out of the kitchen.

The emotional upsets during the early interviews with suicidal patients and their families are *not* undesirable events to be prevented, but rather opportunities for the therapist to intervene and transform negative communications into positive ones. Accusations and expressions of rage and blame have a very different meaning in a therapist's office than they do at home. At some level, the participants in the family meeting are airing their thoughts, feelings, and grievances with a therapeutic intent.

How the therapist responds to these outbursts is crucial. The first principle of therapy with the family with a suicidal member is to maintain an attitude of positive emphasis and regard. For example, the therapist can listen to the blaming, scapegoating, and accusations with concern and interest. Then, at the right time, the therapist commends the participants for being so open with each other; they are good patients.

When outbursts, accusations, double-binding communications, and other seemingly destructive interchanges occur, they tell me that the patient will get better and the family more functional, because they have been more open and trusted me enough to let their guards down. It is the quiet and well-behaved family who have no problems—except that one of their members happens to be suicidal—that gives me cause to worry. However, I accept the family as it is, whatever the members say and do.

During the initial phase of the crisis intervention interview, I listen and encourage interaction between the suicidal person and family. During the second half of the crisis intervention interview, I intervene more actively. I monitor the major danger signs in the person and family, including the presence of depression and suicidal feelings, the exhaustion of resources, feelings of being burdened, and the expression of death wishes. Angry outbursts or interchanges between the suicidal person and the family, followed by monitoring and then procedures such as relabeling or reinterpretation constitute an effective series of procedures. At the end of the assessment interviews, and on the basis of all the data, I make a decision regarding the treatment plan and disposition.

One of the primary decisions made early in the process is whether to hospitalize. Although outpatient crisis intervention (e.g., as described by Langsley,

Kaplan, et al., 1968) may suffice, hospitalization may be necessary. The three major criteria on which the decision to hospitalize is based are (a) high levels of unresolved stress accompanied by symptoms of decompensating defenses and ego weakening in the suicidal person, (b) loss of impulse control in the suicidal person, and (c) the lack of a supportive family or social support system.

Clinical wisdom indicates that, when it occurs with the proper timing and skill, hospitalization can save lives. This is especially true when admission is performed in a competent and sensitive manner, the patient and family are adequately prepared, and contact with the family is maintained throughout the inpatient treatment.

However, hospitalization does not prevent all suicides. The population of hospitalized patients has one of the highest risks of suicide, so it is not surprising that a suicidal person who has been hospitalized may proceed to commit suicide. When a suicide does occur, it is essential to learn from such tragic events.

For example, a 76-year-old man was admitted to a hospital with the chief complaints of anxiety and suicidal ideation. After a few weeks, the hospital staff gave him a weekend pass to be home with his wife. He went home on Friday and jumped from the roof of their apartment house to his death.

The wife had made other plans for that weekend and had not wanted him home. She had earlier confided to a social worker that she felt trapped and had no choice but to spend time with her husband, and she felt that the hospital had manipulated her. Unfortunately, the social worker had not notified anyone of this conversation, and there had been no family discussion of the weekend pass.

Although the tragedy was not prevented, it may be hoped the hospital staff learned to evaluate properly not only the patient, but also the situation to which the patient returns. I cannot emphasize sufficiently that professionals must do more than mourn and declare that the death was inevitable. If we do not, the result may be more such deaths.

Most hospitals organize a meeting of the ward staff, and sometimes the patients, after a suicide has occurred on a ward. Such meetings should take place not only after a completed suicide, but after a suicide attempt as well. In either case, one meeting is not sufficient. The staff and therapists must be prepared for the cluster phenomenon, the tendency for suicidal acts to occur in bunches, and for one suicide to be followed by another or by other forms of symptomatic and disturbed behavior.

These recommendations extend beyond the hospital to the problem of suicide in all types of therapeutic practice. Suicide by a client or patient is a traumatic event for the therapist. Self-help groups for therapists when a suicide occurs can be enormously helpful and therapeutic, as they can be for family survivors of suicide. The groups can help turn the grief experience into a growth experience, which can help make for better therapists and fewer suicides.

THE THERAPEUTIC RELATIONSHIP

The therapeutic relationship includes a caring attitude and a commitment to the patient. That is why it is countertherapeutic for a therapist with suicidal patients to have too large a caseload. Because suicidal people and their families tend to be crisis prone, the therapist must be available when the crisis occurs. Continuity of care is part of this availability.

The importance of continuity is becoming increasingly recognized in all therapy. It is unfortunate, therefore, that many training institutions do not recognize its importance. Teaching centers often assign suicidal patients to trainees who, once a therapeutic relationship has been established, must leave. The relationship with the therapist should not become just another experience of separation and loss for the suicidal person.

What Is the Preferred Treatment Modality?

A positive doctor–patient relationship is necessary even when the treatment is exclusively biological. Individual, group, and family therapies, and often some combination of these, can all help restore social competence as well as individual functioning. Psychotherapy is valuable for establishing an intimate yet nonthreatening relationship with the suicidal person, who often feels alone, lost, and alienated.

There have been some efforts to devise treatment methods specifically for the suicidal person. The cognitive–behavioral therapy of Beck, Rush, Shaw, and Emery (1979) and the interpersonal therapy of Klerman, Weissman, Rounsaville, and Chevron (1984) were developed for the psychotherapy of depression. However, they also contain many features that are applicable to the treatment of suicidal persons. Gallagher and Thompson (1993) have addressed the use of cognitive–behavioral therapy for the suicidal elderly. The gist of their findings is that elderly suicidal patients responded positively and were well suited for cognitive–behavioral treatment.

The Menninger model was developed for the psychodynamic treatment of the younger suicidal patient (Richman & Eyman, 1990; Smith & Eyman, 1988), but the approach is equally applicable to the older patient. The model includes a sensitive awareness of transference and countertransference and the importance of a therapeutic environment with a therapist who is a good parent figure.

Maltsberger (1986) has made distinguished contributions to the treatment of suicidal people ever since the pioneering paper he coauthored on countertransference (Maltsberger & Buie, 1974). Recently, he applied an "ego deficit" model of suicide by the elderly, which recognizes the suicidal older person's need for support and outside resources (Maltsberger, 1991). A particularly positive feature of this model is its recognition of the importance of the therapist's warmth, encouragement, and availability.

Because the family often responds with fear and feelings of threat to the possibility of the suicidal member's engaging in individual therapy, and because of the intense alienation felt by the suicidal elderly, group therapy and family therapy are particularly valuable. They need not be used in place of individual therapy. On the contrary, I agree with Zimmerman and LaSorsa (1992) that a combination of procedures is most desirable.

What Is the Preferred Treatment Style?

Every skilled therapist develops the approach that works best for him or her. In my own work, I am client and family centered, and avoid being intrusive. I accept the patient and family as they are, and let them go at their own pace. Good timing, that is, knowing when to listen and when to intervene, is essential.

Two exceptions to client-centered principles are necessary when working with suicidal persons, however. First, the therapist is not neutral, but places him- or herself on the side of life and does not see suicide as a solution. Second, a thorough and competent assessment is necessary, combined with the continuing monitoring of potential risk factors and the application of tension reduction procedures. With these exceptions, the approach I take is the Rogerian approach, with its positive emphasis and acceptance.

The largely unconscious forces that complicate the transference and the therapeutic relationship include separation and death anxiety; a preoccupation with past, present, and future losses; unfinished bereavement; and the belief that the family must be protected from perceived threats to its integrity or existence. The resulting transference and countertransference manifestations are intrinsic to the success and failure of the therapeutic enterprise.

Cultivating Professional Skills

The qualities of the therapist who can work successfully with suicidal patients are similar to those required for success with patients in general. These include warmth, acceptance, accurate empathy, and genuineness (Truax & Carkhuff, 1967). In addition, the best therapists for suicidal patients are those who have gone through such an experience, have overcome their destructive and self-destructive urges, and have emerged stronger and more compassionate. This is similar to the observation that the best counselors for treating alcoholics are recovering alcoholics who have overcome their compulsion to drink. For the suicidal elderly patient, the best counselor is the one who is aware of the person's assets, no matter how buried or unavailable they may be at the moment; respects the person's wisdom and experience; and realizes how much he or she has to offer.

A prerequisite is for the therapist to represent a good parent. The inability of suicidal persons to tolerate separation, loss, and death touches on the earliest experiences of the infant–mother relationship. Consequently, the therapist, whether female or male, represents the good mother who will symbolically feed and love the suicidal patient and help him or her grow, mature, and develop. Suicidal people must also be treated by those who are trained in suicidology or are provided with competent supervision and consultation.

The therapist is well advised to expect stumbling blocks. The patient's seemingly paradoxical negative reaction to positive and successful experiences during treatment is actually a predictable reaction, regardless of the treatment modality or age of the patient. It occurs because successful therapy implies change, and change poses the threat of unbearable loss or separation that cannot be avoided.

Another stumbling block to establishing a therapeutic relationship is the myth of exclusiveness, the belief, often held by families, that there can be only one close relationship at a time. Therefore, the establishment of a working alliance and positive relationship with a suicidal person, without the involvement or permission of the family, is perceived as a threat, not a promise. Even when the treatment is exclusively individual, an initial interview that includes the family is important. The early reduction of separation and death anxiety will not prevent the negative therapeutic reaction, but it will facilitate success in its management.

CONCLUSION

I have surveyed the use of psychotherapy for the suicidal elderly person and its implications for teaching, treatment, and prevention. Treatment should be comprehensive and multidisciplinary, including the family and social network, as well as the individual. It must also include efforts to modify internalized social attitudes that are inimical to a caring and healing attitude toward ill, aged, and disabled persons.

Many people do not realize that suicidal states are treatable. Universal education and the cooperation of the news and popular media in disseminating information may become important suicide prevention measures. Professional training programs are necessary, but they are not sufficient. Outreach services and a creative use of volunteers are among the developments that hold promise for suicide prevention in the elderly.

It is my hope that health professionals will renew their commitment to healing and service rather than placing an emphasis upon reimbursement. The goal of our endeavors is not only to prevent death, but also to replace a self-destructive act with an act imbued with that touch of the divine in human affairs known as love.

REFERENCES

Beck, A. T., Rush, A. J., Shaw, B. R., & Emery, G. (1979). *Cognitive therapy of depression*. New York: Guilford Press.

Bongar, B. (1991). *The suicidal patient.* Washington, DC: American Psychological Association.

Chance, S. (1992). *Stronger than death.* New York: Norton.

Clark, D. (1992, April). *Narcissistic crises of aging and elderly suicide.* Presidential Address at the 25th Annual Conference of the American Association of Suicidology, Chicago.

Gallagher, D. E., & Thompson, L. W. (1993, April). *Cognitive behavior therapy with the suicidal elderly.* Paper presented at the 26th Annual Conference of the American Association of Suicidology, San Francisco.

Herbert, T. B., & Cohen, S. (1993). Depression and immunity: A meta-analytic review. *Psychological Bulletin, 113,* 472–486.

Klein, M. (1975). A contribution to the psychogenesis of manic-depressive states. *Love, guilt, and reparation and other works. 1921–1945* (pp. 262–289). New York: Delacorte Press Seymour Lawrence. (Original work published in 1935)

Klerman, G. L., Weissman, M. M., Rounsaville, B. J., & Chevron, E. S. (1984). *Interpersonal psychotherapy of depression.* New York: Basic Books.

Kobler, A. L., & Stotland, E. (1964). *The end of hope.* New York: Free Press.

Langsley, D. G., Kaplan, D. M., et al. (1968). *The treatment of families in crisis.* Orlando, FL: Grune & Stratton.

Lettieri, D. J. (1972). Suicide in the aging: Empirical prediction of suicidal risk among the aging. *Journal of Geriatric Psychiatry, 6,* 7–42.

Maltsberger, J. T. (1986). *Suicide risks: The formulation of clinical judgment.* New York: New York University Press.

Maltsberger, J. T. (1991). Psychotherapy with older suicidal patients. *Journal of Geriatric Psychiatry, 24,* 217–234.

Maltsberger, J. T., & Buie, D. H. (1974). Countertransference hate in the treatment of suicidal patients. *Archives of General Psychiatry, 30,* 625–633.

Richman, J. (1986). *Family therapy with suicidal persons.* New York: Springer Publishing Company.

Richman, J. (1993). *Preventing elderly suicide: Overcoming personal despair, professional neglect, and social bias.* New York: Springer Publishing Company.

Richman, J., & Eyman, J. R. (1990). Psychotherapy of suicide: Individual, group, and family approaches. In D. Lester (Ed.), *Current concepts of suicide* (pp. 139–158). Philadelphia: Charles Press.

Smith, K., & Eyman, J. (1988). Ego structure and object differentiation in suicidal patients. In H. Lerner & P. Lerner (Eds.), *Primitive mental states and the Rorschach* (pp. 175–202). Madison, CT: International Universities Press.

Truax, C. G., & Carkhuf, R. R. (1967). *Toward effective counseling and psychotherapy: Training and practice.* Chicago: Aldine.

Zimmerman, J. K., & LaSorsa, V. A. (1992, April). *Being the family's therapist: An integrative approach.* Paper presented at the 25th Annual Conference of the American Association of Suicidology, Chicago.

Zuk, G. H. (1990). Conflict cycle in family therapy. *The Family Psychologist, 6*(3), 38, 45.

Chapter 9

Gender Issues in the Treatment of Suicidal Individuals

Silvia Sara Canetto

Historically, the literature on the treatment of suicidal behavior has not given explicit consideration to gender issues (e.g., Birtchnell, 1983; Kiev, 1975; R. S. Mintz, 1961; Moss & Hamilton, 1956; Salkovskis, Atha, & Storer, 1990). There are, however, several important reasons for considering the influence of gender in the treatment of suicidal individuals. First, women's patterns of suicidal behavior are different from those of men (Canetto, 1991; Canetto & Lester, in press). Second, reasons for suicidal behavior are often assumed to vary by gender (for reviews, see Canetto, 1992–93; Kushner, 1985; Kushner, in press). Third, gender has been recognized as having an impact on the dynamics of psychotherapy (Bograd, 1990; Brown, 1986, 1990; Hare-Mustin, 1987; Kaplan, 1979, 1987; Lerner, 1984; L. B. Mintz & O'Neil, 1990; Sherman, 1980; Wilcox & Forrest, 1992).

This review of the literature focuses on gender issues relevant to psychotherapy with suicidal adults. First, patterns of suicidal ideation and behaviors in women and in men are reviewed. Differences and similarities between women and men in motivations for suicide are then discussed. Finally, gender issues bearing on the initiation and goals of psychological treatment are addressed.

I am grateful to Jeremy Gersovitz, Patricia Kaminski, Tammy Maglia, and David Wohl for comments and suggestions. I also thank the editors for their input.

115

Throughout this discussion, suicidal behaviors are defined in terms of outcome rather than intent. The term *nonfatal suicidal behavior* is used to refer to suicidal acts that did not result in deaths, in lieu of the more common *suicide attempt; fatal suicidal behavior* is used to refer to suicidal acts that resulted in death. One advantage of this descriptive nomenclature is that it does not make assumptions about the suicidal person's intent. Not all persons who engage in nonfatal suicide acts actually wish to survive; conversely, not all suicidal deaths are intended. The term *suicidal behavior* is used to refer to either fatal or nonfatal suicidal behavior, or whenever outcome information is not available (see Canetto, 1992, Lester, 1989, for discussions of suicidal behavior terminology).

GENDER AND THE EPIDEMIOLOGY OF SUICIDAL IDEATION AND BEHAVIORS

According to a survey of suicidal feelings in the general population of the United States (Paykel, Myers, Lindenthal, & Tanner, 1974), suicidal ideation is more prevalent among women than among men. Individuals experiencing suicidal feelings are typically socially isolated and have experienced a number of recent stressful events. In addition, in a recent study of high school students (ages 14–19), girls reported greater suicidal ideation than did boys (Rich, Kirkpatrick-Smith, Bonner, & Jans, 1992).

Women also commit a greater number of suicidal (fatal and nonfatal) acts than do men (Lester, 1990). Women's suicidal behavior is typically nonfatal (for recent reviews, see Canetto, 1991, 1992–93; Canetto & Lester, in press; Jack, 1992). For example, in a review of national and international studies, Weissman (1974) found that women outnumbered men in rates of nonfatal suicidal behavior by an average ratio of 2:1 in all industrialized countries surveyed, except Poland and India. Similarly, a multicenter World Health Organization/European survey (Platt et al., 1992) of nonfatal suicidal behavior in selected European catchment areas during 1989 revealed that women were more likely to engage in acts of nonfatal suicidal behavior than were men in all catchment areas except one (Helsinki).

In the United States, the typical person who survives a suicidal act is a depressed European-American woman under the age of 30 who is of low socioeconomic status and educational achievement, and who has a history of troubled personal relationships (Canetto & Lester, in press; Weissman, 1974). Rates of nonfatal suicidal behavior diminish with age (Wilson, 1981). Women with alcohol abuse problems and a history of paternal alcoholism have higher rates of nonfatal suicidal behavior than do nonalcoholic women of similar age and socioeconomic status (Gomberg, 1989).

The choice of suicide method is influenced by cultural and historical circumstances (Marks & Abernathy, 1974; Marks & Stokes, 1976). Familiarity and accessibility play a role. The method most frequently used in acts of nonfatal suicidal behavior is the ingestion of medically prescribed psychotropic drugs. This choice of suicidal method is not surprising, given that in many countries, including the United States, women are more likely to be prescribed and to take psychotropic drugs, especially sedative-hypnotics (Cooperstock, 1982; Fidell, 1982).

The phenomenon of nonfatal suicidal behavior is sizable. Linehan (1981) estimated that in the United States, 50,000–200,000 persons engage in acts of nonfatal suicidal behavior per year, a figure two to eight times greater than the number of fatal suicidal acts. McIntosh (1985) suggested that as many as 5,000,000 persons had engaged at some time in acts of nonfatal suicidal behavior. According to Jack (1992), "every year in Great Britain as many as 215,000 people deliberately poison themselves with drugs" (p. 1).

A greater number of deaths by suicide is typically found among men than among women (for a recent review of official national and international suicide mortality statistics, see Diekstra, 1990). In the United States, men are three times more likely than women to die from suicide (Frederick, 1978; McIntosh & Jewell, 1986).

The typical suicide fatality in the United States is an unmarried (single, separated, divorced, or widowed), European-American man, age 60 or older, who is unemployed or retired and socially isolated (Canetto, 1992; Stenback, 1980). In recent decades, the rate of death by suicide has been declining among elderly men and increasing among young adult men (McCall, 1991). The well-known association between suicidal behavior and alcohol abuse (Frances, Franklin, & Flavin, 1987; Petronis, Samuels, Moscicki, & Anthony, 1990) may be particularly significant for men, who are more likely to be diagnosed as having an alcohol disorder than are women (Russo, 1990). For some men, alcoholism may be a form of indirect suicidal behavior (Canetto, 1991).

As noted above, suicide methods are influenced by cultural and historical circumstances. In the United States, guns are the method most frequently used in fatal suicidal acts (Frederick, 1978), especially among males (McIntosh & Santos, 1985–86). This is not surprising, given that males are more likely to be socialized in the handling of firearms. Variations in gender and ethnic socialization regarding firearms appear to influence the choice of suicide method. For example, Marks and Abernathy (1974) found that firearms were the most common method of suicide for both women and men living in the southern regions of the United States. Among acculturated cohorts of Asian-Americans, suicidal deaths by firearms are replacing suicidal deaths by hanging (McIntosh & Santos, 1985–86).

According to official national statistics for 1988, men's rate of mortality by suicide was 20.1 per 100,000, compared with women's rate of 5 per 100,000 (National Center for Health Statistics, 1990). Because men's suicide mortality rate reaches its highest level in late life, whereas women's suicide mortality rate decreases after midlife, the gender differential is greatest during late adulthood and smallest at midlife (usually at ages 45–54) (McIntosh, 1991, 1992). The 1988 rate for men age 65 or older was 41.9, compared with 6.6 per 100,000 for elderly women (McIntosh, 1992).

GENDER AND THE REASONS FOR SUICIDAL BEHAVIOR

Historically, the reasons for suicidal behavior have been assumed to vary by gender (Canetto, 1992–93; Kushner, 1985, in press). In this section, theories and evidence regarding the motivations for suicidal behavior in women and men are reviewed.

Why Are Women Suicidal?

Two themes predominate in the literature on women's suicidal behavior (for reviews, see Canetto, 1992–93; Canetto & Feldman, 1993; Cloward & Piven, 1979; Kushner, 1985, in press). First, it is assumed that women become suicidal in response to problems in personal relationships. Second, it is postulated that suicidal women pathologically identify with their relationships. Women's suicidal acts are often conceptualized as private, emotional, irrational responses to relationship troubles. A woman's suicide is seen as a symptom of individual psychopathology, which is usually defined as an immature, passive, dependent, hysterical, or borderline personality.

Recent reviews of the literature on women's nonfatal suicidal behavior (Canetto, 1992–93; Canetto & Lester, in press; Jack, 1992; Linehan, 1981), however, reveal a different picture. The recurring themes in suicidal women's lives appear to be not love and dependence, but socioeconomic disadvantage, unemployment, hostile relationships, and a history of suicidal behavior among family and friends. With respect to socioeconomic disadvantage, Jack (1992) noted that in Western societies, self-poisoning is a "predominantly working class, female phenomenon" (p. 3). Canetto (1992–93), Canetto and Lester (in press), and Linehan (1981) cited evidence indicating that unemployment enhances the risk for nonfatal suicidal behavior in women. The same authors also described studies suggesting that women who engage in nonfatal suicidal behavior often experience hostility and even physical violence in their personal relationships. Finally, Jack and Linehan reported evidence of a higher than expected incidence of suicidal behaviors among family and friends of suicidal individuals. According to Linehan, "exposure to suicidal models may be important in terms of acquisition of the suicidal response and development of outcome expectations" (p. 241). For some individuals, Jack stated, self-poisoning may represent " 'a language' . . . a generally well understood signal" (p. 24) through which distress is communicated.

Why Are Men Suicidal?

The predominant themes in the literature on men's suicidal behavior (for reviews, Canetto, 1992, 1992–93, 1994; Kushner, in press) are, first, that men become suicidal in response to external impersonal stresses (e.g., retirement) and, second, that men's suicides can be rational. Men's suicidal acts are often conceptualized as understandable responses to powerful social or physical calamities or, as Kushner (1985) put it, as "a barometer of national economic and social well being" (p. 541). Men's suicidal acts may even be assumed to be a sign of strength. For example, in a study of attitudes toward suicidal behavior among young adults by Deluty (1988–89), men's committing suicide was rated as less foolish and less weak than women's committing suicide. In sum, men who kill themselves may be portrayed as heroic victims of powerful negative circumstances.

Recent reviews of the literature (Canetto, 1992, 1992–93, in press) highlight some neglected, but recurring, features of men's suicidal behavior. One is that men who kill themselves are often socially isolated. Elsewhere, I have suggested that social isolation in older men—the age cohort most vulnerable to death by suicide—may be the result of a lifetime lack of relationship responsibilities (i.e., being responsible for caring for and nurturing others), rather than simply the outcome of retirement (Canetto, 1992). Thus, the key to older men's survival may not be deferred retirement, as some have proposed (e.g., Lyons, 1984), but a lifetime of relationship responsibilities: If a man feels responsible for another person's well-being, he may reject suicide if only to avoid causing distress to another person.

Another observation emerging from a recent retrospective study (Clark, 1991, 1992) of elderly (mostly male) fatal suicidal behavior is that these men had a fundamental and persistent incapacity to adapt to ordinary life events. This observation challenges the long-held view that suicidal behavior in men is mostly a function of overwhelmingly stressful external events. Thus, questions of personality style may need to be addressed when assessing the risk for suicidal behavior in men.

GENDER AND PSYCHOLOGICAL TREATMENT

Gender and the Initiation of Psychological Treatment

Women are more likely than men to admit feeling suicidal and to engage in nonfatal acts of suicidal behavior. Women also make up the majority of those who contact suicide prevention services (Heilig, 1968; Tekavcic-Grad, Farberow, Zavasnik, Mocnik, & Korenjak, 1988; Wolfersdorf, Nelson, & Dalton-Taylor, 1989). Although women in general are more likely than men to use outpatient psychotherapy (see Russo, 1990, for a review), psychotherapists may not be the first care providers women contact before acting out their suicidal ideation. According to a British study (Hawton & Blackstock, 1976), physicians were the health professionals most commonly visited by women who later (within a month of the visit) poisoned themselves. Most of these women had reported depression and family difficulties and many had been prescribed psychotropic drugs (usually tranquilizers and sedatives), which they used to overdose on.

Although men are less likely than women to contact suicide prevention centers, they often seek, as women do, the attention of medical professionals before engaging in a suicidal act. For example, in several studies (e.g., Barraclough, 1971; Miller, 1978) a majority of elderly men who committed suicide visited their physicians within a month of killing themselves, often with a report of vague physical complaints (Essa & Howell-Burke, 1984; Victoroff, 1984). Given the association between suicidal behavior and alcoholism (Frances et al., 1987; Petronis et al., 1990), and the fact that men predominate among inpatients diagnosed with an alcohol disorder (Russo, 1990), some suicidal men may be found among those hospitalized for alcoholism treatment.

In sum, for most individuals, it is the general physician who has the first chance to assess suicidal intention and to make a referral for treatment. Women call suicide prevention centers and use outpatient psychotherapy more frequently than do men, whereas men are more likely to use inpatient alcohol disorder facilities than women. By inference, the suicidal person in outpatient psychotherapy is likely to be a woman. Therefore, outpatient psychotherapists may be more familiar with the phenomenology of women's suicidal ideation and behavior than with men's. Outpatient psychotherapists assessing suicidal risk in women should take into consideration that many women have access to potentially lethal prescription drugs. On the other hand, psychotherapists assessing suicidal risk in men should be mindful that men may not report their suicidal feelings or actions for fear of social disapproval (Rich et al., 1992) and the perceived femininity of nonfatal suicidal behavior (for reviews, see Canetto, 1992–93, in press). Finally, because other men are most critical of men who survive a suicidal act (Canetto, 1992–93, in press), male clinicians may be at a greater disadvantage than female clinicians in trying to assess suicidal ideation and behavior in male clients because suicidal male clients may fear that the male clinician will view them as unmasculine.

Gender and the Goals of Psychological Treatment

Psychotherapists' assumptions about the women's and men's natures and about the gender dynamics of suicidal behaviors are likely to have a strong influence on many aspects of psychotherapy. Of interest is how assumptions about gender affect the goals psychotherapists set in their treatment of suicidal women and men.

Therapists may define different treatment goals for women and men on the basis of what they consider "natural" for women and men. As Turner and Troll (1982) noted, the "goals of treatment are, of course, inseparable from norms of appropriate sex-role behavior" (p. 424). Uncritical adoption of cultural norms regarding "appropriate sex role behavior" may lead to a failure to discuss with clients the maladaptive consequences of rigid conformity to masculinity and femininity. For example, therapists may not recognize or question their suicidal male clients' intense self-absorption, stoicism, overachievement, or disengagement from family responsibilities, because these behaviors may strike them as quite natural in men. Psychotherapists who conceptualize certain thoughts and behaviors as unfeminine or unmasculine may exacerbate their clients' conflicts and inhibitions about gender identity. Finally, psychotherapists who label some suicidal behaviors as manipulative (e.g., Stengel, 1964) fail to recognize that suicidal individuals, especially suicidal women, often find themselves in relationships in which their ability to negotiate is progressively restricted until suicide becomes the only culturally sanctioned behavior possible (Canetto & Feldman, 1993; Canetto, Feldman, & Lupei, 1989; Counts, 1987; Kirsch, 1982; Sefa-Dedeh & Canetto, 1992).

Psychotherapists' assumptions about the gender dynamics of suicidal behaviors also affect the goals of treatment. As discussed earlier, it is commonly assumed in the clinical literature that women are suicidal because of problems and losses in relationships. It is also assumed that their personality is to blame for the relationship problems. Psychotherapists who uncritically subscribe to these assumptions may recommend that suicidal women aim solely at personal change through individual insight-oriented psychotherapy (e.g., Simpson, 1976). If this intervention goal is promoted exclusively, it can have negative consequences for a suicidal woman. First, the woman's often highly developed inward focus and self-critical attitude may be reinforced, thereby enhancing depression (Nolen-Hoeksema, 1987). Second, individual psychotherapy may perpetuate the suicidal woman's social isolation, a condition that is associated with increased risk for suicidal ideation and behaviors (Lettieri, 1974; Paykel et al., 1974). Third, the external factors that contribute to suicide behavior, including unemployment and hostility from significant others, may remain unrecognized and unaddressed. It is unlikely that mental health professionals will direct a suicidal woman toward potentially therapeutic opportunities, such as education or employment, or seek to assess the quality of her interpersonal environments, if they believe that the woman's main problem is her personality.

The most common assumption in the clinical literature is that men's suicidal behavior is primarily a response to external, impersonal events such as loss of income, employment, or health. Psychotherapists who uncritically adopt these assumptions may recommend to their male suicidal clients that they attempt to change their external circumstances, for example, by regaining employment. If promoted exclusively, such intervention goals can have negative consequences for the suicidal man. First, the psychotherapist's focus on external, impersonal factors may make it difficult for the man to voice his relationship concerns and needs. Second, an external orientation in psychotherapy may reinforce the man's socially supported emotional detachment and focus on outward action (L. B. Mintz & O'Neil, 1990; O'Neil, 1981; Pasick, Gordon, & Meth, 1990), at a time when external solutions, such as regaining employment, may simply be unfeasible. Third, the personal and interpersonal factors contributing to the man's suicidal behavior may remain unrecognized and unaddressed. It is unlikely that mental health professionals will encourage their suicidal male clients to focus on their emotional growth and personal relationships if they believe that employment and income are of primary importance to a man's well-being.

CONCLUSION

Gender socialization experiences affect the way people think, feel, and behave (Brown, 1986, 1990; Kaplan, 1979, 1987; L. B. Mintz & O'Neil, 1990). Gender socialization experiences have an impact on both clients and counselors.

Competent and effective psychological treatment should include consideration of how gender socialization influences a client's suicidal behavior. Psychotherapists working with suicidal individuals should be informed about gender patterns in the epidemiology of suicidal behaviors. Psychotherapists should also be aware of gender theories of suicidal behavior, and that these theories have often overlooked the similarities in the motivations and needs of suicidal women and men.

Sensitivity to gender issues should translate to an awareness of gender dynamics in treatment, namely, the initiation of care and the establishment of the goals of therapy. The gender-sensitive clinician ensures that the goals of psychotherapy are not dictated by stereotyped notions of femininity and masculinity, nor by biased assumptions about the needs of suicidal women and men.

REFERENCES

Barraclough, B. M. (1971). Suicide in the elderly. In D. W. Kay & A. Walk (Eds.), *Recent developments in psychogeriatrics* (pp. 87–97). Ashford, England: Hedley.

Birtchnell, J. (1983). Psychotherapeutic considerations in the management of the suicidal patient. *American Journal of Psychotherapy, 37*, 24–36.

Bograd, M. (1990, May/June). Women treating men. *The Family Therapy Networker*, pp. 54–58.

Brown, L. S. (1986). Gender-role analysis: A neglected component of psychological assessment. *Psychotherapy, 23*, 243–248.

Brown, L. S. (1990). Taking account of gender in the clinical assessment interview. *Professional Psychology: Research and Practice, 21*, 12–17.

Canetto, S. S. (1991). Gender roles, suicide attempts, and substance abuse. *Journal of Psychology, 125*, 605–620.

Canetto, S. S. (1992). Gender and suicide in the elderly. *Suicide and Life-Threatening Behavior, 22*, 80–97.

Canetto, S. S. (1992–93). She died for love and he for glory: Gender myths of suicidal behavior. *Omega, 26*, 1–17.

Canetto, S. S. (1994). Gender issues in counseling the suicidal elderly. In D. Lester & M. Tallmer (Eds.), *Now I lay me down: Suicide in the elderly* (pp. 88–105). Philadelphia: Charles Press.

Canetto, S. S. (in press). Elderly women and suicidal behavior. In S. S. Canetto, & D. Lester (Eds.), *Women and suicidal behavior*. New York: Springer.

Canetto, S. S., & Feldman, L. B. (1993). Overt and covert dependence in suicidal women and their male partners. *Omega, 27*, 177–194.

Canetto, S. S., Feldman, L. B., & Lupei, R. A. (1989). Suicidal persons and their partners: Individual and interpersonal dynamics. *Suicide and Life-Threatening Behavior, 19*, 237–248.

Canetto, S. S., & Lester, D. (in press). The epidemiology of women's suicidal behavior. In S. S. Canetto & D. Lester (Eds.), *Women and suicidal behavior*. New York: Springer.

Clark, D. C. (1991, January). *Suicide among the elderly*. Unpublished final report to the AARP Andrus Foundation, Rush Presbyterian–St. Luke's Medical Center, Chicago.

Clark, D. C. (1992, April). *Narcissistic crises of aging and suicidal despair*. Paper presented at the 25th Annual Conference of the American Association of Suicidology, Chicago.

Cloward, R. A., & Piven, F. F. (1979). Hidden protest: The channeling of female innovation and resistance. *Signs: Journal of Women in Culture and Society, 4*, 651–669.

Cooperstock, R. (1982). Research on psychotropic drug use: A review of findings and methods. *Social Science and Medicine, 16*, 1179–1196.

Counts, D. A. (1987). Female suicide and wife abuse: A cross-cultural perspective. *Suicide and Life-Threatening Behavior, 17*, 194–204.

Deluty, R. L. (1988–89). Factors affecting the acceptability of suicide. *Omega, 19*, 315–326.

Diekstra, R. F. W. (1990). An international perspective on the epidemiology and prevention of suicide. In S. J. Blumenthal & D. J. Kupfer (Eds.), *Suicide over the life cycle: Risk factors, assessment, and treatment of suicidal patients* (pp. 533–569). Washington, DC: American Psychiatric Press.

Essa, M., & Howell-Burke, D. (1984). Toward reducing the morbidity and mortality of the elderly bereaved. *Nebraska Medical Journal, 69*, 272–274.

Fidell, L. S. (1982). Gender and drug use and abuse. In I. Al-Issa (Ed.), *Gender and psychopathology* (pp. 221–236). San Diego, CA: Academic Press.

Frances, R. J., Franklin, J., & Flavin, D. K. (1987). Suicide and alcoholism. *American Journal of Alcohol and Drug Abuse, 13*, 327–341.

Frederick, C. J. (1978). Current trends in suicidal behavior in the United States. *American Journal of Psychotherapy, 32*, 172–200.

Gomberg, E. S. L. (1989). Suicide risk among women with alcohol problems. *American Journal of Public Health, 79,* 1363–1365.

Hare-Mustin, R. (1987). The problem of gender in family therapy theory. *Family Process, 26,* 15–27.

Hawton, K., & Blackstock, E. (1976). General aspects of self-poisoning and self-injury. *Psychological Medicine, 6,* 571–575.

Heilig, S. M. (1968). The Los Angeles Suicide Prevention Center. In N. L. Farberow (Ed.), *Proceedings of the Fourth International Conference for Suicide Prevention* (pp. 18–21). Los Angeles: Delmar.

Jack, R. L. (1992). *Women and attempted suicide.* Hillsdale, NJ: Erlbaum.

Kaplan, A. G. (1979). Toward an analysis of sex-role related issues in the therapeutic relationship. *Psychiatry, 42,* 112–120.

Kaplan, A. G. (1987). Reflections on gender and psychotherapy. In M. Braude (Ed.), *Women, power and therapy* (pp. 11–24). New York: Haworth Press.

Kiev, A. (1975). Psychotherapeutic strategies in the management of depressed and suicidal patients. *American Journal of Psychotherapy, 29,* 245–355.

Kirsch, N. L. (1982). Attempted suicide and restrictions in the eligibility to negotiate personal characteristics. *Advances in Descriptive Psychology, 2,* 249–274.

Kushner, H. I. (1985). Women and suicide in historical perspective. *Signs: Journal of Women in Culture and Society, 10,* 537–552.

Kushner, H. I. (in press). Women and suicidal behavior: Epidemiology, gender and lethality in historical perspective. In S. S. Canetto & D. Lester (Eds.), *Women and suicidal behavior.* New York: Springer.

Lerner, H. E. (1984). Special issues for women in psychotherapy. In P. Perry Rieker & E. H. Carmen (Eds.), *The gender gap in psychotherapy* (pp. 271–284). New York: Plenum.

Lester, D. (1989). The study of suicide from a feminist perspective. *Crisis, 11,* 38–43.

Lester, D. (1990). If women are more often depressed, why don't more of them kill themselves? *Psychological Reports, 66,* 258.

Lettieri, D. (1974). Suicidal death prediction scales. In A. T. Beck, H. L. P. Resnick, & D. J. Lettieri (Eds.), *The prediction of suicide* (pp. 163–192). Bowie, MD: Charles Press.

Linehan, M. M. (1981). A social-behavioral analysis of suicide and parasuicide: Implications for clinical assessment and treatment. In J. F. Clarkin & H. I. Glazer (Eds.), *Depression: Behavioral and directive intervention strategies* (pp. 229–294). New York: Garland Press.

Lyons, M. J. (1984). Suicide in later life: Some putative causes with implications for prevention. *Journal of Community Psychology, 12,* 379–388.

Marks, A., & Abernathy, T. (1974). Toward a sociocultural perspective on means of self-destruction. *Suicide and Life-Threatening Behavior, 4,* 3–17.

Marks, A., & Stokes, C. S. (1976). Socialization, firearms and suicide. *Social Problems, 5,* 622–639.

McCall, P. L. (1991). Adolescent and elderly white male suicide trends: Evidence of changing well-being? *Journal of Gerontology, 46,* S43–S51.

McIntosh, J. L. (1985). *Research on suicide: A bibliography.* New York: Greenwood Press.

McIntosh, J. L. (1991). Middle-age suicide: A literature review and epidemiological study. *Death Studies, 15,* 21–37.

McIntosh, J. L. (1992). Epidemiology of suicide in the elderly. *Suicide and Life-Threatening Behavior, 22,* 15–33.

McIntosh, J. L., & Jewell, B. J. (1986). Sex differences trends in completed suicide. *Suicide and Life-Threatening Behavior, 16,* 16–27.

McIntosh, J. L., & Santos, J. F. (1985–86). Methods of suicide by age: Sex and race differences among the young and old. *International Journal of Aging and Human Development, 22,* 123–139.

Miller, M. (1978). Geriatric suicide: The Arizona study. *The Gerontologist, 18,* 488–495.

Mintz, L. B., & O'Neil, J. M. (1990). Gender roles, sex, and the process of psychotherapy: Many questions and few answers. *Journal of Counseling and Development, 68,* 381–387.

Mintz, R. S. (1961). Psychotherapy of the suicidal patient. *American Journal of Psychotherapy, 15,* 348–350.

Moss, L. M., & Hamilton, D. M. (1956). Psychotherapy of the suicidal patient. *American Journal of Psychiatry, 112,* 814–820.

National Center for Health Statistics. (1990). Advance report of final mortality statistics, 1988. *NCHS Monthly Statistics Report, 39* (7, Suppl.), 37–38.

Nolen-Hoeksema, S. (1987). Sex differences in unipolar depression: Evidence and theory. *Psychological Bulletin, 101,* 259–282.

O'Neil, J. M. (1981). Patterns of gender role conflict and strain: Sexism and fear of femininity in men's lives. *Personnel and Guidance Journal, 60,* 203–210.

Pasick, R. R., Gordon, S., & Meth, R. L. (1990). Helping men understand themselves. In R. L. Meth & R. S. Pasick (Eds.), *Men in therapy* (pp. 152–181). New York: Guilford Press.

Paykel, E. S., Myers, J. K., Lindenthal, J. J., & Tanner, J. (1974). Suicidal feelings in the general population: A prevalence study. *British Journal of Psychiatry, 124,* 460–469.

Petronis, K. R., Samuels, J. F., Moscicki, E. K., & Anthony, J. C. (1990). An epidemiologic investigation of potential risk factors for suicide attempts. *Social Psychiatry and Psychiatric Epidemiology, 25,* 193–199.

Platt, S., Bille-Brahe, U., Kerkhof, A., Schmidtke, A., Bjerke, T., Crepet, P., De Leo, D., Haring, C., Lonnqvuist, J., Michel, K., Philippe, A., Pommereau, X., Querejeta, I., Salander-Renberg, E., Temesvary, B., Wasserman, D., & Sampaio Faria, J. (1992). Parasuicide in Europe: The WHO/EURO multicentre study on parasuicide. I. Introduction and preliminary analysis for 1989. *Acta Psychiatrica Scandinavica, 85,* 97–104.

Rich, A. R., Kirkpatrick-Smith, J., Bonner, R. L., & Jans, F. (1992). Gender differences in the psychosocial correlates of suicidal ideation among adolescents. *Suicide and Life-Threatening Behavior, 22,* 364–373.

Russo, N. F. (1990). Overview: Forging research priorities for women's mental health. *American Psychologist, 45,* 368–373.

Salkovskis, P. M., Atha, C., & Storer, D. (1990). Cognitive-behavioural problem solving in the treatment of patients who repeatedly attempt suicide: A controlled trial. *British Journal of Psychiatry, 157,* 871–876.

Sefa-Dedeh, A., & Canetto, S. S. (1992). Women, family and suicidal behavior in Ghana. In U. W. Gielen, L. L. Adler, & N. Milgram (Eds.), *Psychology in international perspective* (pp. 299–309). Amsterdam: Swets & Zetlinger.

Sherman, J. A. (1980). Therapist attitudes and sex-role stereotyping. In A. Brodsky & R. Hare-Mustin (Eds.), *Women and psychotherapy* (pp. 35–66). New York: Guilford Press.

Simpson, M. A. (1976). Self-mutilation and suicide. In E. S. Shneidman (Ed.), *Suicidology: Contemporary developments* (pp. 281–315). New York: Grune & Stratton.

Stenback, A. (1980). Depression and suicidal behavior in old age. In J. E. Birren & B. Sloane (Eds.), *Handbook of mental health and aging* (pp. 616–652). Englewood Cliffs, NJ: Prentice Hall.

Stengel, E. (1964). *Suicide and attempted suicide.* Harmondsworth, England: Penguin.

Tekavcic-Grad, O., Farberow, N. L., Zavasnik, A., Mocnik, M., & Korenjak, R. (1988). Comparison of the two telephone crisis lines in Los Angeles (USA) and in Ljubljana (Yugoslavia). *Crisis, 9,* 146–157.

Turner, B. F., & Troll, L. (1982). Sex differences in psychotherapy with older people. *Psychotherapy: Theory, Research and Practice, 19,* 419–428.

Victoroff, V. M. (1984). Depression in the elderly. *Ohio State Medical Journal, 80,* 180–187.

Weissman, M. M. (1974). The epidemiology of suicide attempts, 1960 to 1971. *Archives of General Psychiatry, 30,* 737–746.

Wilcox, D. W., & Forrest, L. (1992). The problems of men and counseling: Gender bias or gender truth? *Journal of Mental Health Counseling, 14,* 291–304.

Wilson, M. (1981). Suicidal behavior: Toward an explanation of differences in female and male rates. *Suicide and Life-Threatening Behavior, 11,* 131–139.

Wolfersdorf, M., Nelson, F., & Dalton-Taylor, B. (1989). Who calls? A comparison of callers of the telephone service at the Suicide Prevention Center, Los Angeles, CA, USA, and the callers of the "Telephonseelsorge," Ravensburg, FRG. *European Journal of Psychiatry, 3,* 33–48.

Chapter 10

Suicide and Terminal Illness

Peter M. Marzuk

Until recently, suicide in terminally ill patients was not well studied, both because the concept of suicide in the end stages of life was poorly defined and because suicide prevention had little meaning for those who would die in a few months anyway. In recent years, however, the study of suicide in the terminally ill has radically evolved as a result of three important trends that are likely to alter profoundly the field of suicide research in general. First, through earlier diagnosis and improved palliative care, many terminal illnesses are becoming more chronic, revolutionizing the concept of terminality. Thus, many patients with illnesses such as AIDS and cancer are living longer and dying more protracted deaths. Second, the euthanasia movement, through the efforts of the Hemlock Society and individuals such as Dr. Jack Kevorkian, has rekindled the public's interest in physician-assisted suicide and voluntary euthanasia among the terminally ill. Third, the development of serologic tests to diagnose terminal illnesses such as AIDS or Huntington's disease at an early, asymptomatic phase has raised concern about the suicide potential in populations at risk for these diseases.

This research was supported in part by an Aaron Diamond grant and a National Institute on Drug Abuse Grant DA-06534.

METHODOLOGICAL ISSUES

It is important to clarify what is meant by terminal illness and suicide in the context of terminal illness. First, terminal illness must be distinguished from chronic, debilitating disorders that ultimately end in death. Few would consider diabetes terminal per se, yet it can be associated with a slow deterioration that may ultimately lead to death. HIV illnesses are classically considered terminal, but they involve many asymptomatic years with life satisfaction superior to that found in quadriplegia, which is not considered terminal. It may therefore be preferable to speak of the *terminal stage* of an illness, rather than necessarily classifying certain diseases as terminal.

Second, what a physician considers terminal may differ from what a patient considers terminal (Breitbart, Levenson, & Passik, 1993). Physicians often consider an illness terminal when they have exhausted all curative options and resort to palliation (Breitbart et al., 1993). On the other hand, patients with a chronic, serious illness often consider that their illness has become terminal when their medical condition suddenly deteriorates (Breitbart et al., 1993). Some patients are told, in effect, that they are terminal; others enter an end stage precipitously and rapidly deteriorate beyond the point where the label "terminal" carries any psychological meaning. For practical purposes, it may be useful to consider an illness terminal if life expectancy is less than 1 year. These distinctions are important because they determine how the individual and the family perceive their situation, which has an important bearing on suicide risk. In addition, the varying definitions of terminality or disease staging may explain differences in suicide rates reported by different researchers. In summary, the terminal stage is as much a state of mind as it is a poorly defined time period.

The uncertain definition of suicide in the context of a terminal illness raises difficulties in research and clinical practice. There is an increasingly blurred line between the irrational self-destructive behavior considered suicide and the carefully considered self-destructive action in a terminal state termed *rational suicide* by the euthanasia movement.

First, many self-inflicted deaths among terminally ill patients are never reported as suicides. Physicians may unwittingly certify the deaths of such patients as natural or, occasionally, may actually collude with the patient and the family to conceal a suicide. Thus ascertainment bias takes on momentous proportions in research on terminally ill populations.

Second, people hold different notions about what constitutes suicide in the terminal phases of a disease, and this affects their ability to recognize suicide risk and prevent premature death. For the purposes of this discussion, I limit the definition of suicide to the active and willful use of lethal means to bring about one's death. This definition excludes the refusal of treatment, withholding of nutrition, or removal of life support.

EPIDEMIOLOGY OF SUICIDE AMONG THE
TERMINALLY ILL

The epidemiology of suicide among the terminally ill can be approached from two viewpoints:

Diagnosis—those diseases that are specifically associated with increased risk

Characteristics—those aspects common to terminal illnesses that seem to be correlated with increased risk.

From the perspective of diagnosis, cancer, AIDS, and Huntington's chorea have been the most studied of the terminal illnesses. Systematic studies from Finland (Louhivuori & Hakama, 1979), Connecticut (Fox, Stanek, Boyd, & Flannery, 1982), Denmark (Storm, Christensen, & Jensen, 1992), and Sweden (Boland, 1985a, 1985b) suggest the risk of suicide among cancer patients compared with that among the general population was 0.9–1.9 for women and 1.3–2.9 for men. The most common method, particularly among women, is lethal overdose with sedatives or analgesics used at home (Boland, 1985a, 1985b), although more violent means, such as hanging, jumping, or shooting, have been reported for men and hospitalized patients. Patients with oropharyngeal, lung, breast, gastrointestinal, and urogenital cancers appear to be at greater risk of suicide than those with disease at other sites (Boland, 1985a, 1985b; Farberow, Ganzler, Cutter, & Reynold, 1971). Surprisingly, pancreatic cancer, long associated with profound depression, is not overrepresented among cancer suicides (Van Praag, 1982).

HIV illnesses have also been associated with increased suicide risk. Men with AIDS have been shown to have a 20–36 times greater risk of suicide than men in the general population (Kizer, Green, Perkins, Doebbert, & Hughes, 1988; Marzuk et al., 1988). A more recent national assessment showed the risk was only sevenfold greater and reported a downward trend (Cote, Biggar, & Dannenberg, 1992). However, this study used only national death certificate data and probably underestimated the true rate. Although initial reports suggested suicides among persons with AIDS were largely limited to homosexual white males, the percentage of AIDS-related suicides among intravenous drug abusers is probably underestimated and is increasing (Marzuk, Tierney, Tardiff, Morgan, & Mann, 1988). Overdoses with medications, particularly barbiturates, appear to be the most common lethal method (Cote et al., 1992). Studies of suicide risk among asymptomatic HIV-positive individuals are actually more important than research on suicide risk among persons with AIDS, because of the larger reservoir of individuals affected and the potentially greater number of years of productive life that would be saved through suicide prevention in this group (Marzuk, 1991). However, asymptomatic HIV seropositivity does not define a terminal phase.

Increased risk of suicide has also been reported for persons with Huntington's chorea, particularly at the time of onset of symptoms and before severe motor dysfunction or delirium occur. The risk compared with the general population reportedly ranges from 7 to 200 (Dewhurst, Oliver, & McKnight, 1970; Farrer, 1986; Hayden, Ehrlich, Parker, & Ferera, 1980).

MECHANISMS

Because the mechanism of enhanced suicide risk is not known, suicide in terminal illness may be seen as the outcome of the convergence of multiple biological, psychological, and social stressors on a dying person. The relative importance of any one determinant has not been established. Although terminal illnesses share many characteristics, the rates of suicide among them are quite variable. In addition, most individuals with terminal illness do not commit suicide, despite overwhelming physical and social stressors. Thus, there are undoubtedly important individual differences in response to stress, perceived or real social support, and preexisting psychopathology.

Many characteristics of terminally ill patients are independent risk factors for suicide in their own right. These include altered mental states, such as depression, anxiety, psychosis, and delirium; hopelessness; pain and deterioration; social isolation; and stressors that include dependency, moving away from home, and financial insolvency (Derogatis et al., 1983; Perry, 1990).

Terminal illnesses may affect demographic groups that are already at high risk for suicide, such as older men or substance abusers. Some illnesses, or the drugs used to treat them, may affect the central nervous system. Altered serotonergic functioning has been shown to enhance suicide risk, but the effects of HIV, metastatic brain neoplasms, or Huntington's disease on serotonergic neurons remain to be elucidated (Mann & Stanley, 1986).

CLINICAL ASSESSMENT OF SUICIDE RISK

The assessment of suicide risk in the terminally ill patient proceeds much as it would for the physically healthy psychiatrically ill patient. That is, the psychiatric consultant first determines how the individual's epidemiological profile correlates with known risk factors and then evaluates the patient's current mental status.

Epidemiological risk profiles for suicide are well known. In addition, a premorbid history of an underlying psychiatric disorder, a history of suicide attempts, or a family history of suicide raises the risk of suicide in a terminally ill patient (Roy, 1983). Both AIDS and terminal cancers are associated with high rates of anxiety, depression, and delirium (Bukberg, Penman, & Holland, 1984;

Holland, 1989; Massie, Holland, & Glass, 1983; Miller & Riccio, 1990). These symptoms or syndromes may represent the exacerbation of premorbid psychiatric disorders; the new onset of mental disorder; or the result of hypoxia, sepsis, pain, or medications.

The psychiatric consultant must also explore the patient's current thoughts and intentions regarding suicide in a direct, open, and empathic way. Is the purpose of suicide to liberate the patient from pain and suffering, to spare relatives of a costly and draining burden, or to engender sympathy or attention? Often what initially appeared to be a suicidal preoccupation is only a patient's way of communicating distress and is not serious intent for self-harm. Other patients speak about powerlessness and dependency, with suicide serving as a metaphor for achieving control over their destiny. The consultant should ask also about the duration and intensity of suicidal thoughts, the development of a suicidal plan, and the availability of means of injury.

Although this strategy for assessing suicide risk is straightforward, the evaluation of the terminally ill patient presents particular challenges, discussed in the following sections.

Realistic Preoccupations with Death or Suicide

Physically healthy depressed patients often are preoccupied with death; have fantasies about dying, their funeral, or the afterlife; or report they are writing wills, giving away possessions, or saying goodbye, all of which are considered worrisome indicators of suicide risk. However, in terminally ill patients, preoccupation with dying or realistic planning for death may not be a true indicator of suicidal intent.

The predictive value of frank suicidal ideation in the terminally ill is unknown. Although almost all cancer patients have transient thoughts of suicide at some point, surprisingly few studies report frequent suicidal ideation among cancer patients. For example, only 0–2% of cancer patients interviewed in two studies expressed suicidal thoughts (Achte & Vanhkouen, 1971; Silberfarb, Maurer, & Cronthamel, 1980). Among 185 cancer patients with pain, only 17% expressed suicidal ideation (Saltzburg et al., 1989). In another study, 25% of terminally ill patients who were suicidal were clinically depressed (Brown, Henteleff, Barakat, & Rowe, 1986). Thus, suicidal ideation may be more indicative of depression than of desire to commit suicide.

Diagnostic Difficulties

Almost all patients who commit suicide have depression either as a syndrome or a symptom. Yet, the signs and symptoms of mood disorders overlap with those of physical illnesses. For example, nondepressed medically ill patients may report anorexia with weight loss, insomnia, anergia, fatigue, poor concentration, and physical distress. Thus, the cognitive and affective symptoms must be relied on more heavily than the physical symptoms to make a diagnosis of depression (Endicott, 1984; Massie & Holland, 1984). Hopelessness has been shown to be a predictor of suicide (Beck, Kovacs, & Weissman, 1975), yet many terminally ill persons have little realistic hope of recovery. Hopefulness is best assessed in this population by inquiring about upcoming plans, visits by relatives, or tasks to be done.

Role of Delirium

Many patients who have a terminal illness suffer from intermittent delirium. The prevalence of organic mental syndromes among those with terminal cancer may be as high as 85% (Massie et al., 1983) and may be even higher for those with AIDS (Perry, 1990). This not only makes interviewing these patients difficult, but also increases these patients' impulsivity and unpredictability, making assessment of suicide risk difficult.

Physical Discomforts and Deterioration

The physical discomfort of the terminally ill patient may trigger suicidal thoughts, as well as rendering interviewing difficult. The consultant should assess whether any of these discomforts are reversible.

Pain is the most important of reversible discomforts. It has been estimated that 15% of patients with localized cancer have significant pain (Daut & Cleeland, 1984) with the percentage rising to 60–90% of those with advanced metastic disease (Cleeland, 1984). Many cancer suicides have occurred among individuals whose pain was poorly tolerated and insufficiently controlled (Boland, 1985a, 1985b). The prevalence of pain varies with cancer site. Thus only 5% of leukemia patients may experience pain during their illness, whereas 50–75% of patients with bone, gastrointestinal, or urogenital cancer have significant pain (Foley, 1979). The relationship between cancer pain and suicide risk is not a simple one, however (Breitbart, 1990). For example, in one study, suicidal ideation was related not to the intensity of cancer pain, but to the degree of depression (Saltzberg et al., 1989).

Other physical discomforts that may contribute to suicide risk and that may be reversible include dyspnea, cough, nausea, constipation, intractable hiccuping, pruritus, and insomnia (Breitbart et al., 1993). Irreversible physical deterioration includes impaired mobility, failing eyesight or hearing, amputation, paralysis, dyphagia, and incontinence (Breitbart et al., 1993). Cancer patients and, presumably, individuals with AIDS are at increased risk for suicide if they are experiencing these problems, particularly if they are psychologically distressed.

Burden of Social Stressors

The terminal phase of AIDS or cancer is marked by a convergence of social stressors within several months that is unparalleled in the years of most person's lives (Faulstich, 1987). Many patients have had to leave their homes, relying constantly on others in hospitals, hospices, or nursing homes. Many have run out of insurance, exhausted their savings, and incurred debt. They are often stigmatized. They may be bereaved by the loss of friends who had AIDS, and they may view themselves as a draining burden on their families or friends. In the face of these multiple stressors, suicide may be seen as the only solution.

Personal Style and Interaction with Caregivers

Much useful information about suicide risk can be gained by observation of interactions between terminally ill patients and their caregivers. For example, in one study, cancer patients who were likely to commit suicide were often hostile, sarcastic, immature, and demanding (Farberow, Shneidman, & Leonard, 1963). Interpersonal relationships often deteriorate significantly as medical staff or family members tire of the patient's relentless demands. Patients who need to control every detail of their medical care at higher risk of suicide than those who are flexible and adaptable (Farberow et al., 1963). Similarly, risk is lower among those who have learned to readjust their expectations about life (Marshall, Burnett, & Brosure, 1983).

CLINICAL MANAGEMENT

The management of the suicidal terminally ill patient begins during the assessment phase. That is, the psychiatric consultant's frank, supportive, nonjudgmental exploration of the individual's suicidal intent should have a therapeutic effect that allows the person to feel understood and supported; helping the patient achieve this feeling is the first step in reducing suicide risk. After the patient's safety has been ensured, suicidal episodes may be managed through standard crisis intervention techniques. In addition, the consultant may encourage the primary professional caregivers to treat pain or dyspnea more aggressively or help with sedation. Psychiatric symptoms or disorders may be treated with empathic supportive psychotherapy and the judicious use of antidepressants, neuroleptics, or benzodiazepines. Social stressors may be reduced by a social worker's referrals for help with financial debt, health insurance, or home care.

Timing Interval

Because of the limited life span of terminally ill patients, it is often impractical to wait weeks or months before trials of antidepressants for depression or anxiety disorders are completed. It may be necessary to provide more symptomatic relief through the use of benzodiazepines for anxiety or psychostimulants for depression (Breitbart et al., 1993).

Setting

Terminally ill patients' medical conditions often dictate that they be treated on an acute medical ward, in a hospice, or at a nursing home. Thus many of these patients cannot be treated in the relative safety that a psychiatric hospital offers. Some may require one-to-one observation in these settings. Others may be reluctant to leave their homes. Committing a terminally ill patient with only several weeks of life remaining to a psychiatric ward raises important ethical dilemmas. Such patients may need to be managed at home after the family has been educated about suicide risk.

Availability of Lethal Means

Most terminally ill patients have large quantities of analgesics or sedatives on hand, which can be used for suicide. The consultant may need to enlist the family's help in dispensing medications.

Underlying Medical Condition

Many drugs used to treat depression or anxiety are problematic because of their side effects, their interactions with other drugs, or their potential to precipitate delirium or because of unreliable intravenous administration. As Breitbart et al. (1993) pointed out, treating delirium in suicidal terminally ill patients differs from treating delirium in nonterminal patients, because the delirium is usually multifactorial and irreversible. Treatment is also limited by the setting and the patient's willingness to undergo additional uncomfortable diagnostic procedures. Thus, delirium may be controlled symptomatically, but definitive treatment may be reserved for cases in which an etiology can be readily reversed.

Strain on Family Supports

The management of the suicidal patient usually involves mobilizing family members and friends to support the patient during the suicidal crisis. However, the psychological resources of some family members may already be drained, and these persons may be unable to provide the level of support required. Some may themselves be suicidal. Patients with AIDS may receive little support from some relatives because of the stigma attached to homosexuality and drug abuse. Others may have few surviving friends.

Concepts of Suicide and Euthanasia

In the absence of family psychopathology, most family members are usually appalled by a terminally ill relative's desire to commit suicide and are willing to express hopefulness and encouragement. Similarly, most treating physicians help in managing a suicidal patient by seeking psychiatric consultation. In some cases, however, family members and physicians may be hopeless about the terminally ill patient's condition and see little reason to prevent a suicide. Others may favor euthanasia and view the psychiatrist's interventions to prevent suicide as intrusive, unwarranted, or even unethical. Psychiatrists, themselves, may be unwilling to prevent suicide in someone who displays intolerable suffering.

ROLE OF SEROLOGIC TESTING AND PROGNOSIS

Cancer patients commit suicide most frequently in the advanced stages of the disease, when the prognosis is poor (Boland, 1985a, 1985b; Fox et al., 1982; Louhivuori & Hakama, 1979). For example, Farberow et al. (1963) found that 86% of cancer suicides occurred in the preterminal or terminal stage of the illness. The development of new curative or palliative treatments will undoubtedly make cancer a more chronic disease and reduce the risk of suicide in the early phases. However, there are few tests that reliably predict an individual's susceptibility to cancer. In recent years, serologic tests have been devised for HIV infection (Popovic, Sarngadharan, Read, & Gallo, 1984) and Huntington's chorea (Conneally, Wallace, Gusella, & Wexler, 1984) that can accurately predict whether an individual will contract the symptomatic form of the disease. It is too early to tell if these tests have resulted in increased suicide risk. The psychological effects of these tests are not fully known. Nevertheless, some information is available.

A study of the effect of HIV testing on suicide risk found no significant increase in suicide ideation immediately after and 6 months after the test in either group who tested positive or the group who tested negative for the virus (Perry, Jacobsberg, & Fischman, 1990). However, 15% of both groups did maintain suicide ideation long after testing, suggesting a high prevalence of psychiatric morbidity in the population at risk for developing AIDS (Perry et al., 1990).

The likelihood of suicide after testing in persons at risk for Huntington's disease is more problematic to estimate than the likelihood of suicide after HIV testing. Many of the individuals at risk for Huntington's disease have strong family or personal histories of suicide ideation, attempts, or completions, and fewer persons at risk of Huntington's disease than persons at risk of HIV infection have undergone testing. In surveys of individuals at risk for carrying the gene but who had not undergone testing, as many as 15% have stated they would consider killing themselves if they were found to be positive, but most suggested they would do so only after disabling symptoms began (Kessler, 1987; Mastromauro, Myers, & Berkman, 1987). Studies of individuals tested for carrier status have found no suicides immediately after notification of test results (Brandt et al., 1989; Meissen et al., 1988). The risk of suicide among those who test negative and might therefore incur survivor guilt remains to be established (Tibben et al., 1992).

CONCLUSION

The assessment and management of suicidal terminally ill patients pose many challenges. Although much has been learned about suicide risk through the study of cancer patients, and AIDS shares many characteristics with terminal cancer, significant differences also exist between these populations that require investigation. The relative importance of the biological, psychological, and social determinants of suicide, as well as the role of preexisting psychopathology and varying vulnerability to stressors, remains to be established. The development of new serologic tests that allow early diagnosis and new treatments that allow prolonged life has forced a reevaluation of the concept of terminality. Likewise, the public's increased interest in assisted suicide and euthanasia has resulted in a blurring of the line between suicide and rational self-inflicted death.

REFERENCES

Achte, K. A., & Vanhkouen, M. L. (1971). Cancer and the psyche. *Omega, 2*, 46–56.

Beck, A. T., Kovacs, M., & Weissman, A. (1975). Hopelessness and suicidal behavior: An overview. *Journal of the American Medical Association, 234*, 1146–1149.

Boland, C. (1985a). Suicide and cancer: I. Demographic and social characteristics of cancer patients who committed suicide in Sweden 1973–1976. *Journal of Psychosocial Oncology, 3*, 17–30.

Boland, C. (1985b). Suicide and cancer: II. Medical and care factors in suicides by cancer patients in Sweden, 1973–1976. *Journal of Psychosocial Oncology, 3*, 31–52.

Brandt, J., Quaid, K. A., Folstein, S. E., Garber, P., Maestri, N. E., Abbott, M. H., Slavney, P. R., Franz, M. L., Kusch, L., and Kazazian, H. H. (1989). Presymptomatic diagnosis of delayed-onset disease with linked DNA markers: The experience in Huntington's disease. *Journal of the American Medical Association, 261*, 3108–3114.

Breitbart, W. (1990). Cancer pain and suicide. In K. M. Foley, J. J. Bonica, V. Ventafridda, and M. V. Callaway (Eds.), *Advances in pain research and therapy* (Vol. 16, pp. 399–412). New York: Raven Press.

Breitbart, W., Levenson, J. A., & Passik, S. D. (1993). Terminally ill cancer patients. In W. Breitbart and J. C. Holland (Eds.), *Psychiatric aspects of symptom management in cancer patients* (pp. 173–230). Washington. DC: American Psychiatric Press.

Brown, J. H., Henteleff, P., Barakat, S., & Rowe, J. R. (1986). Is it normal for terminally ill patients to desire death? *American Journal of Psychiatry, 143*, 203–211.

Bukberg, J., Penman, D., & Holland, J. (1984). Depression in hospitalized cancer patients. *Psychosomatic Medicine, 46*, 199–212.

Cleeland, C. S. (1984). The impact of pain on patients with cancer. *Cancer, 54*, 263–267.

Conneally, P. M., Wallace, M. R., Gusella, J. F., & Wexler, N. S. (1984). Huntington disease estimation of heterozygote status using linked genetic markers. *Genetic Epidemiology, 1*, 81–88.

Cote, T. R., Biggar, R. J., & Dannenberg, A. L. (1992). Risk of suicide among persons with AIDS: A national assessment. *Journal of the American Medical Association, 268*, 2066–2068.

Daut, R. L., & Cleeland, C. S. (1982). The prevalence and severity of pain in cancer. *Cancer, 50*, 1913–1918.

Derogatis, L. R., Morrow, G. R., Fetting, J., Penman, D., Piasetsky, S., Schmale, A. M., Henrichs, M., and Carnicks, C. L. (1983). The prevalence of psychiatric disorders among cancer patients. *Journal of the American Medical Association, 249*, 751–757.

Dewhurst, K., Oliver, J. E., & McKnight, A. L. (1970). Sociopsychiatric consequences of Huntington's disease. *British Journal of Psychiatry, 116*, 255–258.

Endicott, J. (1984). Measurement of depression in patients with cancer. *Cancer, 53*, 2243–2248.

Farberow, N. L., Ganzler, S., Cutter, F., & Reynold, D. (1971). An eight year survey of hospital suicides. *Suicide and Life-Threatening Behavior, 1*, 184–201.

Farberow, N. L., Shneidman, E. S., & Leonard, C. V. (1963). Suicide among general medical and surgical hospital patients with malignant neoplasms. *Medical Bulletin, Veteran's Administration, 9:*1–11. (Available from U.S. Veteran's Administration, Washington, DC.)

Farrer, L. A. (1986). Suicide and attempted suicide in Huntington disease: Implications for preclinical testing of persons at risk. *American Journal of Medical Genetics, 24*, 305–311.

Faulstich, M. E. (1987). Psychiatric aspects of AIDS. *American Journal of Psychiatry, 144*, 551–556.

Foley, K. M. (1979). Pain syndromes in patients with cancer. In J. J. Bonica & V. Ventafridda (Eds.), *Advances in pain research and therapy* (Vol. 2, pp. 59–75). New York: Raven Press.

Fox, B. H., Stanek, E. J., Boyd, S. C., & Flannery, S. T. (1982). Suicide rates among cancer patients in Connecticut. *Journal of Chronic Disease, 35*, 85–100.

Hayden, M. R., Ehrlich, R., Parker, H., & Ferera, S. J. (1980). Social perspectives in Huntington's chorea. *South African Medical Journal, 58*, 201–203.

Holland, J. (1989). Anxiety and cancer: The patient and the family. *Journal of Clinical Psychiatry, 50*, 20–25.

Kessler, S. (1987). Psychiatric implications of presymptomatic testing for Huntington's disease. *American Journal of Orthopsychiatry, 57*, 212–219.

Kizer, K. W., Green, M., Perkins, C. I., Doebbert, G., & Hughes, M. J. (1988). AIDS and suicide in California. *Journal of the American Medical Association, 260*, 1881.

Louhivuori, K. A., & Hakama, M. (1979). Risk of suicide among cancer patients. *American Journal of Epidemiology, 109*, 59–65.

Mann, J., & Stanley, M. (Eds.). (1986). Psychobiology of suicidal behavior. *Annals of New York Academy of Sciences, 487*.

Marshall, J. R., Burnett, W., & Brosure, J. (1983). On precipitating factors: Cancer as a cause of suicide. *Suicide and Life-Threatening Behavior, 13*, 15–27.

Marzuk, P. M. (1991). Suicidal behavior and HIV illness. *International Review of Psychiatry, 3*, 365–371.

Marzuk, P. M., Tierney, H., Tardiff, K., Gross, E. M., Morgan, E. B., Hsu, M. A., and Mann, J. J. (1988). Increased risk of suicide in persons with AIDS. *Journal of the American Medical Association, 259,* 1333–1337.

Marzuk, P. M., Tierney, H., Tardiff, K., Morgan, E., & Mann, J. (1988, May). *AIDS is associated with an increased risk of suicide.* Abstract presented at the annual meeting of the American Psychiatric Association, Montreal.

Massie, M. J., & Holland, J. C. (1984). Diagnosis and treatment of depression in the cancer patient. *Journal of Clinical Psychiatry, 42,* 25–28.

Massie, M. J., Holland, J. C., & Glass, E. (1983). Delirium in terminally ill cancer patients. *American Journal of Psychiatry, 140,* 1048–1050.

Mastromauro, C., Myers, R. H., & Berkman, B. (1987). Attitudes toward presymptomatic testing in Huntington's disease. *American Journal of Medical Genetics, 26,* 271–282.

Meissen, G. J., Myers, R. H., Mastromauro, C. A., Koroshetz, W. J., Klinger, K. W., Farrer, L. A., Watkins, P. A., Gusella, J. F., Bird, E. D., and Martin, J. B. (1988). Predictive testing for Huntington's disease with use of a linked DNA marker. *New England Journal of Medicine, 318,* 535–542.

Miller, D., & Riccio, M. (1990). Nonorganic psychiatric and psychosocial syndromes associated with HIV-1 infection and disease. *AIDS, 4,* 381–388.

Perry, S. W. (1990). Organic mental disorders caused by HIV: Update on early diagnosis and treatment. *American Journal of Psychiatry, 147,* 696–710.

Perry, S., Jacobsberg, L., & Fischman, B. (1990). Suicidal ideation and HIV testing. *Journal of the American Medical Association, 263,* 679–682.

Popovic, M., Sarngadharan, M. G., Read, E., & Gallo, R. (1984). Detection, isolation, and continuous production of cytopathic retrovirus (HRV-111) from patients with AIDS and pre-AIDS. *Science, XX,* 497.

Roy, A. (1983). Family history of suicide. *Archives of General Psychiatry, 40,* 971–974.

Saltzburg, D., Breitbart, W., Fishman, B., Stiefel, F., Holland, J., & Foley, K. (1989, May). *The relationship of pain and depression to suicidal ideation in cancer patients.* Abstract presented at the annual meeting of the American Society of Clinical Oncologists, San Francisco.

Silberfarb, P. M., Maurer, L. H., & Cronthamel, C. S. (1980). Psychosocial aspects of neoplastic disease: I. Functional status of breast cancer patients during different treatment regimens. *American Journal of Psychiatry, 137,* 450–455.

Storm, H. H., Christensen, N., & Jensen, O. (1992). Suicides among Danish patients with cancer: 1971–1986. *Cancer, 69,* 1507–1512.

Tibben, A., Vegter-van der Vlis, M., Skraastad, M. I., Frets, P. G., Van de Kamp, J. J. P., Niermeijer, M. F., Van Ommen, G. J. B., Roos, R. A. C., Rooijmans, H. G. M., Stronks, D., and Verhage, F. (1992). DNA-testing for Huntington's disease in the Netherlands: A retrospective study on psychosocial effects. *American Journal of Medical Genetics, 44,* 94–99.

Van Praag, H. M. (1982). Depression, suicide, and the metabolism of serotonin in the brain. *Journal of Affective Disorders, 4,* 275–290.

Part IV

Psychiatric Issues

Although suicidal pain is often readily accessible to psychotherapeutic influence, medication and hospitalization should not be eschewed by any competent mental health professional. Today we know that suicide is multidetermined. Many factors, including biogenetic factors, may contribute to elevated suicide risk. Medication may be essential in many cases, as is hospitalization during periods of acute perturbation or heightened lethality. Yet both can add complications to the treatment of suicidal patients. Although the safety needs of a suicidal patient are of utmost importance, the decision whether to admit a suicidal patient is often difficult and vexing, especially in this era of decreased resources. Managing suicidal inpatients demands special care in risk assessment, care, and policies and procedures. In Part IV, these psychiatric issues are discussed. Chapter 11 discusses the psychopharmacotherapy of suicide, Chapter 12 offers an overview of hospitalization issues, and Chapter 13 provides detailed recommendations for managing suicidal inpatients.

Psychopharmacotherapy of Suicide

Andrew Edmund Slaby

Self-inflicted death is a subject of mystery and stigma. Society once condemned posthumously those assumed to have willfully died (Alvarez, 1973). Not until the advent of psychoanalysis and sociology at the end of the 19th century was a more rational and scientific perspective brought to bear on the act deemed willful and therefore sinful.

Today we know that suicide is not determined by a single factor (Slaby, 1993; Valzell, 1981). Many factors converge at one point in time to turn the balance from the natural impulse to survive to a desire to die. In addition to psychosocial factors, existential, genetic, and neurochemical influences can bring about a desire to die. In this chapter, the differential diagnosis of self-destructive behavior (Appendix 1) is discussed in the context of growing awareness of how, when coupled with contributing factors (Appendix 2), these disorders lead to suicide in individuals with the biogenetic basis for self-destructive behavior (Slaby, 1993).

DIFFERENTIAL DIAGNOSIS

The variable that is most consistently associated with and is sufficient for suicide is major psychiatric illness; however, psychiatric illness is not necessary. Suicides do occur in the absence of it. An elderly Jewish couple living in Nazi

Germany, aware that they were about to be deported to a concentration camp where death in the gas chamber was almost certain, and without hope or energy to escape, might have rationally elected to die by their own hands. Comparably, a person with an extremely painful terminal illness, such as cancer with bone metastases or end-stage chronic obstructive lung disease secondary to emphysema, may chose to die. Such suicides are existential choices involving quality of life, individual right to die or refuse treatment, and individual morals. A revolutionary may choose to die in an attempt to kill others by driving a car carrying explosives into a crowd and detonating them, or a soldier may intentionally crash into a shop or other target like a Kamikaze pilot. These suicides are due to cultural and political factors.

Rational, existential, and political suicides represent very few of reported suicides. Most reported suicides are associated with psychiatric illnesses. Bipolar illness, major depression, and schizoaffective disorder account for 60–80% of suicides (Bulik, Carpenter, Kupfer, et al., 1990). When other disorders with a strong depressive component, such as dysthymia, cyclothymia, narcissistic personality, and borderline personality, are included, this percentage swells to as great as 80%. Many psychiatrically ill persons have dual diagnoses: They suffer a psychiatric disorder, such as major depression, that they self-medicate with drugs or alcohol, resulting in a secondary chemical abuse disorder.

Suicide risk among individuals with affective illness is estimated to be 30 times that of those not suffering the disorder, with about 15% of those with major depression taking their own lives (Bulik et al., 1990). The rate for schizophrenic individuals is 20 times greater (Breier & Astrachan, 1984) than that for nonschizophrenic persons, with the 10% or 15% of schizophrenic individuals who ultimately commit suicide dying during the first 10 years of the illness (Cohen, Test, & Brown, 1990). Suicide has so increased among young schizophrenic persons that it is now said to be the leading cause of death in this group. This may be due to (a) a lack of compliance with medication that results from abbreviated hospitalizations, which provide less indoctrination regarding the need for psychopharmacotherapy, and (b) impulsivity due to substance abuse. Hopelessness and depression characterize the subgroup of schizophrenic individuals at greatest risk.

People who experience panic attacks either as part of panic disorder or alone have an increased risk of a suicide attempt, with approximately 20% of the latter and 12% of the former making an attempt (Reich, 1989; Weissman et al., 1989). More than 1.5% of the population is estimated to experience panic disorder sometime during their lives, and two to three times as many experience the attacks without criteria sufficient for the diagnosis (Weissman et al., 1989).

Some individuals suffer double depression; they experience major depressive episodes superimposed on an enduring depression. The enduring depression is the result, in some instances, of the failure to identify and treat aggressively affective illness that occurs in adolescence as the personality is developing.

Consequently, depression, low self-esteem, and learned helplessness become personality traits. When another depression occurs later in life, accompanied by neurovegetative signs as sleep, appetite, energy, and sexual interest disturbance, antidepressants may ameliorate the acute symptoms, but those that have become an enduring part of the adult personality (e.g., low self-esteem and helplessness) do not abate as they would be expected to had they first appeared as part of the depression in adult life. Individuals with double depression present a particular management problem, requiring treatment of both acute psychiatric illness and personality traits that enhance helplessness and hopelessness and therefore risk of suicide.

Not all persons who attempt suicide die. Some survive, at times with great disability. Gunshot wounds disfigure. Carbon monoxide poisoning, hanging, and car accidents may result in brain damage in survivors. Early recognition and management of those at risk for suicide therefore are directed at not only saving lives, but also preventing attempts that would result in permanent physical and psychological dysfunction. Only about 1% of those who attempt suicide die by suicide in the ensuing 10 years (Reich, 1989). The same factors associated with violent suicide are associated with violent nonlethal suicidal behavior (Slaby, 1993). Greater depression and hopelessness regarding the resolution of problems have been found in those who repeat a suicide attempt than in single-episode attempters (Sakinofsky et al., 1990). A suicide attempt or completed suicide by another member of the family, stressful life events, and depression predict both attempts and completed suicides in adolescents (McKenny et al., 1982; Slaby, 1993; Tishler, McKenny, & Morgan, 1981).

THE NEUROCHEMICAL BASIS OF VIOLENT BEHAVIOR

Depression, suicidal behavior, thought disturbance, anxiety, and violence directed at others have a neurochemical basis in many instances. In some ways, a suicidal act is similar to a seizure. Most seizures have a biological basis, but not all do. Some are what are called *psychogenic epilepsy* or *pseudoseizures*. These seizures may occur independently of or together with biologically based epilepsy. Similarly, most, but not all, suicidal behavior can be attributed to neurobiologically based disease that results from a genetic predisposition to illness that manifests itself in self-destructive behavior (Slaby, 1993). The drive to live is so great that, with rare exceptions (e.g., existential, cultural, or political suicides), affective illness, with its concomitant alterations in catecholamine and indoleamine metabolism, is at the basis of self-inflicted death. Antidepressants and electroconvulsive therapy appear to work on the aberrations in metabolism found with depression, resulting in a euthymic mood and thereby mollifying one of the single greatest risk factor for suicide: depression. Anxiety disorders appear to involve changes in the locus ceruleus in the brain, the site of action of the benzodiazepines used to treat panic and other anxiety disorders. Asberg (1986) and others have specifically demonstrated that, regardless of diagnosis, violent suicides and suicide attempts are often associated with changes in the metabolism of the indoleamine serotonin. Indoleamines and catecholamines and their metabolites in the cerebrospinal fluid of suicide attempters and the brains of completers, and receptor binding, and measures of cortical and thyroid-releasing hormone in attempters have been studied to support this hypothesis (Slaby, 1993).

The results of these investigations indicate that impulsive violent behavior, be it self or other directed, is associated more with disturbances of serotonin (5-hydroxytryptamine) metabolism in the brain than with mood disorders. Serotonergic mechanisms are involved with fight-or-flight behavior, sexual drive, and affect (Linnoila et al., 1983; Traskman-Bendz, Asberg, & Schalling, 1990), which at times may be manifested as impulsive and self-destructive behavior. Serotonergic aberrations have been reported with suicide, homicide, assaults, rape, and eating disorders (Cohen, Wichel, & Stanley, 1988). Serotonergic dysfunction has also been found in obsessive-compulsive disorder, schizophrenia, and panic disorder (Van de Kar, 1990). Many healthy people also show a decrease in cerebrospinal fluid levels of 5-hydroxyindoleacetic acid (Asberg, Nordstrom, & Traskman-Bendz, 1990), supporting the multifactorial theory of suicide. In addition to biogenetic vulnerability evinced in some instances by changes in serotonin production, situational (e.g., stress, life events, or lack of social support), psychological (e.g., hopelessness or early loss), and existential (e.g., angst) factors play role in compelling a person to take his or her life (Asberg et al., 1990). To maximize reduction of suicidal behavior, psychopharmacotherapy is accompanied by psychotherapy and sociotherapy (Slaby, 1993).

IMPLICATIONS FOR THE TREATMENT OF SUICIDAL PATIENTS

The reported serotonergic dysfunction in patients who are suicidal, particularly those who are impulsively and violently so, indicates need for diagnosis-specific treatment involving use of antidepressants that are specific serotonin reuptake inhibitors, such as fluoxetine (Prozac), paroxetine (Paxel), sertraline (Zoloft), and trazodone (Desyrel). If a patient has a personal history of a suicide attempt or plans to attempt suicide, antidepressants and mood-stabilizing agents (i.e., lithium carbonate, carbamazepine, valproic acid, and calcium channel blockers) restore mood and decrease impulsivity. Not all suicidal plans or feelings are immediate, impulsive, or violent, however. For example, an adolescent who is learning disabled or one who is homosexual may feel hopeless and consider suicide an option but be devoid of either impulsivity or the neurovegetative signs of affective illness. In such cases, a behavioral intervention such as interpersonal or cognitive therapy is more appropriate. For the adolescent with a learning disability, identification of the specific learning disability and remedial education to allow compensation for the disorder are indicated. Clinical management of the homosexual adolescent who is considering suicide, regardless of the need for psychopharmacotherapy for impulsivity or mood disturbance, entails social support and assignment of healthy homosexual role models. Moreover, it is possible that in addition to a learning disability or a sexual orientation issue with or without impulsivity or a psychiatric disorder, a medical disorder such as hyperthyroidism or cardiac arrhythmia exists, creating a feeling of impending doom. The medical disorder may have been triggered by hopelessness, rejection, or low self-esteem, but it nevertheless requires medical treatment specific for it.

Benzodiazepines (e.g., alprazolam [Xanax] and lorazapam [Ativan]) and some antidepressants specifically work to counter panic and other instances of episodic and chronic anxiety. Neuroleptics (e.g., perphenazine [Trilafon] and thiothixene [Navane]), alone or together with mood stabilizers or antidepressants, are required in the management of suicidal schizophrenic persons.

The use of antidepressants with selective neuronal reuptake blockade of serotonin is of particular importance in the psychopharmacotherapeutic management of self-destructive behavior, because these drugs (a) have more specific pharmacological effects and thus cause fewer side effects and (b) are less toxic on overdose than are tricyclics and tetracyclics (Asberg et al., 1986; Asberg, Nordstrom, & Traskman-Bendz 1986). The tendency toward fewer side effects enhances patients' willingness to take medication at therapeutic doses and for a sufficient length of time to allow evaluation of an antidepressant's efficacy in a specific instance. A discussion of possible side effects, their frequency, and their management fosters a therapeutic alliance with the patient, enhancing his or her sense of control and hope.

Although not all depression is responsive to medication, at this time in the history of the understanding of suicidal behavior, serious question may be raised regarding quality of care a suicidal patient is receiving if medical, surgical, and psychiatric disorders with a neurobiological basis are not considered in the evaluation and management of the suicidal behavior. Specifically, affective disorders, schizoaffective disorder, schizophrenia, eating disorders, anxiety disorders, posttraumatic stress disorder, and other psychiatric disorders must be considered, as well as medical and surgical illnesses associated with organic brain disorders. Patients and their families may not always accept state-of-the-art psychopharmacological treatment, but it should be offered together with the rationale for the advised intervention.

Not all depressions that may be predicted to be medication responsive respond to drugs, any more than all cases of hypertension respond to antihypertensive therapy. Strokes and heart attacks may still occur when a patient is on antihypertensive medication, just as suicide occurs in some patients on antidepressants long enough to have appropriate serum levels. The clinician's duty is to provide the best care available for an illness associated with suicide, but the outcome of care cannot be guaranteed.

An example of the need for caution in making claims regarding the effects of a medication is the much-publicized controversy over whether fluoxetine (Prozac) precipitated suicidal ideation, as was reported by Teicher, Glod, and Cole (1990). Obviously, although an increase in suicide impulses may be possible, there are a number of other plausible explanations. First, there generally is not an immediate response to antidepressant psychopharmacotherapy. Antidepressants usually take weeks and even months to have full effect, and suicide may occur before improvement is seen. In addition, a small fraction of patients, as mentioned, will not show any response, and their suicide ideation may increase. In other instances, patients will terminate treatment because they find side effects intolerable before therapeutic effect may occur. Second, an individual who has been prescribed a medication that has the reputation of being a miracle drug may feel more hopeless if he or she does not show some response in the course of therapy. The person may despair of any reprieve of the illness if he or she is among the subpopulation that do not respond. The increased hopelessness could lead to suicide. Third, the side effects that may occur with fluoxetine include lethargy and agitation, which may be construed as a worsening of the depression. Again, this could increase some patients' wish for suicide. Fourth, it has long been known that early in the course of treatment of a depression with medication, energy may return before the feelings of worthlessness, hopelessness, and helplessness abate, giving patients the energy to act on the impulse to kill themselves, whereas before they were too withdrawn. Finally, it is possible that just as other thoughts become clearer with treatment of depression, thoughts of self-destruction become sharper. Patients and their families must be alerted to the possibility of these occurrences and instructed to inform their therapists if the desire for suicide increases early in the course of antidepressant therapy.

SUPPLEMENTS TO PSYCHOPHARMACOTHERAPY

Psychotherapy is an important supplement to psychopharmacotherapy in that it enhances response to medication and facilitates functioning. Cognitive and interpersonal therapy aimed at reducing learned helplessness, enhancing self-esteem and interpersonal skills, and reducing stress is believed to be the most efficacious (Hollon, 1990). In instances where medication is not indicated, cognitive therapy alone may be sufficient (Hollon, 1990). In biologically based depression, cognitive therapy is an important adjunctive treatment in the acute stage because it facilitates response, and it is an important adjunct in the chronic phase because it minimizes exacerbation. The success of cognitive therapy is predicated on the fact that maladaptive information processing and erroneous cognitions play causal roles in the onset and exacerbations of some depressions and in the persistence of learned helplessness after the neurovegetative signs of depression, such as sleep, appetite, energy, and sexual interest disturbances, have abated.

Electroconvulsive therapy is sometimes required, particularly when a patient is severely suicidal, when other treatments have failed, or when medication is contraindicated. Given the safety of the selective serotonin reuptake blockers, this last instance is rare. Even when electroconvulsive therapy is required early in the course, antidepressants are usually necessary to sustain response, because the effects of electroshock generally do not endure longer than 6 months to a year, and if depression remains, it will reemerge unless a person is maintained on medication.

Given the fact that response to medication is not immediate and in some patients no response may be seen or suicidality may increase early in the course of treatment, appropriate safeguards must be provided to prevent self-injury. In the extreme, this includes one-to-one observation and reasonable removal of any means by which a patient could take his or her life.

In cases of dual diagnoses, wherein a patient has abused substances in an attempt to self-medicate a mood, thought, or anxiety disorder, enrollment in a chemical dependence program supplements management of the psychiatric disorder. In addition to detoxification, this entails the usual 12-step approach accompanied by family therapy, psychopharmacotherapy, and appropriate diagnostic-specific treatment.

Acutely suicidal patients must be hospitalized (Roy, 1989), although some caution is warranted. Institutionalization is not without negative effects. Characterologically disturbed patients with narcissistic or borderline personality disorders are at times unpredictably suicidal. Hospitalization of these patients may reinforce self-destructive patterns and increase, rather than diminish, maladaptive behavior patterns. Monamine oxidase inhibitors (e.g., tranylcypramine [Parnate]) have been found to affect the sustained depression of some of these patients. In many instances, depression is reported to have endured as long as a patient can remember. Any of the drugs that have been reported to reduce impulsivity may be considered. These include, in addition to the serotonin agonists, lithium carbonate, valproic acid, diphenylhydantoin, clonazepam, and carbamazepine.

All illnesses are family illnesses; that is, when one member of the network of those we love hurts, we all hurt. We are fearful when there is the possibility of death, particularly self-inflected death. Family therapy not only counters the pathological family dynamics of dependency and enabling that result when an individual's functioning has long been compromised because of an affective illness, but also teaches the family productive ways of living with a depressed and often angry person who may threaten to take his or her life or may do so without any warning. Families must understand how pharmacotherapy works and what to do if it does not work or if complications or side effects arise. Suicidal patients frequently come from families that not only are more talented and creative than those not so affected, but also are, because of the depressive diathesis, more sensitive to their own and others' feelings. People who are slightly depressed listen more carefully to what is said—and not said. If a medication is prescribed that may be addictive (e.g., benzodiazepine for anxiety disorders), families as well as patients must be informed of the risk and taught the signs that indicate that addiction is occurring or exists. Supportive psychotherapy should be afforded both the family and the patient to enhance compliance with treatment when the side effects of psychopharmacotherapy loom greater than the promise of recovery.

When a response does not appear after a patient has been at a therapeutic dosage of medication for a sufficient period of time, the problem may be due to individual variations in pharmacokinetics or the fact that the patient is using other medications or recreational drugs (e.g., alcohol) that affect the metabolism of the antidepressant. Serum level may prove to be inadequate for response despite an oral dosage that may be in the toxic range. In most instances of nonresponsiveness to antidepressant therapy, a patient has not been on an adequate dose, has not been on an adequate dose for a sufficient period of time, or lacks a therapeutic serum level despite adequate oral dosage.

SUMMARY

Most, but not all, impulses to commit suicide are due to neurochemical changes in the brain at a synaptic level. These changes involve aberration in amine metabolism, particularly indoleamine synthesis. The predisposition to these changes is genetically determined. In individuals thus predisposed, stressors precipitate a change, resulting in an initial episode or exacerbation of psychiatric illness that includes suicide as one of its clinical manifestations. Management of these patients involves diagnosis-specific treatment using psychotropic medication with adjunctive cognitive and interpersonal therapy.

REFERENCES

Alvarez, D. (1973). *The savage god: A study of suicide*. New York: Bantam Books.
Asberg, M. (1986). Biochemical aspects of suicide. *Clinical Neuropharmacology, 9* (Suppl. 4), 374–376.
Asberg, M., Ericksson, B., Martensson, B., et al. (1986). Therapeutic effects of serotonin uptake inhibitors in depression. *Journal of Clinical Psychiatry, 40* (Suppl. 4), 23–35.
Asberg, M., Nordstrom, P., & Traskman-Bendz, L. (1986). Biochemical factors in suicide. In A. Roy (Ed.), *Suicide*. Baltimore: Williams & Wilkins.
Asberg, M., Nordstrom, P., & Traskman-Bendz, L. (1990). Cerebrospinal fluid studies in suicide: An overview. *Annals of the New York Academy of Sciences, 487*, 243–255.

Breier, A., & Astrachan, B. M. (1984). Characterization of schizophrenic patients who commit suicide. *American Journal of Psychiatry, 141,* 206–209.

Bulik, C. M., Carpenter, L. L., Kupfer, D. J., et al. (1990). Features associated with suicide attempts in recurrent major depression. *Journal of Affective Disorders, 18,* 29–37.

Cohen, L. J., Test, M. A., & Brown, R. L. (1990). Suicide and schizophrenia: Data from a prospective community treatment study. *American Journal of Psychiatry, 147,* 602–607.

Cohen, L. S., Whichel, R. M., & Stanley, M. (1988). Biochemical markers of suicide risk and adolescent suicide. *Clinical Neuropharmacology, 2,* 423–435.

Hollon, S. D. (1990). Cognitive therapy and pharmacotherapy for depression. *Psychiatric Annals, 20,* 249–258.

Linnoila, M., Virkkunnen, M., Scheimin, M., et al. (1983). Low cerebrospinal fluid 5-hydroxyindoleacetic acid concentration differentiates impulsive from non-impulsive violent behavior. *Life Sciences, 33,* 2609–2614.

McKenny, P. C., Tishler, C. C., & Kelly, C. (1982). Adolescent suicide: A comparison of attempters and nonattempters in an emergency room population. *Clinical Pediatrics, 21,* 266–270.

Reich, P. (1989). Panic attacks and the risk of suicide. *New England Journal of Medicine, 321,* 1269–1261.

Roy, A. (1989). Suicide. In H. Kaplan & B. Sadock (Eds.), *Comprehensive textbook of psychiatry/V* (5th ed.). Baltimore: Williams & Wilkins.

Sakinofsky, I., Roberts, R. S., Brown, Y., et al. (1990). Problem resolution and repetition of parasuicide: A prospective study. *British Journal of Psychiatry, 156,* 395–399.

Slaby, A. E. (1993). *The handbook of psychiatric emergencies* (4th ed.). New York: Appleton & Lange.

Teicher, M. H., Glod, C., & Cole, J. O. (1990). Emergence of intense suicidal preoccupation during fluoxetine treatment. *American Journal of Psychiatry, 147,* 207–210.

Tishler, C. L., McKenny, P. C., & Morgan, K. C. (1981). Adolescent suicide attempts: Some significant factors. *Suicide and Life-Threatening Behavior, 11,* 86–92.

Traskman-Bendz, L., Asberg, M., & Schalling, D. (1990). Serotonergic function and suicidal behavior in personality disorders. *Annals of the New York Academy of Sciences, 147,* 168–174.

Van de Kar, L. D. (1990). Neuroendocrine aspects of the serotonergic hypothesis of depression. *Neuroscience and Biobehavioral Reviews, 13,* 237–246.

Valzell, L. (1981). *Psychobiology of aggression and violence.* New York: Raven Press.

Weissman, M. M., Klerman, G. L., Markowitz, J. S., et al. (1989). Suicidal ideation and suicide attempts in panic disorder and attacks. *New England Journal of Medicine, 321,* 1209–1214.

Appendix 11-1   The Differential Diagnosis of Self-Destructive Behavior

Adjustment disorders
Anxiety disorders
Bipolar disorder
Brief reactive psychosis
Delusional (paranoid) disorder
Dysthymic disorder
Impulse control disorder
Major depression
Organic mental disorders associated with physical disorders or
   conditions
Personality disorders
Posttraumatic stress disorder
Psychoactive-substance-induced organic mental disorders
Schizoaffective disorder
Schizophrenia

Appendix 11-2 Contributing Factors in Self-Inflicted Death

Access to means of suicide
Age
Anomie
Command hallucinations
Family history
Gender
Generation in country
Homicide
Homosexual or bisexual orientation
Hypochondriasis
Insomnia
Intelligence
Amount of social support
Learning disorders
Marital status
Number of generations after immigration to country
Occupation
Physical and psychological disabilities
Physical illness
Psychiatric disorders
Previous attempt
Religion
Race
Socioeconomic status
Stressful life events
Substance abuse
Suicide of significant others
Unemployment
Urban versus rural origin

Chapter 12

Hospitalization of the Suicidal Patient

Mark J. Goldblatt

GENERAL CONSIDERATIONS

Safety is usually foremost in the mind of the clinician who treats a suicidal patient. However, when the physical safety of the patient preoccupies the therapist, he or she may lose sight of other important aspects of treatment (e.g., reality testing in psychotic patients, analysis of defenses in neurotic patients, pathological personality styles and interpersonal relationships, or the prescription of medication where indicated). Nevertheless, the principal reason for hospital admission, with few exceptions, is to protect against suicide. When should a patient be admitted to a psychiatric unit? What negotiations are involved in arranging voluntary and involuntary admissions? What are the available resources, and how are they best used? These questions are examined from three perspectives: (a) issues related to the patient, (b) issues related to the therapist, and (c) issues related to the interaction between the patient and the therapist.

Hospitalization has long been a trusted standby in the psychiatric treatment of suicidal patients. Admitting a patient to a psychiatric unit when the danger of suicide was discovered was almost a clinical reflex, under all circumstances. In fact, most early treatment protocols assumed that all treatment of suicidal patients took place in an inpatient setting (Stone & Shein, 1968). In the past, inpatient resources were more plentiful, the costs of these facilities more manageable, the legal obstacles fewer, and physician authority not so questioned as one finds today. Each of these considerations, once of seemingly small importance, has now grown into a thorny problem. In addition, clinicians have come to believe that for some suicidal patients inpatient care can be more hurtful than helpful. The traditional dogma that all suicidal patients are better off in the hospital is no longer accepted without question.

Generally, suicidal patients are probably better off in an inpatient setting. A psychiatric unit provides safety for patients when they or their families and friends are unable to provide such a holding environment themselves. The psychiatric unit is indispensable as a safe place where caring clinicians provide support, empathic attunement, limit setting, and counseling. Where but in a psychiatric unit can patients who are unable to care for their own safety be monitored? Because ward staff are closely observing patients' physical and emotional states, they are alert to possible danger and can prevent acts of self-destruction.

The psychiatric unit is, of course, useful for other purposes too. It provides the clinician access to study a patient over a prolonged period of time, amassing essential details of the patient's psychological distress, psychiatric illness, and interpersonal style. In addition, the inpatient unit provides a safe setting in which psychological testing can be done to increase understanding of deeper processes; families and friends can be involved in treatment in new ways to bring about psychological shifts; and new drugs or electroconvulsive therapy can be started to alter a dangerous mental state. Placement of a patient in a hospital setting also allows for the expansion of the treatment team to include inpatient psychiatrists, psychologists, social workers, nurses, and occupational workers who can provide much-needed collaboration, consultation, and support in dealing with difficult issues.

Inpatient admission, however, also has its negative consequences. First, there is the patient's loss of freedom. Regression often follows the surrender of adult independence, and in some patients this may increase the danger of self-destructiveness. Second, when the therapist assumes the authority of knowing what's right for the patient, the therapeutic alliance is invariably strained. When the admission is against the patient's own judgment, the alliance may in fact break down. It is rare for the therapeutic alliance to survive when the admission is involuntary. The breakdown of the therapeutic alliance is frequently the price paid for forced hospitalization.

The appropriate psychiatric unit where the patient can be safe and treatment issues can be addressed is not always immediately available; the best units are often crowded or have waiting lists. No admission may at times be preferable to admission into an ill-conducted unit. Funding for inpatient treatment, either directly from patients and their families or indirectly through third-party payers or state and federal agencies, is not always readily available. Insurance company reviewers (managed care consultants) often refuse to authorize inpatient treatment as appropriate and may not agree to pay. No hospitalization is sometimes preferable to one that will decimate a family's savings and force them into bankruptcy.

Deciding whether to hospitalize is complicated. There are risks and benefits involved on each side of the decision. Only by thinking through the various aspects of the problem in each individual case can the clinician discern the appropriate action. True therapeutic action arises from balancing issues related to the particular patient (diagnosis, transference, and available resources), issues related to the therapist or treatment team (clinical level of expertise, past therapeutic experience, countertransference issues, and sense of support or conflict among members of the treatment team), and issues related to the interaction between the patient and therapist or treatment team.

PATIENT-RELATED ISSUES

Diagnosis

The patient's diagnosis is a major factor in formulating plans for hospitalization.

Depression   Studies have shown that approximately 70% of people who commit suicide suffer from affective disorders (Barraclough, Bunch, Nelson, & Sainsbury, 1974; Dorpat & Ripley, 1960; Robins & Murphy, 1959). Depressed suicidal patients account for the majority of situations in which the question of hospitalization arises, and depression is also implicated in many suicides where the primary diagnosis is schizophrenia, alcoholism, or personality disorder. The revised third edition of the *Diagnostic and Statistical Manual of Mental Disorders (DSM-III-R;* American Psychiatric Association, 1987) is helpful in clarifying the diagnosis of major depression; however, not all patients who meet *DSM-III-R* criteria for this illness are best treated as inpatients.

In making the decision regarding hospitalization, what the patient says about his current state of suicidal danger should be taken most seriously. Patients with major depression often think of taking their lives. They usually are able to discuss their suicidal plans and ideas and are remarkably candid about how they see their options. Patients who unambivalently plan to commit suicide soon should be immediately admitted to the hospital. However, in those depressed patients whose immediate resolve for suicidal action is uncertain, estimation of safety is less clear-cut. In these cases, the immediate need for hospitalization is often ambiguous.

Several factors are critical in determining the acute risk for suicide in response to the current exacerbation. These are (a) a past history of significant depression, (b) a past history of suicide attempts, (c) a family history of suicide, and (d) the severity of the current stressors (Maltsberger, 1992a). Other factors play a role in deciding the need for admission to the psychiatric unit for the current exacerbation. These factors are as follows.

1 Severity of the illness. How depressed is the patient? How much are sleep and appetite disturbed? To what extent is daily functioning impaired?

2 Feelings of mental anguish. These states are frequently expressed in terms of panic or agitation. Patients with panic attacks have been reported to be at increased risk for suicidal actions (Weissman, Klerman, Markowitz, & Ouellette, 1989). This was also empirically observed in a recent study by Fawcett et al. (1990), who noted an association between suicides occurring in the first year followng hospitalization and severe psychic anxiety, panic attacks, diminished concentration, global insomnia, moderate alcohol abuse, and severe loss of interest or capacity for pleasure. Shneidman (1993) referred to "psychache," as the "hurt, anguish, soreness, aching, psychological pain in the psyche, the mind" (p. 147). Suicide occurs when this psychache becomes unbearable (Shneidman, 1993).

3 Degree of hopelessness and despair. Pessimism about the future and doubts about improvement appear to be significant long-term predictors of suicidal action (Beck, Steer, Kovacs, & Garrison, 1985).

4 Psychodynamic forces exerted on the individual. Through clinical observation, the therapist assesses the patient's characterlogical defenses; his ability to deal with stress, including loss; and his ability to react to injury. Narcissistic strengths and self-sustaining capacities are used to combat affects of rage, self-hatred, and depression. When the patient is not able to sustain a positive self-image in the face of such anxiety, through his own inner mechanisms, then exterior sustaining resources are needed. These resources usually take the form of a positive relationship to a family member, spouse, or friend or to work. However, if these relationships are unavailable, or if the patient is not able to connect to them as a result of his own defensiveness or psychosis, then the patient is left narcissistically bereft and imminently suicidal. By taking into account these forces (i.e., characterlogical defenses, ego strength, exterior sustaining resources, and mental state factors) in the face of narcissistic vulnerability, stress, and loss, the clinician is better equipped to evaluate suicidal decompensation and recommend interventions that are best suited to supporting a renewed capacity to cope with loss and stress.

The level of need for hospitalization depends on these factors, as well as on the clinician's ability to recognize and intervene. Psychodynamic formulation plays a critical role in the assessment of current suicidality and prediction of future safety considerations (Maltsberger, 1986).

Depression with Psychotic Features A notable subset of depressed patients are those whose depressions are complicated with psychotic features (e.g., major depression with psychotic features, bipolar disorder, depressed, and schizoaffective disorders). Some controversy remains about whether patients with delusional depressions are more likely to succumb to suicide than those diagnosed with depression without psychotic features. Roose and his colleagues (1993) reported on a retrospective analysis of patients who had died by suicide, and found that there was a significant association between delusions and suicide. Another study by Robins (1986) found that in 19% of a series of completed suicides, the individuals had been psychotic at the time of suicide. Although some authors have raised questions about the association between delusional depression and suicide (Kleespies, 1993), it is apparent that this subgroup of patients presents a great challenge to the clinician.

Therapists may neglect to search for psychosis in "normal-appearing" depression. In examining patients for signs of psychosis, the clinician should be on the lookout for the different manifestations of psychotic process. The presence of hallucinations (usually auditory) may be missed unless the clinician specifically asks about them. Delusions, usually mood-congruent beliefs associated with excessive guilt, death, or punishment, may be strong, yet remain hidden because patients are ashamed of them. A formal thought disorder, as evidenced by loose associations, thought blocking, or neologisms, may be subtle and requires deliberate examination and attentiveness to detail. Each of these symptoms of psychosis should be searched for in the clinical examination, because subtle signs may elude even experienced clinicians, and patients may deny the presence of psychosis out of shame or as a result of some other prohibitory force.

When the patient conceals symptoms or does not volunteer information about psychotic phenomena, and the therapist fails to search for them, the likely result is a treatment impasse, with a concomitant rise in suicide risk. When such potent forces go unrecognized, the patient's safety is precarious. Psychotic depression demands vigilant clinical engagement; hospital admission is almost always necessary to protect the patient from impulsive responses to command hallucinations or delusional convictions. In addition, prompt hospitalization is expeditious for electroconvulsive therapy to be speedily undertaken, when appropriate, in the safety of a hospital setting. Unfortunately, in some extreme cases of depression with psychotic complications, even inpatient hospitalization may be insufficient to prevent a suicide attempt. Clinicians should always be alert to the danger of psychotic disintegration and narcissistic collapse.

Schizophrenia   Patients diagnosed with schizophrenia account for about 10% of suicides (Barraclough et al., 1974; Dorpat & Ripley, 1960; Robins & Murphy, 1959). Hospitalization can be of great help to these patients, especially during an acute psychotic episode. Any patient who hears voices demanding suicide should be hospitalized at once. Even when patients minimize the importance or malice of these voices, the clinician's objective knowledge should alert him to the clinical danger. Patients often report hearing voices that order them to do things they do not quite understand or find confusing. When such commands involve violence, the need for immediate hospitalization is great.

Command hallucinations have traditionally been considered to have a malignant connotation. Recently this has become a subject of some debate. Hellerstein, Frosch, and Koenigsberg (1987) reviewed consecutive inpatient admissions and found that patients with command hallucinations were not significantly different from other psychotic patients, and that "command hallucinations alone may not imply greater risk for acute life-threatening behavior" (p. 219). However, Rogers, Gillis, Turner, and Frise-Smith (1990) noted that compared with other patients with psychotic impairments, those with command hallucinations showed "more aggression, dependency and self-punishment themes in their hallucinations, and . . . frequently responded to these hallucinatory commands with unquestioned obedience" (p. 1304). Rogers et al. also noted that such patients were reluctant to reveal their hallucinations and that in "approximately one half of the sample population the command hallucinations went undetected by the clinical staff" (p. 1305). Without doubt, hallucinations and delusions are unpredictable and destabilizing. If they have shameful or conflicted feelings about such symptoms, patients may retreat into silence or withdrawal. These psychotic disturbances play a powerful role in patients' thought processes and may remain hidden if the patient is embarrassed, paranoid, or lacking in insight.

Schizophrenic patients often suffer superimposed depressions that color their view of the future, especially their hope for recovery. When these patients begin to come to terms with their realistically constricted future prospects, the clinician should be alert for subtle signs of giving up. Sometimes hospitalization helps patients reengage in the struggle against withdrawal, loneliness, and despair. Hospitalization at such times can reaffirm supportive relationships with the treatment team, fellow patients, or family members and provide a holding environment while new medications are tried or solutions to other problems are attempted.

Alcohol and Drug Abuse   Alcohol or drug abuse is the primary diagnosis in about 15–28% of suicides (Barraclough et al., 1974; Dorpat & Ripley, 1960; Robins & Murphy, 1959), and alcohol abuse has been reported to be associated with up to 50% of all suicides (Frances, Franklin, & Flavin, 1987). Most patients, whatever their primary diagnosis, are to some extent intoxicated when attempting suicide. When drug or alcohol abuse is out of control, suicidal patients should be confined in a safe environment until they are sober. Often this sort of protection can be arranged outside a formal psychiatric setting. Most of these patients recover their sobriety with minimal supervision in a detoxification unit, but there are several risks to be weighed, especially during the withdrawal period. At great risk are those who, grasping the enormity of some drunken behavior and its consequences, are overcome with shame and become suicidal. Such patients would obviously be better off in a secure psychiatric facility, by court order if necessary, where suicide precautions may be enforced.

Personality Disorders   It is often difficult to decide whether to hospitalize patients with personality disorders. The indications for and against hospitalization often seem conflictual and complex. In addition, these patients usually arouse strong feelings, often of a highly aversive nature, at every level. These admissions may be quite ambiguous and may stir up the most intense feelings, not only in the patient, but in staff too.

Patients with borderline personality disorder often feel suicidal and out of control. They are often morbidly preoccupied and may cut, burn, or otherwise hurt themselves. Their moods and behavior are mercurial; these patients can spiral out of control, giving the therapist increasing cause to worry about their safety and the need for external limits. It may be difficult to distinguish between life-threatening situations that require hospitalization and other, less destructive regressions that may be managed outside the hospital. This is especially troublesome in the early stages of treatment, when the therapist does not know the patient very well and the therapeutic alliance remains tentative and is being tested. The presence of a major depression worsening an already bleak dysphoric state, in the face of poor impulse control, complicates the issue and invites hospitalization. Much may be accomplished when patient and therapist agree on admission to a psychiatric unit for assessment and treatment.

The Therapeutic Alliance

At minimum, a basic commitment between the patient and therapist to work together toward certain agreed upon goals is necessary for therapeutic growth to occur. This commitment to treatment goals forms a basis for the patient and therapist to meet consistently, in a structured and respectful manner, so that the patient's anguish or conflicts may be resolved. Freud (1937/1964) described this in his early technical papers: "The analytic situation consists of our allying ourselves with the ego of the person under treatment, in order to subdue portions of his id which are uncontrolled—that is to say to include them in the synthesis of his ego" (p. 235). Zetzel (1970) clarified this relationship as "the therapeutic alliance," which she described as "a working relationship between patient and analyst" (p. 182). She suggested that "resolution of psychic distress . . . is contingent on sufficient success at a pre-oedipal level, for the patient to establish and maintain a secure basic relationship which recognizes the integrity of separate individuals" (p. 184–185). Although both Freud and Zetzel were referring to the analysis of neurotic patients, such an alliance is a necessity in the treatment of suicidal patients of all diagnoses. Thus the therapeutic alliance also requires the patient to be able to work with the therapist toward a common goal, with safety mutually understood to be of primary importance, so that dangerous fantasies and acting out may be promptly and aggressively addressed in therapy (Stone & Shein, 1968).

The capacity to form an alliance, to work with the therapist toward common goals, cannot be taken for granted. In the early stages of treatment, the therapist may not yet be sufficiently important to the patient that his judgment and perspectives seem to matter. Patients whose thought processes are impeded by psychosis (especially if they are paranoid) may also have difficulty in forming a therapeutic alliance. Those patients who are withdrawn and inhibited by depression, and those whose capacity for object relatedness is slight or limited by organic impairment, may also be severely restricted in their ability to develop a therapeutic alliance. Patients with severe personality disorders also have great impediments in forming close treatment alliances.

When the therapeutic alliance has become sufficiently strong, patients can often tolerate fearful and painful thoughts and feelings and remain engaged with their therapist to accomplish difficult psychological work. However, the therapist should not be lulled into thinking that the therapeutic alliance will prevent the patient from *ever* doing anything self-destructive. The alliance is no stronger than the ego that binds it; it may crumble under pressure from increased mental pain, symptoms, frustrations, or psychosis. Experienced therapists are cognizant of the therapeutic alliance when considering hospitalization of a suicidal patient and realize the contribution it makes as part of the bigger picture, not as an omnipotent force, acting alone to keep the patient alive.

THERAPIST-RELATED ISSUES

The therapist's past experiences with suicidal patients and his feelings about the current ongoing treatment invariably play a role in the decision to hospitalize. The clinician's unconscious thoughts and feelings are of critical importance in the treatment of suicidal patients, and they remain so in the decision-making process regarding hospitalization. Countertransference is an inherent part of psychological treatment and may be constructively employed when the therapist is fully conscious of his feelings toward the patient and the reactions that follow. These responses in the therapist may arise from any source, not only from repressed memories pertaining to previous patients' suicide, but also from the therapist's personal development, especially in the area of loss, abandonment, and sadism. Buie (1982) described one motivation for psychotherapists as the need to be sustained—"consciously or unconsciously to be relieved of his sense of aloneness" (p. 227). "The holding environment that the therapist provides for the patient serves to hold the therapist as well" (p. 231). Rejection of the therapist by the patient (signaled by suicide or threats of suicide) precipitates separation anxiety, depression, and rage in the therapist. The transference hate of borderline and psychotic patients is related to their great difficulty in dealing with aloneness, hostility, and sadism (Maltsberger & Buie, 1974). This inevitably stirs up countertransference hate in the therapist. As Maltsberger and Buie (1974) described, this reaction is likely to be very intense in the treatment of suicidal patients and, if not handled appropriately, can lead to the therapist's acting out in the countertransference, precipitating suicidal crises: "While we do not believe it is possible to treat any patient without countertransference, and, in the case of suicidal patients, without countertransference hate, clearly the discharge of countertransference hate in the therapeutic relationship is noxious and sometimes fatal for the patient" (p. 627).

Awareness of these countertransference issues and, wherever possible, resolution of these conflicts are critical to the progress of treatment with suicidal patients. Countertransference issues may be resolved through the therapist's own analysis, self-analysis, or sometimes in supervision.

Therapists who have lost patients to suicide regularly report the pain of such losses. Those stung once by suicide often shun such cases later. Those who do continue to treat suicidal patients often shift their therapeutic style to favor hospitalization sooner or on the basis of less objective data than previously. At issue is the therapist's countertransference, that is, feelings of guilt and narcissistic injury, as well as masochistic and other impulses, which if not fully conscious, can lead to the therapist's avoiding certain patients or treating suicidal patients in overly conservative modalities that may precipitate further crises (Maltsberger, 1992b).

The therapeutic milieu of an inpatient service often provides support to the therapist dealing with suicidal patients. However, when this milieu alters, and a split develops such that the therapist is scapegoated by the staff, the therapy can be undone as the alliance is destroyed and negative transference trends are validated. This is particularly likely to occur in the course of treatment of patients with borderline personality organization (Kernberg, 1975). Similar misadventures can also occur outside the hospital, in the context of an ill-conceived consultation. Although peer supervision and collaboration are extremely useful in treating difficult patients, inappropriate public peer criticism and judgment can be extremely harmful. The therapist may respond with depression and appear to the patient to abandon hope, with the result that the patient's risk of suicide rises. Nevertheless, sophisticated and constructive consultation and supervision are reliable aids in these difficult cases (Maltsberger, 1984–85).

INTERACTION BETWEEN THE PATIENT AND THERAPIST

Contracts

The use of verbal or written no-suicide contracts in the treatment of suicidal patients is controversial, and the literature regarding such contracts is sparse. Because few studies exist to substantiate the efficacy of no-suicide contracts, their true usefulness and reliability are unknown. Although some authors (e.g., Drye, Goulding, & Goulding, 1973) advocate the use of no-suicide contracts, few clinicians would rely completely on the suicidal patient's ability to contract against self-destruction when weighing factors regarding hospitalization.

The therapeutic dialogue involved in the no-suicide contract can serve several useful purposes. It offers an entry into the patient's inner state and a way of conducting a mental status examination about suicidality. It can also help the therapist and patient formulate ways of dealing with increasing levels of dangerousness and devise plans to ensure safety. Although some clinicians believe that no-suicide contracts provide documentation that would be helpful for forensic purposes, this has not been proven. Often, the no-suicide contract serves merely to reduce the anxiety of the clinician. In such cases, real danger may be missed as the clinician attempts to gain some distance from the patient's intense pain and violence.

The clinician who uses a no-suicide contract should be aware of why he is negotiating such a contract, for whose benefit it is, and what the contract means to the patient and to the therapist. When making decisions regarding hospitalization, it is unwise to depend too heavily on a no-suicide contract, because these agreements have been notoriously unreliable and have no proven ability to prevent self-destruction. The psychodynamic formulation of stressors and defenses provides a more salient assessment of the patient's potential for self-harm and is a more trustworthy guide in making decisions regarding hospitalization.

Security

Therapists should always take seriously threats of violence that emerge in the context of psychotherapy or treatment evaluation. When patients report suicidal plans, the clinician should immediately consider the necessary safety countermeasures. Threats of self-destruction require urgent assessment and treatment responses. Most patients will cooperate and even appreciate the doctor's help in acquiring a safe environment in the hospital. However, there are times when the patient's capacity for self-observation is overextended, and he is unwilling to cooperate with hospitalization. On these occasions, the clinician must consider how to diminish the likelihood of violence and ensure safety for all concerned, even by reaching beyond the patient's level of cooperation.

When a patient says he is planning to kill himself, the clinician may infer some ambivalence. Some part of the patient is asking for help; another part is determined to die. Some patients may reject the offer of safe haven in the hospital. Some may try to run away; a few will attack the therapist verbally or, rarely, physically. Given the volatility of such an impasse, good security planning can be the most basic intervention of treatment. Various degrees of security planning may be needed. For example, the clinician may simply ask family members whom the patient respects to stay in the room for the evaluation and recommendation for hospitalization. If the assessment is taking place within a hospital system, the clinician may inform the hospital security system that a crisis is near at hand and request that assistants stand by.

When a new patient is examined in the emergency room, security personnel play a critical role in allowing the clinician to interview the patient safely, knowing that physical support is near at hand. Some patients may feel uneasy if security personnel are too conspicuous, but, under optimal circumstances, discreet placement of security personnel should not detract from the usefulness of the protection they provide.

When the therapist is dealing with a suicidal patient outside of a hospital-based office, the local police or emergency medical technicians may sometimes be needed to provide necessary security. Obviously, such interventions should be handled with great care and consideration. It is an extreme violation of boundaries to send the police to force open the locked door of a patient's home on the grounds that the patient has been suicidal lately and now does not answer the telephone. Yet, when there is sufficient clinical backing for such concern, it may in fact be a life-saving intervention. There remains the risk of disturbing the therapeutic alliance, which is probably already on shaky grounds, given the clinician's concerns about the patient's reliability and cooperation.

The absolute need to maintain the safety of the clinician and the patient, especially in the evaluation stage, clearly supersedes other clinical considerations. Although the use of external security agents is not ideal, it does provide a pathway toward safety when all other avenues point to violence. In such cases, getting the dangerous patient into the hospital in a safe and prompt manner is the overriding concern. Clarification and working through this experience can take place at a later stage, once the safety of the inpatient unit has been reached.

CONCLUSION

Many issues are involved in the decision to hospitalize a suicidal patient. Of great concern is the ability of the patient and therapist to work together to decide on the appropriate level of help necessary to ensure the patient's safety during a suicidal crisis. When resources are limited, it may be appropriate for the patient and therapist to work toward providing an outpatient support system sufficient to support the patient through a time-limited crisis. However, hospitalization is indicated when the external holding environment is insufficient, or when there is doubt as to the patient's ability to use such a supportive outpatient network.

The decision to hospitalize is based on issues related directly to the patient, including diagnosis, available support system, past history of suicidality, and current stressors; as well as considerations relating to the therapist such as experience, expertise, and countertransference. The therapeutic alliance and the patient's ability to accept the support provided by the therapist are the final components in this complicated decision process.

Even today, when resources are scarce and hospital admissions are emotionally and financially costly, it is almost always better for the clinician to err on the side of conservative management with early use of inpatient hospital units, rather than to attempt heroic measures that involve a high degree of risk and set the stage for disappointment, rejection, and blame when disaster occurs. It is foolhardy for any clinician to assume that he can provide the perfect holding environment to prevent suicide because his intentions are pure. Treatment of suicidal patients requires that the clinician be aware of potential dangers and find ways of lessening the patient's burden by increasing supports, in particular from inpatient staff and hospitals. It is far more cost-effective, and indeed more humane, to use hospitals for assessment of safety. Patients may be discharged once the crisis has ended. The therapist must guard against denying the severity of distress or falsely exaggerating his capacity to maintain the patient's will for life in the face of overwhelming stressors.

REFERENCES

American Psychiatric Association. (1987). *Diagnostic and statistical manual of mental disorders* (3rd ed., rev.). Washington, DC: Author.

Barraclough, B., Bunch, J., Nelson, B., & Sainsbury, P. (1974). A hundred cases of suicide: Clinical aspects. *British Journal of Psychiatry, 125,* 355–373.

Beck, A. T., Steer, R. A., Kovacs, M., & Garrison, B. (1985). Hopelessness and eventual suicide: A 10-year prospective study of patients hospitalized with suicidal ideation. *American Journal of Psychiatry, 142,* 559–563.

Buie, D. H. (1982). The abandoned therapist. *International Journal of Psychoanalytic Psychotherapy, 9,* 227–231.

Dorpat, T. L., & Ripley, S. R. (1960). A study of suicide in the Seattle area. *Comprehensive Psychiatry, 1,* 349–359.

Drye, R. C., Goulding, R. L., & Goulding, M. E. (1973). No-suicide decisions: Patient monitoring of suicidal risk. *American Journal of Psychiatry, 130,* 171–174.

Fawcett, J., Scheftner, W. A., Fogg, L., Clark, D. C., Young, M. A., Hedeker, D., & Gibbons, R. (1990). Time related predictors of suicide in major affective disorder. *American Journal of Psychiatry, 147,* 1189–1194.

Frances, R. J., Franklin, J., & Flavin, D. K. (1987). Suicide and alcoholism. *American Journal of Drug and Alcohol Abuse, 13,* 327–341.

Freud, S. (1964). Analysis terminable and interminable. In J. Strachey (Ed. & Trans.), *The standard edition of the complete psychological works of Sigmund Freud* (Vol. 23, pp. 235). London: Hogarth Press (Original work published in 1937).

Hellerstein, D., Frosch, W., & Koenigsberg, H. W. (1987). The clinical significance of command hallucinations. *American Journal of Psychiatry, 144,* 219–222.

Kernberg, O. F. (1975). *Borderline conditions and pathological narcissism.* New York: Jason Aronson.

Kleespies, P. M. (1993). Letter to the editor. *Suicide and Life-Threatening Behavior, 23, 1,* 67–71.

Maltsberger, J. T. (1984–85). Consultation in a suicidal impasse. *International Journal of Psychoanalytic Psychotherapy, 10,* 131–158.

Maltsberger, J. T. (1986). *Suicide risk: Formulation of clinical judgment.* New York: New York University Press.

Maltsberger, J. T. (1992a). The psychodynamic formulation: An aid in assessing suicide risk. In R. W. Maris, A. L. Berman, J. T. Maltsberger, & R. I. Yufit (Eds.), *Assessment and prediction of suicide* (pp. 25–49). New York: Guilford Press.

Maltsberger, J. T. (1992b). The implications of patient suicide for the surviving psychotherapist. In D. Jacobs (Ed.), *Suicide in clinical practice* (pp. 169–182). Washington, DC: American Psychiatric Press.

Maltsberger, J. T., & Buie, D. H. (1974). Countertransference hate in the treatment of suicidal patients. *Archives of General Psychiatry, 30,* 625–633.

Robins, E. (1986). Psychosis and suicide. *Biological Psychiatry, 21,* 665–672.

Robins, E., & Murphy, G. E. (1959). Some clinical considerations in the prevention of suicide based on a study of 134 successful suicides. *American Journal of Public Health, 49,* 888–889.

Rogers, R., Gillis, J. R., Turner, R. E., & Frise-Smith, T. (1990). The clinical presentation of command hallucinations in a forensic population. *American Journal of Psychiatry, 147,* 1304–1307.

Roose, S. P., Glassman, A. H., Walsh, B. T., Woodring, S., & Vital-Herne, J. (1983). Depression, delusions and suicide. *American Journal of Psychiatry, 140,* 1159–1162.

Shneidman, E. S. (1993). Suicide as psychache. *Journal of Nervous and Mental Disease, 181,* 147–149.

Stone, A. A., & Shein, H. M. (1968). Psychotherapy of the hospitalized suicidal patient. *American Journal of Psychotherapy, 22,* 15–25.

Weissman, M. M., Klerman, G. L., Markowitz, J. S., & Ouellette, R. (1989). Suicidal ideation and suicide attempts in panic disorder and attacks. *New England Journal of Medicine, 321,* 1210–1214.

Zetzel, E. R. (1970). The therapeutic alliance in the psychoanalysis of hysteria (1958). In *The capacity for emotional growth* (pp. 182–196). New York: International Universities Press.

Chapter 13

Managing Suicidal Inpatients

Lloyd I. Sederer

The suicidal patient is the most common and the vexing clinical challenge for the staff on an inpatient unit. First, clinicians' capacity to predict suicide is woefully limited (Goldstein, Black, Nasrallah, & Winokur, 1991). Second, not all that appears to be suicidal behavior is truly the pursuit of a deadly outcome. Third, even when clinicians know a patient is truly suicidal, they cannot ensure a sanguine outcome, because of the limits of the security measures and therapeutic tools at their disposal and, in some instances, the sheer determination to die on the part of the patient. In fact, as many as 5% of deaths by suicide in the United States annually have occurred on psychiatric inpatient units (Crammer, 1984). Finally, work with the suicidal patient may evoke intense and irrational feelings in the clinician, not the least of which are fear of failure and consequent humiliation or litigation. It is no surprise, therefore, that many clinicians find work with suicidal patients disturbing or aversive.

In this discussion, I address three topics in the treatment of the suicidal psychiatric inpatient: the assessment of risk, the need to differentiate among various characteristics of the suicidal crisis, and institutional suicide policies and procedures.

RISK ASSESSMENT

Although suicide definitely cannot be predicted, the clinician cannot eschew the most diligent of efforts to determine whether a patient is in a life-threatening condition. The assessment of risk proceeds along three principal tracks: patient demographics, past history, and the present-day assessment.

Demographic risk factors have been identified through studies of completed and attempted suicides (Jacobs, 1992; Klerman, 1987). Older age is associated with risk for completed suicide, whereas younger age, 20–30, is associated with suicide attempts. Men are far more likely to complete suicide, whereas women are more likely to have unsuccessful tries. Regarding completed suicides, Native Americans carry the highest risk, followed by whites and then blacks (although accidental deaths and homicides should have us rethink this ranking). Being single, widowed, or divorced or living alone is correlated more highly than being married with completed suicide, whereas divorce is associated with suicide attempts (Schrut & Michels, 1974). Urban professionals have higher rates of completed suicide, and unemployment in men is associated with suicide attempts. Finally, completed suicide in the United States is most commonly associated with the ownership and use of firearms, whereas suicide attempts are most commonly by drug ingestion.

The assessment of the patient's history must include a psychiatric history, a medical history, a family history, and a careful review of past suicidal behavior (Goodwin & Runck, 1992; Jacobs, 1992; Lepine, Chignon, & Teherani, 1993). A history of affective illness or panic disorder carries the highest lifetime risk of suicide, which has been estimated to be 15%. Schizophrenia carries a 10% lifetime risk, although death is not associated with acute psychotic episodes or with command hallucinations. Substance abuse has been identified to carry a 3% lifetime risk, and this risk is heightened by a comorbid psychiatric disorder; by active abuse of substances; or by loss of any type (recent, imminent, anticipated, or imagined). Active, comorbid medical illness has been associated with suicide risk and should be carefully sought and discussed. A family history of suicide or suicide attempts is also associated with risk, through the gene pool, modeling of helplessness or self-destructiveness, or early loss or early abuse. Finally, the best predictor of future behavior is generally past behavior: Patients with past histories of suicidal behavior are at significant risk for repetition. The assessment should determine, to the extent possible, whether past episodes of suicidal behavior carried high risk of lethality and what motivated them (Maltsberger, 1986; Maltsberger & Buie, 1980).

The present-day assessment is a comprehensive study of the patient's current status. Diagnosis, comorbidity, the history of the present illness (HPI), the adequacy of the patient's supports, and the patient's capacity for alliance are the principal dimensions of the assessment.

A psychiatric diagnosis may be the necessary condition for suicide, but a diagnosis of a mental disorder is not itself a sufficient condition for suicide

(Black & Winokur, 1992). The *sufficient condition* refers to those psychological, familial, and biological elements of the patient that release potential into actual destructiveness. The HPI and the mental status examination are the clinician's tools for discovering the presence of the sufficient condition.

In obtaining the HPI, the clinician must pay careful attention to the nature of the patient's recent suicidal behavior, especially method, intent, risk/rescue dimensions, and motives. Did the patient mean to die? What fantasy or need compelled the suicidal behavior, and what effect did the patient fantasize it would have on others? What does the patient imagine it would be like to be dead? Does the patient believe in an afterlife, and, if so, who is believed to inhabit it? Does the patient still want to die? Would the patient change his or her method, and are the means available for the patient to do so?

Hopelessness, severe anxiety or dysphoria, panic, and an experience of psychological disintegration or impending psychosis are especially disturbing findings on the mental status examination. Severe psychic anxiety and panic have been associated with suicide within 1 year, whereas hopelessness has been related to suicide after 1 year, suggesting certain time-related predictors (Fawcett, 1992; Fawcett et al., 1990). Poor ego controls (especially evidenced by impulsivity) or active substance abuse that handicaps ego constraints adds to the patient's risk. An accumulated sense of failure and despair is a worrisome finding in chronic psychotic patients, especially in younger patients who have known some measure of success. A burning wish to inflict suffering on others, particularly through manipulative self-destruction, and a resolute desire for peace or reunion through death are high-risk motives for suicidal behavior.

Several scales are available that can augment the psychiatric interview, but they cannot serve as its replacement. Crucial to the assessment is direct contact by the clinician who demonstrates, through the process of inquiry, a willingness to hear despair and hatred (and other affects) and a capacity to bear, with the patient, such powerful human feelings. Beck and his colleagues have developed the Scales for Suicide Ideation and the Scale for Suicide Intent (Beck, Kovacs, & Weissman, 1979) as well as the Hopelessness Scale (Beck, Weissman, Lester, & Trexler, 1974). These scales are readily available from their authors and can be useful on inpatient units as one method of assessment.

Disturbances, disruptions, or losses in the patient's human milieu are critical in prompting suicidal behavior. Any loss, actual or imagined, is highly destabilizing to the vulnerable patient (Havens, 1963). Even relationships fraught with conflict and pain are more bearable and life-supporting than a life alone, without relief from the panic of aloneness and without some measure of human contact and comfort (Murphy, 1992).

An often omitted aspect of the assessment is the patient's capacity for a therapeutic alliance, however tenuous and transitory. The alliance is a measure of the patient's ability to have an active role in treatment. Alliance is a measure of both the patient's capacity to see someone else as helpful and/or trustworthy and the patient's motivation to improve, rather than to eschew responsibility or pursue gratification. Many inpatient units have turned to contracts as a device to establish a working relationship. Contracts imply mutuality and competence, qualities that are often missing from acutely ill patients, particularly at the outset of a hospitalization. A contract may lull the clinician into thinking that the patient has the capacity to engage in a working alliance when the patient does not have that capacity.

DIFFERENTIATION OF THE CHARACTERISTICS OF THE SUICIDAL CRISIS

By effectively differentiating among certain characteristics of the suicidal crisis, the clinician will be better able to manage the clinical conundrums so common in the treatment of this patient population.

Acute Versus Chronic Suicidality

Acute conditions are, by their nature, state (transitory) disorders. The patient's symptoms are the product of an acute process generated by biopsychosocial disturbances. Acute conditions (a) improve, (b) become persistent or chronic (become trait phenomena), or (c) cause the sufferer to succumb. Acute suicidality conforms to the definition of a state disorder—the unfortunate convergence of mental disorder with personal and/or social vulnerability that has inspired lethal intent. The patient will recover, will incorporate suicidality into his or her adaptational style (become chronically suicidal), or will die by his or her own hand (Havens, 1963). Inpatient units are particularly effective in controlling acute suicidality by treating acute symptoms and by providing temporary safety, support, and hope. Inpatient units are not particularly effective in controlling chronic suicidality, especially in nonpsychotic patients. To paraphrase Gutheil (1985), acute suicidality is a defect in the metabolism of despair, whereas chronic suicidality is a defect in the metabolism of responsibility. I know of no short-term inpatient unit that can significantly alter character or ingrained deficits in individual responsibility.

Ideas Versus Actions

A cornerstone of psychiatric theory and practice is the uncensored expression of ideas and affects. From the outset of hospitalization, the suicidal patient must be told that staff are prepared and able to hear the disturbing ideas and feelings that the patient cannot bear alone and that threaten his or her well-being (Sederer & Thorbeck, 1991). At the same time, staff must convey—clearly and firmly—that suicidal behavior cannot be tolerated. Patient safety is always the first priority of the patient milieu.

Suicide ideation can be understood as the product of despair, as a communication, or even as a form of self-soothing (Buie & Maltsberger, 1983). In all cases, it serves a purpose. The clinician's aim is not to try to take suicide ideation away from a patient, because this would deprive the patient of a necessary mental operation. Instead, the clinician offers the patient both the opportunity not to be alone in despair and the prospect of altering illness and circumstance so that suicide ideation is no longer necessary for psychic equilibrium.

Threats Versus Suicidal Ideation and Intent

A further distinction that the clinician should understand is that between suicide threats and suicide ideation or intention. Suicidal ideation and intention (acute) are symptomatic of illness, despair, or disequilibrium. Suicidal threats are very different. Threats are interpersonal acts meant, consciously or unconsciously, to manipulate someone. That someone, be it family, friend, or the clinician, often cannot marshal empathy and support for the person making the threats, because he or she feels resentment or aversion, the common by-products of the experience of being manipulated. The clinician cannot be hostage to a patient's threats and simultaneously provide what the patient truly needs. As Main (1957) said, "sincerity by all about what can and cannot be given *with good will* offers a basis for management (p. 145, emphasis added).

Parasuicide versus Suicide

Parasuicide refers to behaviors that are equivocally suicidal, such as gestures or self-destructive acts that are not lethal in intent (Kreitman, 1977). Parasuicide is a "non-fatal act in which an individual deliberately causes self-injury or ingests a substance in excess of any prescribed or generally recognized therapeutic doses" (Kreitman, 1977, p. 3). Parasuicide does not have death as its aim, which is what differentiates it from a completed suicide that is not an accident and a serious suicide attempt that is foiled by unexpected discovery and rescue.

Parasuicide has been understood as manipulative, depersonalized, or both (Maltzberger & Lovett, 1991). Manipulative parasuicide aims to control others and is generally inspired by rageful panic or narcissistic shame and injury. Revenge may be the primary motive in manipulative parasuicide. Depersonalized parasuicide aims to relieve the patient of an unbearable numbness, alienation, or derealization. Its method is usually self-mutilation through cutting, burning, banging, or biting.

Parasuicide may not be an adequate indication for hospitalization. If a pattern of increasing self-destructiveness develops, however, hospital-level care may be needed to avert the progression to a lethal outcome. The treatment in such cases differs from that offered in suicidal situations, because the aims and methods of parasuicide do not merit the same safety considerations and therapeutic interventions that apply to the suicidal patient.

POLICIES AND PROCEDURES

All inpatient units must have written and regularly updated policies and procedures for the care of suicidal patients. These policies and procedures may be understood as addressing four principal areas of concern:

- Environmental precautions
- Patient-specific interventions
- Privilege system
- Pass system

Environmental Precautions

An inpatient service that can appropriately accept and contain patients judged to be acutely suicidal must be architecturally equipped for safety (Benensohn & Resnik, 1973; Kroll, 1978; Schoonover, 1982). Windows must have stops to keep them from providing an opening through which a person could escape. Safety screens must be in a place that prevent exit and resist tampering or destruction. Obviously, all doors and other exits from the unit must be locked, equipped with an alarm, or staffed by someone who can prevent egress.

Toxic substances, including detergents and cleaning substances, must be kept in locked boxes, dispersed in limited quantities, and carefully overseen by the cleaning staff who bring these substances by cart onto the unit. Bathroom curtain rods must be designed to break if subject to any significant weight. Closet rods must also meet this specification. Wooden rods harden with age and can bear more weight, making J-hooks a desirable alternative (Libby, 1992). Finally, exposed pipes in low-security areas should be covered or rendered inaccessible.

Units should consider instituting "environmental rounds," in which clinicians and members of the plant and operations department inspect the unit. Established parameters for inspection, including those just mentioned, would be examined and new problems addressed as they arise.

Patient-Specific Interventions

The most intensive level of intervention is seclusion, with or without restraint, with either an open or closed door. Highly specific regulations exist for seclusion and restraint on a state-by-state basis. These regulations serve as the basis of unit procedural requirements.

An important unit procedure is the search of the patient's belongings. Sharps (pointed or bladed instruments) and flames (matches, lighters, and cigarettes) must be confiscated from the suicidal patient. All patients must surrender prescriptions and over-the-counter medications. Suicidal patients must surrender any substances that could be put to deleterious use (e.g., art supplies, detergents, dyes, etc.). Belts, shoelaces, and other articles of apparel represent dangerous devices for suicidal patients. However, staff must weigh the danger of these objects against the dehumanization of stripping patients of everyday elements of attire and convenience.

The use of the body search should be restricted to patients at high risk for suicide. A body search is intrusive and potentially humiliating or stimulating to vulnerable patients. Room searches, on the other hand, may be done with less concern and are one way the staff can demonstrate their rigor and commitment to safety.

Observation of the patient is fundamental to all inpatient units and is typically a dimension of nursing policy and procedure. Increments of observation should be specified and procedures articulated. One-to-one observation (constant observation) should be defined as either "at arm's length" (i.e., immediately next to the patient) or under the continuous eye of the staff. Typical increments of observation then proceed from 5- to 15- to 30-min checks. Checks may be recorded either by staff or by the patient (self-checks), depending on clinical goals. Orders for intensive observation probably would last no longer than 24 hr and, optimally, require daily physician examination of the patient.

Supervision of the patient is different from observation and may warrant its own policy and procedure. Certain patients may require, for safety, supervision of their use of sharps and flames. Other patients may not be safe in the kitchen area because of the many materials and instruments that can be used for self-destruction. Bathroom use will need to be supervised for all patients who are on one-to-one status and for some patients who cannot safely be allowed access to pipes, rods, and pools of water. Finally, some patients may have "open areas" supervision, which indicates that they are safe in public areas where people are present, but they cannot be trusted to not secrete themselves away when alone. Staff supervision can be effective only for limited periods of time (i.e., hours to days) because of the limited capacity to control anyone, and in fact it should be in place for only a limited period of time, because prolonged supervision can invite regression.

Privilege System

A privilege system exists on all inpatient units and varies among hospitals and staffs. Privileges should be clearly defined and require a physician's order. A typical privilege system spans degrees of freedom from restriction to the unit, to permission to go off unit if accompanied (by staff or by family/friend), to permission to go off unit unaccompanied. Some units will differentiate on-grounds from off-grounds privileges.

By definition, privileges must be earned. The patient must demonstrate the clinical capacity to merit the lifting of restriction. Inpatient units are the opposite of a democracy; freedom is not inherent to life on an inpatient unit, especially for the involuntary or dangerous patient. Instead, restriction is normative and freedom is granted as a privilege when the patient has shown alliance, self-control, and responsibility for safety.

The patient's privileges (and passes) should also be consistent with his or her legal status. A patient committed to the unit by court order, for example, should have privileges consistent with the court's action, or there should be documentation as to why privileges do not conform to the court's order.

Pass System

Two types of passes generally are used: therapeutic and nontherapeutic. Therapeutic passes are provided to patients so that diagnostic or treatment plans may be pursued or to test patients' capacity to tolerate increasing degrees of liberty. Nontherapeutic passes may be offered to allow the patient to care for everyday needs (car, bank, or shopping) or for recreational purposes (exercise, entertainment, or socializing). Patients with restricted privileges may receive therapeutic passes; they should not receive passes for convenience or social purposes.

Passes may also be accompanied or nonaccompanied. It is important to distinguish accompaniment for support from accompaniment for safety. Many patients will benefit from pass accompaniment but will not be unsafe without it. Patients who require accompaniment for safety (those at risk of escaping or causing themselves harm) should be accompanied by staff adequate in number and strength to maintain safety.

Summary

No standardized system of policies and procedures exists for the four areas of concern discussed herein. Each hospital or inpatient unit has its own specific resources and concerns, making a universal system undesirable. Nevertheless a core set of policies and procedures is important, for clinical and risk management purposes, for all facilities. The Harvard University hospitals and the Harvard Risk-Management Program are in the process of developing such a set of guidelines for the care of the suicidal patient.

CONCLUSION

Suicidality is the preeminent clinical challenge for hospital-based psychiatric staff. Although full safety for all patients can never be promised, conscientious assessment of risk and thoughtful policies and procedures are the foundations of care for suicidal patients. Staff efforts will keep many of these patients safe from self-destruction.

REFERENCES

Beck, A. T., Kovacs, M., & Weissman, A. (1979). Assessment of suicidal intention: The Scale for Suicide Ideation. *Journal of Consulting and Clinical Psychology, 47,* 343–352.

Beck, A. T., Weissman, A., Lester, D., & Trexler, L. (1974). The measurement of pessimism: The Hopelessness Scale. *Journal of Consulting and Clinical Psychology, 42,* 861–865.

Benensohn, H., & Resnik, H. (1973). Guidelines for "suicide-proofing" a psychiatric unit. *American Journal of Psychotherapy, 27,* 204–212.

Black, D. W., & Winokur, G. (1990). Suicide and psychiatric diagnosis. In S. J. Blumenthal & D. J. Kupfer (Eds.), *Suicide over the life cycle: Risk factors, assessment, and treatment of suicidal patients* (pp. 135–153). Washington, DC: American Psychiatric Press.

Buie, D. H., & Maltsberger, J. T. (1983). *The practical formulation of suicide risk.* Somerville, MA: Firefly Press.

Crammer, J. L. (1984). The special characteristics of suicide in hospital inpatients. *British Journal of Psychiatry, 145,* 460–476.

Fawcett, J. (1992). Suicide risk factors in depressive disorders and in panic disorder. *Journal of Clinical Psychiatry,* 9–13.

Fawcett, J., Scheftner, W. A., Fogg, L., Clark, D. C., Young, M. A., Hedeker, D., & Gibbons, R. (1990). Time-related predictors of suicide in major affective disorder. *American Journal of Psychiatry, 9,* 1189–1194.

Goldstein, R. B., Black, D. W., Nasrallah, A., & Winokur, G. (1991). The prediction of suicide. *Archives of General Psychiatry, 48,* 418–422.

Goodwin, E. F., & Runck, B. L. (1992). Suicide intervention: Integration of psychosocial, clinical and biomedical traditions. In D. G. Jacobs (Ed.), *Suicide and clinical practice* (pp. 1–21). Washington, DC: American Psychiatric Press.

Gutheil, T. G. (1985). Medicolength pitfalls in the treatment of borderline patients. *American Journal of Psychiatry, 142,* 9–14.

Havens, L. L. (1963). The anatomy of a suicide. *New England Journal of Medicine, 272,* 401–410.

Jacobs, D. G. (Ed.). (1992). *Suicide and clinical practice.* Washington, DC: American Psychiatric Press.

Klerman, G. L. (1987). Clinical epidemiology of suicide. *Journal of Clinical Psychology, 48,* 33–38.

Kreitman, N. (1977). *Parasuicide.* New York: Wiley.

Kroll, J. (1978). Self-destructive behavior on an inpatient ward. *Journal of Nervous and Mental Disease, 166,* 429–434.

Lepine, J. P., Chignon, J. M., Teherani, M. (1993). Suicide attempts in patients with panic disorder. *Archives of General Psychiatry, 50,* 144–149.

Libby, M. (1992). Minimizing a facility risk. *Forum: Risk Management Foundation of the Harvard Medical Institutions, 13,* 9–10.

Main, J. F. (1957). The ailment. *British Journal of Medical Psychology, 30,* 144–145.

Maltsberger, J. T. (1986). *Suicide risk: Formulation of clinical judgment.* New York: New York University Press.

Maltsberger, J. T., & Buie, D. H. (1980). The devices of suicide: Revenge, riddance and rebirth. *International Review of Psychoanalysis, 7,* 61–72.

Maltsberger, J. T., Lovett, C. G. (1992). Suicide in borderline personality disorders. In D. Silver (Ed.), *A handbook of borderline disorders* (pp. 335–387). New York: International Universities Press.

Murphy, G. F. (1992). *Suicide in alcoholism.* New York: Oxford University Press.

Schoonover, S. C. (1982). Intensive care for suicidal patients. In E. L. Bassuk, S. C. Schoonover, & A. D. Gill (Eds.), *Lifelines: Clinical perspectives on suicide* (pp. 137–153). New York: Plenum.

Schrut, A., & Michels, T. (1974). Suicidal divorced and discarded women. *Journal of the American Academy of Psychoanalysis, 2,* 329–347.

Sederer, L. L. & Thorbeck, J. (1991). Borderline character disorder. In L. I. Sederer (Ed.), *Inpatient psychiatry: Diagnosis and treatment* (3rd ed., pp. 108–140). Baltimore: Williams & Wilkins.

Part V

Clinical and Legal Issues

Regardless of the treatment model or format used, certain clinical, legal, and ethical issues confront the interventionist working with the suicidal patient. Because the possibility of patient suicide is substantial for practicing professionals, there is a need for clear guidelines for sound assessment and intervention. Legally and ethically, the professional must act in a reasonable and prudent fashion. Yet, clinically, calculated risks must be taken. Whereas discharge from an inpatient setting is therapeutically desirable for some suicidal patients, for others it is not. Nonetheless, economic factors are now making prolonged inpatient care almost impossible for most patients. In the event of postdischarge suicide, the risk of lawsuit is considerable. Medical and mental health professionals must be prepared for this eventuality by avoiding the common pitfalls that compromise the standard of care they provide and place them at greater risk of litigation. Part V outlines the legal, ethical, and clinical issues facing suicide interventionists. Chapter 14 outlines the essential legal issues in work with suicidal patients, Chapter 15 considers the issues involved in calculated risk taking, and Chapter 16 lists the 10 most common errors of suicide interventionists.

Essential Clinical and Legal Issues When Working with the Suicidal Patient

Bruce Bongar
Sheila A. Greaney

The average professional psychologist involved in direct patient care has a greater than 20% chance of losing a patient to suicide at some time during his or her professional career, with the odds being greater than 50% for psychiatrists (Chemtob, Hamada, Bauer, Kinney, & Torigoe, 1988; Chemtob, Hamada, Bauer, Torigoe, & Kinney, 1988). Because a patient's committing suicide is not a rare event in psychological practice, it must be considered a real occupational hazard for those clinicians involved in direct patient care (Chemtob, Hamada, Bauer, Torigoe, & Kinney, 1988). This hazard encompasses not only the threat of malpractice action, but also the intense emotional toll that a patient's suicide can take on the survivors (including the clinician).

At the present time, malpractice actions against clinicians for the death of a patient are relatively rare, although they are increasing in frequency. Summary data provided by the American Psychological Association's Insurance Trust (1990) indicate that the suicide of a patient was the sixth most common category for a claim (5.4% of all claims), but the money paid in this category ranked second in percentage (10%) of the total money paid on claims. However, as clinicians (e.g., psychologists and social workers) seek expanded professional privileges, such as hospital staff membership and admission and discharge privileges, they will find themselves exposed to many of the same malpractice liabilities to which psychiatrists are exposed (Gutheil & Appelbaum, 1982). In malpractice actions for the death of a patient, two criteria are used in the evaluation of negligence in the standard of care: the ability to foresee and causation. Given that current case law provides a limited view of the total malpractice picture, it is difficult to discern clear legal guidelines for what constitutes an adequate standard of care for the suicidal patient (Harris, 1988). Hence, clinicians should anticipate that there may be a conflict between the clinical and legal standards of care (Bongar, 1991). The best response to this conundrum is a sound risk management approach.

Six tasks form the basis of a professionally sound risk management approach for the clinician working with suicidal patients. The clinician must have an understanding of the legal perspectives of suicide; must know the legal definition of negligence and the common causes of malpractice actions; must be knowledgeable about his or her duty to prevent suicide through the use of reasonable care and skill; and must understand assessment, intervention, and postvention procedures. In this discussion, we focus primarily on the first three tasks and briefly introduce the reader to the risk management activities of assessment, intervention, and postvention.

LEGAL PERSPECTIVES OF SUICIDE

Simon (1988) reported that the most common interjection of the law into health care practice may be a patient's suing a practitioner for malpractice. Hence, an essential element in effective risk management and high-quality clinical care in professional psychological practice is the possession of a basic working knowledge of the legal system and understanding of contemporary legal views on standards of care. Until the 1970s, the incidence of lawsuits against mental health professionals was quite low, especially when compared with what the courts regard as other medical specialties (Robertson, 1988). Although a review of case law (cases that go to trial and to appeal) indicates that the majority of cases that go to trial deal with issues of inpatient management and treatment (Bongar, 1991; Litman, 1982), today, outpatient therapists are as likely as inpatient practitioners to be the targets of suits (Bongar, Maris, Berman, & Litman, 1992).

Lawsuits over suicide usually fall into one of three legal fact patterns. Psychotherapists or institutions may be sued (a) when an inpatient commits suicide, with survivors claiming that the facility failed to provide adequate care and supervision; (b) when a recently released patient commits suicide; or (c) when an outpatient commits suicide (VandeCreek, Knapp, & Herzog, 1987). Perr (1979) and Meyer, Landis, and Hays (1988) noted that mental health clinicians carry a tremendous legal burden when it comes to patient suicide, because, to put it simply, the clinician is asked to be responsible for someone else's behavior. Although generally the law does not hold any person responsible for the actions of another, suicidal and other self-destructive acts are a clear exception.

The therapist's duty to exercise adequate care and skill in diagnosing suicidality is well established (*Meier v. Ross General Hospital*, 1968). When the risk of self-injurious behavior is identified, an additional duty to take adequate precautions arises (*Abille v. United States*, 1980; *Pisel v. Stamford Hospital*, 1980). When the psychotherapist fails to meet these responsibilities, he or she may be liable for injuries that result (Meyer et al., 1988).

Further obfuscating the issue is a discrepancy between clinical and legal philosophies: Psychotherapists "on the one hand are told . . . not to hospitalize unless the need is blatantly clear; on the other, they are threatened with legal liability if they do not do so and thus minimize a patient's ability to kill himself" (Perr, 1979, p. 91).

Understandably, many practitioners are reluctant to work with suicidal patients for fear of being sued if a patient commits suicide, although courts have usually maintained that the clinician is not liable if he or she has maintained adequate care of the patient (Kermani, 1982). For both the inpatient and outpatient settings, the clinician's legal liability for patient suicide is clustered into three general categories: (a) failure to assess properly the potential and severity of suicide risk, (b) failure to use reasonable treatment interventions and precautions, and (c) failure to carry out treatment reasonably (Simon, 1992). Moreover, Simon (1992) noted,

> In all three, liability is fundamentally based on a clinician's failure to act *reasonably* to provide appropriate care to the patient. What is reasonable treatment depends on what is likely to happen with the patient. *Foreseeability* of suicide is often a central issue in patient suicides that lead to wrongful death or personal injury lawsuits. Was there sufficient evidence to suggest to a reasonable clinician, making a reasonable assessment, that suicide was foreseeable? (pp. 40–41)

A review of case law indicates that a number of legal theories have bearing on the liability of mental health professionals (Robertson, 1988).

Failure To Diagnose Properly

If the clinician had taken ordinary and accepted care in making a diagnosis, he or she would have ascertained that the patient was suicidal (*Dillman v. Hellman*, 1973).

At the present time, much of the case law on suicide is based on claims that allege liability for a misdiagnosis or lack of prediction of the risk of suicide (Swenson, 1986; VandeCreek et al., 1987). Most suits brought on this basis are directed against hospitals and institutions for clinical care and involve either inpatients or recently discharged patients (Rachlin, 1984). However, the potential certainly exists for an increase in suits involving outpatient care. One authority, Perr (1985), in his review of suicide litigation and risk management, pointed to a study (Farberow, 1981). of completed suicide in Veterans Administration patients in which 65% of the suicides were found to have occurred outside the hospital.

Failure To Take Adequate Protective Measures

The clinician must take adequate precautions against patient suicide, consistent with accepted psychotherapeutic practices and based on his or her knowledge and assessment of the patient (*Bellah v. Greenson*, (1978); *Dimitrijevic v. Chicago Wesley Memorial Hospital*, 1968; *Meier v. Ross General Hospital* 1968; *Topel v. Long Island Jewish Medical Center*, 1981).

Both Swenson (1986) and VandeCreek and Knapp (1989) cited the case of *Dinnerstein v. United States* (1973), which held that clinicians are liable when a treatment plan overlooks or neglects the patient's suicidal tendencies. VandeCreek and Knapp (1989) also pointed out that courts will generally not find a psychotherapist liable when the patient's suicide attempt was not foreseeable.

The courts have tended to be less stringent in evaluating cases of outpatient suicide in the absence of clear signs of foreseeability, because of the obvious increased difficulty in controlling the patient's behavior (Fremouw, de Perczel, & Ellis, 1990; Simon 1988). The case law seems to put forward the basic rule that the clinician needs to recognize the risk of suicide and to balance it against the benefits of greater control through hospitalization (Simon, 1987, 1988, 1992). Furthermore, VandeCreek and Knapp (1983) noted that although only a few cases have dealt with outpatient suicide, the principles are the same as for inpatient cases, namely, that clinicians must use reasonable care in the diagnosis of suicidal intent and in the development and implementation of the treatment plan. Although the courts have not imposed a Tarasoff-type duty to warn relatives of potential suicide risk (*Bellah v. Greenson*, 1978), it remains an option that clinicians should consider seriously when a patient presents as at risk (Fremouw et al., 1990). Lastly, when a suicide attempt is foreseeable, the treatment provided must be consistent with professional standards (VandeCreek & Knapp, 1983).

Early Release of Patient

A clinician may be found liable for the death of a patient if release from the hospital is negligent and not a valid exercise in professional judgment (Robertson, 1988). Fremouw et al. (1990) pointed out that when a clinician makes a reasonable assessment of danger and believes that a risk no longer exists, he or she is not held liable for the postdischarge death of a patient.

Failure To Commit

In making the decision whether to commit a patient, the clinician is responsible for taking a complete history and making a thorough examination of the patient's status and then exercising sound judgment in making the decision (Robertson, 1988). The more "obvious the suicidal intent, the greater will be the practitioner's liability" for his or her failure to take this elevated risk into account in the treatment plan (VandeCreek & Knapp, 1983, p. 276).

Liability of Hospitals

Malpractice law regarding hospitals is a complex and ever-changing field, making a review of the liability of hospitals beyond the scope of this discussion (a bibliography on the subject is available from B. B.). However, as VandeCreek and Knapp (1983) underscored, psychotherapists should know that malpractice actions for inpatient suicides could be directed against them or the hospital, or both. Malpractice actions can be brought against psychiatrists or psychologists within the hospital setting, provided they have staff or hospital privileges.

The hospital's duty in the care of a patient can best be defined as the generally accepted standard that reasonable care must be used in the treatment of a patient (Robertson, 1988). "If, however, the hospital is on notice that a patient has suicidal tendencies, then the hospital also assumes the duty of safe guarding the patient from self-inflicted injury or death" (Robertson, 1988, p. 193). Thus, as it is in judgments of the practitioner's behavior, the issue of foreseeability is crucial in judgments of the hospital's behavior. Even when the patient is under the care of a private psychotherapist, the hospital staff must perform the proper evaluation and observation (and take affirmative action if necessary).

Robertson (1988) stated that hospitals generally have not been held liable when a physician has determined that surveillance was adequate or when staff followed proper procedures. He further noted that "psychiatric hospitals can be found liable when adequate standards for the protection of patients were not followed" (Robertson, p. 197), referring practitioners to the Joint Commission on Accreditation of Hospitals's Guidelines for Nursing and Safety Standards for a definition of adequate standards for protection.

In considering malpractice actions against hospitals, the courts have slowly moved the standard of liability away from the custodial model to more of an open-door model (VandeCreek & Knapp, 1983). In the traditional custodial model, the purpose of the hospital was to diagnose suicidal intentions correctly and then to monitor the patient so closely that an attempt would be impossible. In recent years, however, hospitals have implemented so-called open-door policies, decreasing the restrictions they place on patients' behavior and encouraging patients to assume more responsibility for their treatment. The courts have observed such changes in psychotherapeutic policies, recognizing that "some of the traditional policies harmed patients because they engendered feelings of helplessness" (VandeCreek & Knapp, 1983, p. 277). Indeed, as VandeCreek and Knapp (1983) observed, courts no longer require strict observation in all suicide cases:

> The law and modern psychiatry have now both come to the conclusion that an overly restrictive environment can be as destructive as an overly permissive one. . . . Now the courts recognize that the therapist must balance the benefits of treatment against the risks of freedom. (p. 277)

Yet as Gutheil (1990) remarked, hospitalization has its drawbacks. Although laypersons may perceive hospitalization as a panacea (and plaintiffs' attorneys may present it as such), experienced clinicians are aware that a psychiatric hospitalization presents some clear risks, including regression, dependency, loss of time from work or studies, and considerable stigma.

In summary, clinicians who are mindful of maintaining a coherent treatment philosophy with their suicidal patients are protected to the extent that they demonstrate their best professional judgment in assessing the therapeutic risks of freedom. They also must carefully assess decisions (their own and others') to reduce the level of supervision of suicidal patients, whether those decisions involve discharge, transfer, decision to commit, or other actions (VandeCreek & Knapp, 1983). However, it is critical to remember that when a "patient is dangerously suicidal, hospitalization and close supervision are clearly indicated—an 'open door' policy does not mean an open window policy for highly suicidal patients" (VandeCreek & Knapp, p. 77).

Abandonment

Once a professional relationship has been established, a clinician is required to provide treatment until the relationship is properly terminated. Abandonment can be overt, or it can be implied, for example, by a failure to be available or to monitor the patient adequately. VandeCreek and Knapp (1983) noted that the therapist may not terminate the therapeutic relationship unless treatment is no longer necessary, the relationship has been terminated by the patient, or the therapist has given suitable notice that gives the patient adequate time to engage another therapist. Typically, abandonment is based on two theories:

1   If a therapist errs in the judgment that treatment is no longer needed, he or she may be liable for negligence under the criteria for malpractice. Usually, this is decided by expert witnesses after the fact.

2 If a therapist willfully terminates or withholds treatment knowing that further care is needed or that a referral is indicated, he or she may be liable for intentional abandonment.

The circumstances under which liability could be determined are fairly explicit, especially if a crisis occurs or is foreseeable. Clinicians face charges of abandonment when they fail to provide patients with a way of contacting them after hours, between sessions, and when they are on vacation or leave and when they fail to provide adequate coverage when they are on vacation or leave. Also, reasonable contact must be maintained with hospitalized patients (Simon, 1988; VandeCreek & Knapp, 1983).

Only if there is not an emergency or threatened crisis (e.g., threatened suicide or danger to the public), may a therapist safely terminate a relationship with a patient. Termination is done by "giving reasonable notice, assisting the patient in finding another therapist, [and] insuring that appropriate records are transferred to the new therapist, as requested by the patient" (Simon, 1988, pp. 11–12).

LEGAL DEFINITION OF NEGLIGENCE AND COMMON CAUSES OF MALPRACTICE ACTIONS

The key issue that underlies malpractice actions against mental health professionals is the concept of negligence (Robertson, 1988; Simon, 1988). Simon (1988) pointed out that negligence on the part of a mental health professional can be "described as doing something which he or she should not have done [commission] or omitting to do something which he or she should have done [omission]" (p. 3). The fact that a mental health professional's act is a consequence of carelessness or ignorance rather than will does not excuse him or her from liability (Robertson, 1988; Simon, 1988). The law "presumes and holds all practitioners and psychotherapists to a standard of reasonable care when dealing with patients" (Robertson, 1988, p. 7).

Sadoff noted that there are four essential legal elements in establishing negligence, which "may be remembered by the 4D mnemonic: Dereliction-of-Duty-Directly-causing-Damages" (cited by Rachlin, 1984, p. 303). To prevail against a clinician in a malpractice action, the plaintiff must prove by a preponderance of evidence that

1 There was a clinician–patient relationship that created a duty of care,
2 The clinician breached the duty of care that was owed to the patient,
3 The patient was damaged,
4 The damage was proximately caused by the clinician's negligence (Simon, 1992, p. 41).

The simple fact that the patient was receiving any psychological treatment makes a relation between the two parties such that a legal duty of care is created. In determining whether a patient was damaged, a key issue is whether, and with what degree of medical certainty, the suicide or suicide attempts could have been foreseen or predicted (Maris, Berman, Maltsberger, & Yufit, 1992). However, because suicide is a rare event, its prediction is extremely difficult and results most often in false, not true, positives (Pokorny, 1983). At issue is the relative benefit of a standard of care that necessitates great health care expense and yet provides a large number of false positives. Because suicide is a multifaceted, multicausal outcome (Shneidman, 1985), it is extremely difficult to determine whether a therapist's actions, failures to act, decisions, and so forth actually caused a suicide. Bongar et al. (1992) noted that

> suicide prevention is an ideal, that the responsibility of the clinician or institution is to follow acceptable standards of care, and that these standards of care are dynamic and ever changing. Clinicians must understand that there is no magical "right" way to act in every clinical situation and that for every decision in clinical practice there are always potential risks and benefits. (pp. 459–460)

The threat of litigation exacerbates the burden that a patient's death creates for the clinician (Rachlin, 1984). In a general clinical practice setting, patient suicide is always a possibility: In a recent review of risk assessment and treatment procedures for suicidal patients, Brent, Kupfer, Bromet, and Dew (1988) estimated that 10–15% of patients with major psychiatric disorders (i.e., affective disorder, substance abuse, and schizophrenia) will die by suicide. Brent et al. (1988) asserted unequivocally that the assessment and diminution of suicide potential among psychiatric patients should be tasks of the highest priority for the mental health professional.

Malpractice actions against mental health professionals are also "plagued by such issues as what constitutes an acceptable level of care in suicide treatment and who is qualified as an expert witness to testify to the reasonableness of deviations from that standard" (Berman & Cohen-Sandler, 1983, p. 6). Furthermore, mental health and legal professionals have not yet been able to settle such basic issues as

> who legitimately may decide what constitutes standard or acceptable care in the treatment of suicidal patients, and what level of quality should be considered standard; that is, ought we to demand some minimum degree of care or, instead, more optimal care? (Berman & Cohen-Sandler, 1982, p. 115)

Moreover, what seem to be the pivotal elements in most cases of malpractice and suicide are the twin issues of the ability to foresee and causation (Bongar, Peterson, Harris, & Aissis, 1989; Perr, 1979, 1988; Rachlin, 1984; Simon, 1988;

VandeCreek & Knapp, 1989; VandeCreek et al., 1987). Generally, in grappling with these two important issues in cases of suicide (Simon, 1988), the courts have focused on whether the clinician should have predicted the suicide and whether there was sufficient evidence for an identifiable risk of harm. Ultimately, the clinician, the institution, or both will be judged according to whether enough was done to protect the patient (VandeCreek et al., 1987). Negligence is typically indicated only when, on the basis of expert testimony, the treatment or assessment of the patient is found to be unreasonable (Berman & Cohen-Sandler, 1982). Berman and Cohen-Sander (1982) noted that although failures in treatment are often blamed on the patient, mental health professionals often play a significant role in the suicidal deaths of their patients.

Demonstrated negligence requires evidence that the patient was clearly identifiable as suicidal on the basis of the recognized criteria used by most clinicians of the same training (Meyer et al., 1988).

STANDARD OF THE "REASONABLE AND PRUDENT PRACTITIONER"

Until the present time, the courts have not been consistent in defining a standard of care for the suicidal patient (Bongar, 1991). What, then are some options for care that are available to the reasonable and prudent clinician who assesses and treats suicidal patients?

Rachlin (1984) suggested that the following practices will minimize the clinician's risk of being found negligent as a result of a patient's suicide:

- Careful documentation of decisions to grant the patient increased freedom,
- Detailed documentation of the specifics of suicide precautions,
- Consultation from supervisors or colleagues, and
- Outreach to survivors.

There will always be areas of indecision—fuzzy areas where clinicians will disagree, resulting in differences of opinion among both treating clinicians and expert witnesses (Sadoff, 1985). "A key element (in the context of the legal system that provides confusing or even contradictory rules) has been attributing to professional people the capacity to predict and control the behavior of the mentally ill" (Perr, 1988, p. 4). Although a patient's suicide is not always preventable, clinicians' only course is to integrate appropriate guidelines within their treatment plans, in good faith that they will prevail in convincing the court that no liability need be attached to the patient's demise.

Bongar et al. (1992), in accord with Berman and Cohen-Sandler (1982), asserted that it is the duty of a clinician or institution to prevent suicide through the use of reasonable care and skill.

"Reasonable" is considered by law to be the "average standard of the profession"—
"the degree of learning, skill, and experience which ordinarily is possessed by others
of the same profession" (American Jurisprudence, 1981). . . . The average standard
is essentially defined by the legal system through decisions rendered in malpractice
cases, which, in turn, determine completely the liability of the clinician who treats
suicidal patients. (Berman & Cohen-Sandler, p. 116)

For every patient seen in professional psychological practice, there are a
number of important steps the clinician can take to reduce dramatically his or
her exposure should a malpractice action be brought. These steps are encom-
passed within the clinical phases of assessment, intervention, and postvention.
Should a malpractice action be brought, the clinician's and/or institution's decisions and actions during these phases of treatment will be scrutinized by plaintiff attorneys with 20/20 hindsight.

ASSESSMENT AND INTERVENTION

A discussion of sound risk management procedures in the assessment and intervention phases is beyond the scope of this discussion. However, some general
comments about assessment and intervention that apply to both inpatients and
outpatients may be beneficial. Risk assessment is a multidetermined decision,
based both on the unique characteristics of the patient and his or her social matrix
and on the therapist's equally unique capabilities and tolerances for stress and
uncertainty (Bongar et al., 1992). Clinicians and hospitals should assiduously
assess their patients' suicidal potential and carefully implement affirmative treatments (Bongar, Maris, Berman, Litman, & Silverman, in press). For each patient, the risk of suicide should be noted regularly in the management plan and
should be reevaluated at each significant turning point in treatment and whenever
important management decisions are to be made (Simon, 1992; VandeCreek &
Knapp, 1983). Furthermore, a new evaluation should be made whenever family,
staff, and other significant persons provide new information (see Farberow,
1981, for additional information on this point). For a preliminary discussion of
risk assessment, risk management policies, intervention procedures, and standards of care, the reader is directed to the works of Bongar (1991), Bongar et
al. (1992), Maris and Berman (1992), and Simon (1987, 1988, 1992).

POSTVENTION

Postvention consists of activities that can help reduce the aftereffects of a traumatic event in the lives of the survivors, including the clinician. "Its purpose is
to help survivors live longer, more productively, and less stressfully than they
are likely to do otherwise" (Shneidman, 1981, p. 350). A complete discussion
of the voluminous clinical literature on postvention is beyond the scope of this

article. As a starting point, readers should consult the works of Bongar (1991); Cotton, Drake, Whitaker, and Potter (1989); Dunne, McIntosh, and Dunne-Maxim (1987); Friedman (1989); Litman (1965); and Shneidman (1981). However, a few general comments about postvention work with survivors may be helpful. First, outreach to survivors is both ethically necessary and clinically crucial (Gutheil, 1988, 1990). Furthermore, because malpractice actions often result from a combination of bad outcome and bad feelings, the clinician who initiates postvention immediately and does not leave the surviving family members with a feeling of being abandoned is practicing sound risk management (Ruben, 1990). Finally, the most important step that a clinician can take after a patient's suicide is to consult a knowledgeable senior colleague about postvention steps. "From their different perspectives, the clinician and the consultant can better formulate plans for immediate postvention efforts with the patient's family, as well as reach out to other friends and members of the interpersonal matrix" (Bongar, 1991, p. 192).

Stromberg et al. (1988) noted that in serious circumstances such as suicide, a clinician should be aware that every statement he or she makes can be subjected to later judicial scrutiny: "A routine expression of sympathy ('I'm really sorry this happened; I feel so bad') may be characterized later as an admission of legal liability. Therefore, the psychologist should be careful about what is said" (p. 496).

Bongar (1991) cautioned the clinician that "any discussion with a colleague, or even with one's own family or friends, of the deceased patient's care is usually considered nonprivileged information that is open to the legal discovery process." That is, the plaintiff attorneys will subpoena the clinician's colleagues and ask them what the clinician told them about his or her concerns regarding the patient's suicide. Discussions of feelings and concerns regarding possible errors in management or treatment should always be confined to the context of a psychotherapeutic or legal consultation (Ruben, 1990). In particular, clinicians should refrain from making self-incriminating statements to other concerning "their role or responsibility for the patient's death" (Ruben, 1990, p. 623).

SUMMARY GUIDELINES[1]

The following guidelines are adapted from *The Suicidal Patient: Clinical and Legal Standards of Care,* Bongar (1991, pp. 202–204) for clinicians wishing to take a sound risk management approach in working with suicidal patients.

1 For each patient seen as part of a clinician's professional practice activities, there must be an initial evaluation and assessment, regular ongoing clinical evaluations and case reviews, consultation reports and supervision reports (where

[1]Portions of this section are adapted from Bongar, B. (1991). *The suicidal patient: Clinical and legal standards of care.* Washington, DC: American Psychological Association. Copyright American Psychological Association. Reproduced by permission.

indicated), and a formal treatment plan. All of these activities need to demonstrate specifically a solid understanding of the significant factors used to assess elevated risk of suicide and how to manage such risk—with a documented understanding of the prognosis for the success (or possible paths to failure) of subsequent outpatient (or inpatient) treatment or case disposition.

2   Clinicians must be aware of the vital importance of documentation. In cases of malpractice, courts and juries often have been observed to operate on the simplistic principle that "if it isn't written down, it didn't happen," no matter what the subsequent testimony or elaboration of the defendant maintains. Defensive clinical notes, written after the fact, may help somewhat in damage control, but there is no substitute for a timely, thoughtful, and complete chart record that demonstrates (through clear and well-written assessment, review, and treatment notes) a knowledge of the epidemiology, risk factors, and treatment literature for the suicidal patient. Such a case record should also include (where possible) a formal informed consent for treatment, formal assessment of competence, and a documentation of confidentiality considerations (e.g., that limits were explained at the start of any treatment).

3   Clinicians must obtain all previous treatment records whenever possible and consult with previous psychotherapists. When appropriate, mental health practitioners should involve the family and significant others in the management or disposition plan. The family and significant others are good sources of information (both current and background) and can serve as an integral and effective part of the support system.

4   Clinicians should routinely obtain consultation and/or supervision (or make referrals) on any case in which suicide risk is determined to be even moderate and after a patient suicide or serious suicide attempt. They also should obtain consultation and/or supervision on (or refer) cases that are outside their documented training, education, or experience, as well as when they are unsure of the best avenue for initiating or continuing treatment. A guiding principle in moments of clinical uncertainty is that two perspectives are better than one.

5   Clinicians should be knowledgeable about the effects of psychotropic medication and make appropriate referrals for a medication evaluation. If the clinician decides that medication is not indicated in the present instance, he or she should thoroughly document the reasoning for this decision in the written case record. Where appropriate, the patient (and, when it is indicated, the patient's family or significant others) should be included in this decision-making process. Clinicians need to know the possible organic etiologies for suicidality and seek immediate appropriate medical consultation for the patient when they detect any signs of an organic condition.

6   Clinicians who see suicidal patients should have access to the full armamentarium of resources for voluntary and involuntary hospital admissions, day treatment, 24-hr emergency backup, and crisis centers. This access can be direct or indirect (e.g., through an ongoing collaborative relationship with a psychologist or psychiatrist colleague).

7   If a patient succeeds in committing suicide or makes a serious suicide attempt, clinicians should be aware not only of their legal responsibilities (e.g., they must notify their insurance carrier in a timely fashion), but, more important,

of the immediate clinical necessity of attending to both the postvention needs of the bereaved survivors and to their own emotional needs. (The clinician must acknowledge that it is both normal and difficult to work through feelings about a patient's death and that he or she, having lost a patient to suicide, is also a suicide survivor.) The concern should be for the living. After consultation with a knowledgeable colleague and an attorney, immediate clinical outreach to the survivors is not only sensitive and concerned clinical care, but, because it helps the survivors deal with the catastrophic aftermath, also effective risk management.

8 Most important, clinicians must be cognizant of all of the standards above and take affirmative steps to ensure that they have the requisite knowledge, training, experience, and clinical resources before accepting high-risk patients into their professional care. All of these mechanisms should be in place *before* the onset of any suicidal crisis.

CONCLUSION

The fear of mental health litigation should not lead to clinicians' responding to suicidal patients with trepidation, defensive practice, or other adversarializing reactions (Gutheil, 1992). Although there is no specific set of clinical practices that can absolutely guarantee a psychologist that he or she will be immune from either losing a patient to suicide or being sued (and being held liable), good clinical care as reviewed herein should provide a solid foundation for reducing the clinician's exposure to malpractice action.

Clinicians are less likely to be sued successfully when they can demonstrate that their decision-making process and management efforts were coherent and appropriate and fell within the guidelines of the profession's standard of care (Bongar, 1991). However, we wish to remind the reader that the information contained here is no substitute for a timely and formal consultation with a knowledgeable attorney and one's professional colleagues. In particular, clinicians with specific questions or those who are threatened with a suit should follow the suggestion of Wright (1981) and VandeCreek and Knapp (1983) that when one has specific legal concerns or has reason to believe that a malpractice suit is imminent, one's first step is quite straightforward: Consult an attorney who is expert in matters of mental health and the law (Bongar, 1991).

REFERENCES

Abille v. United States, 482 F. Supp. 703 (N.D. Cal. 1980).

Bellah, V. Greenson, 146 Cal. 535 (1978).

Berman, A. L., & Cohen-Sandler, R. (1982). Suicide and the standard of care: Optimal vs. acceptable. *Suicide and Life-Threatening Behavior, 12,* 114–122.

Berman, A. L., & Cohen-Sandler, R. (1983). Suicide and malpractice: Expert testimony and the standard of care. *Professional Psychology: Research and Practice, 14,* 6–19.

Bongar, B. (1991). *The suicidal patient: Clinical and legal standards of care.* Washington, DC: American Psychological Association.

Bongar, B., Maris, R. W., Berman, A. L., & Litman, R. E. (1992). Outpatient standards of care and the suicidal patient. *Suicide and Life-Threatening Behavior, 22,* 453–478.

Bongar, B., Maris, R. W., Berman, A. L., Litman, R. E., & Silverman, M. M. (in press). Inpatient standards of care and the suicidal patient: General clinical formulations and legal considerations. *Suicide and Life-Threatening Behavior.*

Bongar, B., Peterson, L. G., Harris, E. A., & Aissis, J. (1989). Clinical and legal considerations in the management of suicidal patients: An integrative overview. *Journal of Integrative and Eclectic Psychotherapy, 8,* 53–67.

Brent, D. A., Kupfer, D. J., Bromet, E. J., & Dew, M. A. (1988). The assessment and treatment of patients at risk for suicide. In A. J. Frances & R. E. Hales (Eds.), *American Psychiatric Press Review of psychiatry* (Vol. 7, pp. 353–385). Washington, DC: American Psychiatric Press.

Chemtob, C. M., Hamada, R. S., Bauer, G. B., Kinney, B., & Torigoe, R. Y. (1988). Patient suicide: Frequency and impact on psychiatrists. *American Journal of Psychiatry, 145,* 224–228.

Chemtob, C. M., Hamada, R. S., Bauer, G. B., Torigoe, R. Y., & Kinney, B. (1988). Patient suicide: Frequency and impact on psychologists. *Professional Psychology: Research and Practice, 19,* 416–420.

Cotton, P. G., Drake R. E., Whitaker, A., & Potter, J. (1989). Guidelines for dealing with suicide on a psychiatric inpatient unit. In D. G. Jacobs & H. N. Brown (Eds.), *Suicide: Understanding and responding: Harvard Medical School perspectives on suicide* (pp. 405–413). Madison, CT: International Universities Press.

Dillman, v. Hellman, 283 So.2d 388 (FL Dist. Ct. App. 1973).

Dimitrijevic v. Chicago Wesley Memorial Hospital, 92 Ill. App. 2d 251, 236 N.E.2d 309 (1968).

Dinnerstein v. State, 486 F.2d 34 (CT, 1973).

Dunne, E. J., McIntosh, J. L., & Dunne-Maxim, K. (1987). *Suicide and its aftermath: Understanding and counseling the survivors.* New York: Norton.

Farberow, N. L. (1981). Suicide prevention in the hospital. *Hospital and Community Psychiatry, 32,* 99–104.

Fremouw, W. J., de Perczel, M., & Ellis, T. E. (1990). *Suicide risk: Assessment and response guidelines.* New York: Pergamon Press.

Friedman, R. S. (1989). Hospital treatment of the suicidal patient. In D. G. Jacobs & H. N. Brown (Eds.), *Suicide: Understanding and responding: Harvard Medical School perspectives on suicide* (pp. 379–402). Madison, CT: International Universities Press.

Gutheil, T. G. (1988, May). *Suicide and suit: Liability and self-destruction.* Paper presented at the annual meeting of the American Psychiatric Association, Montreal.

Gutheil, T. G. (1990). Argument for the defendant-expert opinion: Death in hindsight. In R. I. Simon (Ed.), *Review of clinical psychiatry and the law* (pp. 335–339). Washington, DC: American Psychiatric Association.

Gutheil, T. G., & Appelbaum, P. S. (1982). *Clinical handbook of psychiatry and the law.* New York: McGraw-Hill.

Harris, E. A. (1988, October). *Legal issues in professional practice.* Workshop presented at the annual meeting of the Massachusetts Psychological Association, Northampton, MA.

Kermani, E. J. (1982). Court rulings on psychotherapists. *American Journal of psychotherapy, 36,* 248–254.

Litman, R. E. (1965). When patients commit suicide. *American Journal of Psychotherapy, 19,* 570–576.

Litman, R. E. (1982). Hospital suicides: Lawsuits and standards. *Suicide and Life-Threatening Behavior, 12,* 212–220.

Maris R. W., & Berman, A. L. (1992). Conclusions and recommendations. In R. W. Maris, A. L. Berman, J. T. Maltsberger, & R. I. Yufit (Eds.), *Assessment and Prediction of suicide* (pp. 660–688). New York: Guilford Press.

Maris, R. W., Berman, A. L., Maltsberger, J. T., & Yufit, R. (Eds.). (1992). *Assessment and prediction of suicide.* New York: Guilford Press.

Meier v. Ross General Hospital, 69 Cal. 2d 420, 71 Cal. 903, 445 P.2d 519 (1968).

Meyer, R. G., Landis, E. R., & Hays, J. R. (1988). *Law for the psychotherapist.* New York: Norton.

Perr, I. N. (1979). Legal aspects of suicide. In L. D. Hankoff & B. Einsidler (Eds.), *Suicide: Theory and clinical aspects* (pp. 91–100). Littleton, MA: PSG.

Perr, I. N. (1985). Suicide litigation and risk management: A review of 32 cases. *Bulletin of the American Academy of Psychiatry and the Law, 13,* 209–219.

Perr, I. N. (1988). The practice of psychiatry and suicide litigation. *New Developments in Mental Health Law, 8*(1), 4–19.

Pisel v. Stamford Hospital, 180 Conn. 314, 430 A.2d 1 (1980).

Pokorny, A. D. (1983). Prediction of suicide in psychiatric patients. *Archives of General Psychiatry, 40,* 249–257.

Rachlin, S. (1984). Double jeopardy: Suicide and malpractice. *General Hospital Psychiatry, 6,* 302–307.

Robertson, J. D. (1988). *Psychiatric malpractice: Liability of mental health professionals.* New York: Wiley.

Ruben, H. L. (1990). Surviving a suicide in your practice. In S. J. Blumenthal & D. J. Kupfer (Eds.), *Suicide over the life cycle: Risk factors, assessment, and treatment of suicidal patients* (pp. 619–636). Washington, DC: American Psychiatric Press.

Sadoff, R. L. (1985). Malpractice in psychiatry: Standards of care and the expert witness. *Psychiatric Medicine, 2,* 235–243.

Shneidman, E. S. (1981). Postvention: The care of the bereaved. *Suicide and Life-Threatening Behavior, 11,* 349–359.

Shneidman, E. S. (1985). *Definition of suicide.* New York: Wiley.

Simon, R. I. (1987). *Clinical psychiatry and the law.* Washington, DC: American Psychiatric Press.

Simon, R. I. (1988). *Concise guide to clinical psychiatry and the law.* Washington, DC: American Psychiatric Press.

Simon, R. I. (1992). *Review of clinical psychiatry and the law.* Washington, DC: American Psychiatric Press.

Stromberg, C. D., Haggarty, D. J., Leibenluft, R. F., McMillan, M. H., Mishkin, B., Rubin, B. L., & Trilling, H. R. (1988). *The psychologist's legal handbook.* Washington, DC: Council for the National Register of Health Service Providers in Psychology.

Swenson, E. V. (1986). Legal liability for a patient's suicide. *Journal of Psychiatry and Law, 14,* 409–434.

Topel v. Long Island Jewish Medical Center, 431 NE2d. 293 (1981).

VandeCreek, L., & Knapp, S. (1983). Malpractice risks with suicidal patients. *Psychotherapy: Theory, Research and Practice, 20,* 274–280.

VandeCreek, L., & Knapp, S. (1989). *Tarasoff and beyond: Legal and clinical considerations in the treatment of life-endangering patients.* Sarasota, FL: Professional Resource Exchange.

VandeCreek, L., Knapp, S., & Herzog, C. (1987). Malpractice risks in the treatment of dangerous patients. *Psychotherapy: Theory, Research, and Practice, 24,* 145–153.

Chapter 15

Calculated Risk-Taking in the Treatment of Suicidal Patients: Ethical and Legal Problems

John T. Maltsberger

Psychiatrists traditionally have held that it is their moral duty to prevent suicide by whatever legal means are at their disposal. For many years, this point of view supported the involuntary commitment of suicidal patients when they needed it and underlay older treatment philosophies that emphasized close monitoring and protection of every patient from self-harm (Battin, 1982; Lesse, 1965; Mintz, 1971; Shein & Stone, 1969). Many have observed, however, that whereas an attitude of close watchfulness may be necessary for patients in acute suicidal states, it can impede psychotherapy and recovery for patients who suffer from chronic suicidal character problems (Basecu, 1965; Birtchnell, 1983; Henden, 1981; Lowenthal, 1975; Olin, 1976).

Private and public hospitals no longer support prolonged inpatient treatment, as they did a decade or two ago. Changes in commitment laws that accompanied the libertarian movement of the 1960s and 1970s have made involuntary confinement more difficult (Applebaum & Gutheil, 1991). Psychiatrists are forced

I acknowledge the helpful suggestions of Dr. Margaret Battin and Dr. David Mayo. Although they do not agree with all the statements contained in it, I am in their debt for the removal of a number of infelicities and the clarification of some points.

to rethink whether long hospitalization is always necessary and to plan outpatient care for suicidal patients whenever possible. In some circumstances, where public hospitals bluntly refuse to admit suicidal patients and there is no money for private care, there is no option but discharge.

Most clinicians subscribe to the point of view that a patient in the grip of a major mental illness, especially a major depression or psychosis, is often sufficiently impaired in judgment to justify forced admission and treatment if voluntary hospital admission is refused.

Case Study   Mr. E. was a 50-year-old attorney who had been depressed for some months and whose treatment with psychotherapy and antidepressant drugs had brought minimal improvement. He proposed a suicide pact to his wife, who was also depressed. She, less hopeless than he, brought his invitation to his psychiatrist's attention. Mr. E. acknowledged that he had decided to end his life, but he refused admission to a hospital. He was involuntarily committed, and a court order was obtained to permit electroconvulsive treatment. The patient fully recovered and afterward offered profuse thanks to the physician whose sangfroid had saved his life.

Not every patient's story has such a satisfactory ending. There are those who remain suicidal in spite of every reasonable treatment, and in these cases, the ethical question clouds. Once recovered, we argue, patients will no longer wish to commit suicide; they will be grateful to us for preventing it, as the lawyer was. The difficulty with this position lies in the question, How long must one wait for the expected recovery to take place? The question is most pointed with patients whose prognosis for recovery seems hopeless.

When it no longer seems likely that our treatment interventions are going to change the patient's mind, continuing interference is difficult to justify. There is a growing consensus that in terminally ill cases the moment arrives when medical intervention becomes meddlesome, not therapeutic. Occasionally psychiatrists as well as internists and surgeons may find themselves faced with such choices. There is a parallel between suffering of the incurable physically ill patient kept alive by artificial means and the suffering of the incurable mentally ill patient being kept alive by prolonged hospitalization and close monitoring.

This question is also pointed in the treatment of chronic suicidal personalities who vacillate between whether to live or whether to die. In some cases prolonged hospitalization in the service of suicide prevention can result in a treatment stalemate which Hendin (1981) has called *therapeutic bondage*. The therapist, dominated by his determination to prevent suicide at all costs, takes over so much responsibility that the patient, deprived of reasonable autonomy, regressively retreats more and more into a pattern of suicidal threats and suicide attempts.

PATIENTS FOR WHOM FURTHER TREATMENT OFFERS LITTLE

From time to time a patient's treatment response is poor, and suicide continues in his mind as the best option. The classical example of this difficulty is that of a person only partially recovered from schizophrenia. It has long been argued that in intractable mental illness where suffering is substantial and recovery unlikely, the prevention of suicide is inhumane (Bleuler, 1950).

Case Study Miss C., a 38-year-old, unemployed woman with a diagnosis of chronic schizophrenia complicated with depression and multiple suicide attempts, was readmitted when her auditory hallucinations recurred, once again commanding her to commit suicide. With the help of neuroleptic and antidepressant drugs, the hallucinations disappeared and the depression largely abated, but the patient continued to feel hopeless about her future and to speak ambivalently about suicide. She seemed to have a trusting relationship with her therapist. She had family in the vicinity but was close to none of them. The family had fragmented considerably after the suicide of a brother some years before. Her suspicious, quirky personal style had made it impossible for Miss C. to hold a job, and she was socially quite isolated.

Miss C. wished to leave the hospital. Electroconvulsive treatment was considered but not offered, because she had not responded well to a previous trial. Good outpatient follow-up plans were made, although all concerned were quite aware that suicide was likely sooner or later if Miss C. left the hospital. When asked whether she felt suicidal, she said she was not sure; when asked whether she would call her doctor if she began to feel more suicidal after discharge, she replied, "Maybe." After extensive consultation, it was decided that further hospital care had little to offer Miss C., especially because, as part of discharge planning, she had obtained a part-time job, a step that seemed a hopeful one. The possibility that she might elect to take her own life was never explicitly discussed with her. She was discharged, and a few weeks later she took her life.

Depressed chronic schizophrenic patients are less likely to complain of somatic symptoms (e.g., weight loss, depleted energy) and more likely to complain of psychological symptoms, especially hopelessness (Drake & Cotton, 1986). Some have argued that the hopelessness that afflicts these patients is realistic: After several psychotic episodes the patient correctly grasps that his illness has corroded his powers, devastated his social and personal life, and dashed his hopes for work achievement. Many of these patients are college educated and had realistic, high self-expectations and ambitions before falling ill (Drake, Gates, Cotton, & Whittaker, 1984; Roy, 1986).

One could fairly argue that in Miss C.'s case suicide was an act of voluntary euthanasia on her part, and an act of passive euthanasia on the part of the psychiatric staff. It is disturbing that at the time of the patient's discharge there was no discussion of such an alternative with her. The patient was given to understand that she was being released, but that if she wished to return to the hospital for further care, she might do so. Critics might suggest that to discharge a patient in this way sends a message that suicide is, after all, the best alternative. Her possible choice of suicide was not discussed in the psychotherapy as an acceptable option. The guilt the psychiatric staff experienced silenced them (Birtchnell, 1983; Lowenthal, 1975). Had the patient's choice to live or to die been discussed with her in an empathic but non-interfering way it is possible she might have chosen otherwise. It is well known that emotional isolation is intolerable to suicidal patients (Maltsberger & Buie, 1974).

No doubt the psychiatrists' guilt arose in part from the sense that they were at least partly responsible for the patient's death. It might be argued that although they had appropriately taken responsibility for protecting her life while treatment was being attempted, they quite properly relinquished the responsibility when it was clear further treatment had little to offer, and the patient wished to leave. They believed their decision was humane: not to interfere in suicide if the patient took her life, as they expected she might, but on the other hand, to offer a continuing supportive relationship and the opportunity for readmission to the hospital if she requested it.

A troublesome problem in deciding to give responsibility for living or dying back to a patient arises from the persistence of depression. Much of the literature addressing "rational suicide" overlooks the fact that hardly ever does suicide take place in the absence of major mental illness, most commonly depression (Barraclough, Bunch, Nelson, & Sainsbury, 1974; Dorpat & Ripley, 1960; Robins, Murphy, Wilkinson, Glassner, & Kays, 1959). The treatment refractory patients discussed here are likely to have some persisting degree of depression late in their care when their clinicians contemplate interfering no more. The question arises as to whether a somewhat depressed patient can weigh suicide in a rational way.

To some extent we are caught in a tautology—most diagnostic manuals (e.g., *DSM-III-R*) list suicidal ideation among the criteria for arriving at a diagnosis of depression; hopelessness is a part of depressed mood. It follows that any person who feels hopelessness and entertains thoughts of suicide meets two of the diagnostic criteria for a diagnosis of major depression. Adding any three of the following will satisfy the full definition: sleep difficulty, diminished interest in the circumambient world, self-reproach, lowered energy, difficulty concentrating, an appetite disturbance, or psychomotor agitation or underactivity. The question is clarified when posed in this way: Is a person who feels hopeless and thinks of suicide, experiences a lowering of energy, mild insomnia, and reduced appetite, capable of making a rational decision about suicide (rational euthanasia)? Such a person is technically depressed.

The clinical (and ethical) difficulty is this: Patients are not rational or irrational in an all or nothing way (a fact to which the law seems to be blind).

Irrationality is a matter of degree. Many people who nobody would call irrational suffer from mild depressive disorders (dysthymias in the jargon) and are pessimistic characters. How depressed must a patient be before the clinician decides his mood disorder has impaired his judgement?

This decision ordinarily turns on the clinician's judgement as to whether the patient's hopelessness is congruent in degree to the patient's circumstances and life prospects. In the case of Miss C. there was a clinical consensus that the patient's hopelessness was more than an ordinary mood disturbance secondary to her depressive illness. In the minds of those responsible for her care her hopelessness *might have asserted itself even in the absence of other depressive indicia*. It would seem to follow that a somewhat rational suicide is theoretically possible in the face of a lingering depression—or at least that a more or less reasonable suicide is.

Though to some readers I may seem to beg an issue, I should like to draw a distinction between the terms *rational* and *reasonable*. Though these words are ordinarily synonyms, I believe there is a difference in nuance. From the psychoanalytic viewpoint one could argue that any decision, in order to be fully rational, must not be influenced by unconscious forces out of the decider's awareness. Most patients in deciding to commit suicide are powerfully influenced by unconscious forces, and cannot be described as strictly rational (Maltsberger & Buie, 1980). Indeed, few major life decisions (e.g., the decision to marry, or the decision to choose one profession over another) are rational in this sense. Yet many decisions, examined in the decider's overall life context, may seem reasonable, even though he may not be fully aware of everything that drives his choice. Hence it follows that some suicides may be reasonable but not rational.

A judgment of this kind requires the examiner to put himself in the patient's place psychologically and, on the basis of trial identification with the patient, to form an opinion from what he conceives to be the patient's point of view, or what might be the patient's point of view, were the patient not depressed. In short, it is a judgment based on empathy (Buie, 1981). That his frame of reference may not be sufficiently congruent with that of the patient presents a very substantial difficulty. Because the examiner may not be fully in touch with the patient's life history and enough of its important emotional implications, he may fall into empathic errors.

In discussing rational suicide Siegel (1986) observes that many people experience transitory wishes to die in response to severely stressful events, such as the onset of senescence. She comments that suicidal states arising from stress usually pass off, and that "in the majority of cases these individuals eventually achieve a satisfactory adaptation." The question must arise, Satisfactory to whom? The onset of early senile dementia could devastate a professor of history but his despair could seem inappropriate to an empathically mistuned examiner who failed to grasp the narcissistic importance of vivid memory to such a patient. If this hypothetical professor's hopelessness persisted and did not pass off, how would the mistuned examiner estimate its reasonableness in the context of a persisting wish to die?

What is an intolerable circumstance for a patient may not seem so to the examiner. Furthermore, so idiosyncratic may some patients seem in concluding their life circumstances are intolerable that the ordinary examiner may disagree out of hand. Examiners substitute their own judgments about these matters for the judgments of patients, and usually would not agree that hopelessness was reasonable unless the patient's global circumstances were very grim indeed. Who can say where someone else *reasonably* crosses the line from sufficiently hopeful prospects to insufficiently hopeful prospects? This kind of difficulty has prompted Szasz (1986) to argue that clinicians should not interfere in patients' decisions to commit suicide at all.

The outside observers agreed Miss C.'s suicide took place in objectively hopeless circumstances. If reality-congruent hopelessness drove her suicide, it could be described as fairly rational voluntary autoeuthanasia. The possibility remains nevertheless that her death was not driven by rational considerations, but by the sudden revival of psychosis or a sudden crescendo of depression. Under those circumstances the suicide could not be described as rational. Some would deem it reasonable. In all likelihood there was a mixture of rational and irrational components in the death of this patient.

Not every patient allowed to commit euthanasic suicide has had the best possible care. Binswanger (1958), the existential psychiatrist who discharged his patient Ellen West in the full expectation she would commit suicide (she did), can be faulted for failing to take into account the destructiveness of Mrs. West's husband and family as he planned and carried out her treatment. Extended consultation, often with several others, is always indicated in these cases. Whether other treatments may soon become available to make the patient's prospects more hopeful must also be weighed.

The current litigious climate makes it hazardous to discharge any suicidal patient, whatever the circumstances of the case. Even though to release a patient such as Miss C. may be arguably the more ethical course, plaintiff heirs might later claim that the psychiatrists responsible for her care had been derelict in their duty to protect her from suicide. It is ironic that though the law makes discharging such patients from private institutions too risky, public hospitals frequently send such patients into the street because government institutions and those who practice in them enjoy immunity from the law's reprisals as agents of the government.

PATIENTS WITH CHRONIC SUICIDAL PERSONALITY DISORDERS

Another group of patients who may be discharged from inpatient care while the risk of suicide remains high are those who suffer from chronic suicidal personality disorders.

Case Study Mr. H., a 28-year-old unmarried graduate student, was admitted to a psychiatric hospital for the fifth time in 2 years following an overdose of the antidepressant medicine prescribed by his psychiatrist. He had fallen into a coma and nearly died. Mr. H. had a history of repeated wrist-cutting. He frequently threatened suicide. He suffered from a chronic state of emptiness and aloneness, low self-esteem, and suicidal preoccupation, but he slept well, maintained an interest in his work most of the time, enjoyed a reasonable level of energy, and concentrated without difficulty. There was no psychomotor disturbance. He had no friends and had alienated his family with his cynical attitude and repeated suicidal behavior. He tortured his therapist with suicide threats and non-lethal self-injuries, seeming to enjoy the worry he aroused in others. Without antidepressant drugs he was prone to more profound spells of hopelessness. The patient was given a diagnosis of major depressive illness, partially remitted with treatment, and borderline personality disorder.

His was, in short, a chronic suicidal character; he was a man unable to commit himself fully to living or to dying. His suicide attempts, though often dangerous, were contrived in such a way so that discovery and rescue before death were always probable. In the hospital his suicidal threatening worsened and he appeared more preoccupied with suicide than he had been in previous weeks. A decision was made to discharge Mr. H. to outpatient care even though he remained at risk to end his life.

Mr. H., and other patients like him, having little investment in living, are at risk to becoming habituated to hospital life, surrendering independent functioning, and falling into permanent, deteriorating inpatient careers. When hospital staffs continue over prolonged periods of time to take responsibility for preserving the lives of patients, there is the likelihood that a morbid struggle will blossom: Who will win? The patient engages in a contest, himself on the side of suicide, casting the staff on the side of its prevention. The entanglement that results will reduce the treatment to a struggle for control over the patient's life. Lost in the power fight are three central therapeutic questions: Whose life is it anyway, Who ultimately is responsible for the patient's self care, and Why has the patient abandoned connection and commitment to other people and to meaningful pursuits (Basecu, 1965)?

When we see that continued monitoring, vigilance, and preemptive anti-suicidal intervention is leading to the development of coercive bondage and psychotherapeutic stalemate, giving responsibility back to the patient for the decision whether to live or to commit suicide becomes not only ethically defensible, but therapeutically necessary.

Giving responsibility back to the patient, even though the immediate suicide risk may increase for a time, is the best hope. The turning point in the treatment of a chronically suicidal personality is often the moment when suicidal feelings begin to be communicated freely, the patient asks for help in resisting them when necessary, and reliance on interrogations and externally imposed controls is given up.

Patients such as Mr. H. should be discharged when, in the best judgment of those responsible, keeping the patient in the hospital is likely to result in greater harm over the course of time than discharging the patient, even though at the time of discharge the risk of suicide may be heightened.

In most jurisdictions involuntary commitment to a psychiatric unit requires that the patient suffer from a mental illness. Major affective disorders and the psychoses are generally understood to be mental illnesses of considerable significance in that they interfere with patients' capacity to think rationally. Personality disorder diagnoses and the more minor mood disorders such as "dysthymic disorder" lie somewhere in forensic limbo.

The important question is not diagnosis, but this: Does the patient stand a better long-term chance for living instead of suiciding if he is discharged soon instead of remaining in the hospital? If the answer is yes, ethically he should be discharged, and six important forensic questions arise:

Has the patient been afforded all reasonable treatment for the depressive and/or psychotic aspects of his illness (if there are any)? Because depression and psychosis (delusions, hallucinations, and thought disorder) are likely to interfere with patients' judgment in many sectors, including choosing living over suicide, full psychopharmacological review is desirable as discharge is contemplated. Where the treatment response has been unsatisfactory, electroconvulsive therapy should be considered. In rare instances neurosurgical intervention may be in order.

Is there a reasonable post-discharge treatment plan? Patients should have established a reasonable therapeutic alliance with a clinician who is prepared to assume outpatient treatment as hospital discharge nears. The plan should aim at minimal use of further inpatient treatment; ideally the patient should initiate and consent to hospital readmission. When the therapeutic alliance collapses, or when depression or psychosis increase and overwhelm the patient, the clinician has no choice but to assume responsibility for readmission. Setbacks of this kind are not always avoidable. The therapist should avoid struggles over suicide rescue, attempting to leave it to the patient to decide whether inpatient care is truly necessary whenever possible. The therapist should shun false omnipotent assumptions of responsibility for the patient's life and be prepared to confront the patient with the lack of commitment that his suicidal orientation entails instead. The investigation of the roots of the detachment is most important (Basecu, 1965; Olin, 1976; Hendin, 1981; Schwartz, Flinn, & Slawson, 1974). Family therapy or comparable work with others emotionally close to him are valuable (Birtchnell, 1983); partial programs and support groups are helpful.

Is the patient competent to give informed consent to discharge and to the proposed post-hospital treatment, i.e., does he understand the calculated risk?

While formal competency can only be determined by a court, the clinician needs to make sure, for ethical as well as for legal reasons, that the patient understands and can reasonably cooperate in the proposed treatment (Applebaum & Gutheil, 1991). Should the patient commit suicide at some future time, evidence in the record of carefully documented inquiry to support a view that the patient was competent would be protective in the event of a lawsuit.

The record should show that the plan was fully explained to the patient, as well as alternatives (including chronic state hospital care, should it be obtainable, and the option of no treatment whatever), the risks and disadvantages of continued inpatient treatment (hospitalism and therapeutic bondage) and the risks and advantages of early discharge. The following details (italicized for emphasis) can establish that the patient was competent to give informed consent to the necessary risk hospital discharge entailed should the question arise at a later time. The record should show that the patient *understood* the information and *demonstrated a good grasp of what it implied for his future*. It should reflect that the examiner made sure the patient was not laboring under some incapacity to think clearly and to form rational opinions: A statement is needed that the patient was *free of delusions or hallucinations that would affect the decision*, and that the patient's *mood* was not so disturbed as to affect his capacity to make a good judgement. A note should be included that the patient was *well oriented, had an intact memory, and that his capacity for reasoning was unimpaired*.

Has the patient given consent to the treatment plan? Be sure to ask the patient if he agrees to the treatment proposed and to record the consent in the record.

Has full consultation been obtained in support of the discharge plan? An experienced colleague, whenever possible someone who has worked extensively with patients of this kind, should review the record, interview the patient, and write down his support for the treatment plan, making it plain that he feels taking a calculated risk is in the patient's best interest, and acknowledging the hazards of prolonged hospitalization.

Have those close to the patient been informed of and agreed to the plan? The patient's family and close friends should be invited to a conference in which the projected outpatient treatment program is fully explained, with its risks and its expected benefits. The risks and benefits of prolonged hospital care should also be laid out, and the realities about obtaining and paying for long-term inpatient care explained. The vicissitudes and problems of the state hospital system should be explained. Their agreement to the plan should then be obtained and recorded in the patient's chart.

It is particularly desirable that the patient's immediate heirs, usually the next-of-kin, should be present for this conference. In the event of future suicide it is the heirs who have legal standing to bring negligence actions against clinicians and the hospital. In future legal proceedings, could it be shown that the family had been fully informed of the circumstances and had supported taking the recommended calculated risk, the defendants' position would be strengthened.

CONCLUSION

To discharge a patient unlikely to recover and expected to be near suicide is foolhardy for clinicians not working under the protective umbrella of a government institution. Though patients of this class may wish to leave the hospital and clinicians may believe that compelling them to remain there is not ethical, the legal system stands in the way. A wrongful death action could follow; plaintiff's attorney would argue that the physician had a duty to preserve the patient's life, and knowing that suicide was probable, was derelict in sending the patient out of the hospital.

On the other hand, when on balance the benefits of discharge outweigh the risks of continued inpatient confinement, it is both ethically and legally prudent to discharge patients suffering from chronic suicidal character problems. Careful preparation of the patient and family as well as meticulous documentation of the clinical circumstances are essential for the protection of clinicians and hospitals in the event of future suicide and legal action.

REFERENCES

Applebaum, P. S. & Gutheil, T. G. (1991). *Clinical handbook of psychiatry and the law.* Baltimore: Williams & Wilkins.

Basecu, S. (1965). The threat of suicide in psychotherapy. *American Journal of Psychotherapy, 19,* 99–105.

Barraclough, B., Bunch, J., Nelson, B., & Sainsbury, P. (1974). A hundred cases of suicide: Clinical aspects. *British Journal of Psychiatry, 125,* 355–373.

Battin, M. P. (1982). *Ethical issues in suicide.* Englewood Cliffs, NJ: Prentice Hall.

Binswanger, L. (1958). The case of Ellen West. In R. May, E. Angel, & H. F. Ellenberger (Eds.) and W. M. Mendel & J. Lyons (Trans.), *Existence: A new dimension in psychiatry and psychology* (pp. 237–364). New York: Basic Books.

Birtchnell, J. B. (1983). Psychotherapeutic considerations in the management of the suicidal patient. *American Journal of Psychotherapy, 37,* 24–36.

Bleuler, E. (1950). *Dementia praecox or the group of schizophrenias.* New York: International Universities Press.

Buie, D. H. (1981). Empathy, its nature and limitations. *Journal of the American Psychoanalytic Association, 29,* 281–307.

Dorpat, T. L., & Ripley, H. S. (1960). A study of suicide in the Seattle area. *Comprehensive Psychiatry, 1,* 349–359.

Drake, R., Gates, C., Cotton, P., & Whittaker, A. (1984). Suicide among schizophrenics. Who is at risk? *Journal of Nervous and Mental Disease, 172,* 613–617.

Drake, R. E., & Cotton, P. G. (1986). Depression, hopelessness and suicide in chronic schizophrenia. *British Journal of Psychiatry, 148,* 554–559.

Hendin, H. (1981). Psychotherapy and suicide. *American Journal of Psychotherapy, 35,* 469–480.

Lesse, S. (1965). Editorial comment. *American Journal of Psychotherapy, 19,* 105.

Lowenthal, U. (1975). Suicide—the other side: The factor of reality among suicidal motivations. *Archives of General Psychiatry, 33,* 838–842.

Maltsberger, J. T., & Buie D. H. (1974). Countertransference hate in the treatment of suicidal patients. *Archives of General Psychiatry, 30,* 625–633.

Maltsberger, J. T., & Buie D. H. (1980). The devices of suicide. *International Review of Psycho-Analysis, 7,* 61–72.

Mintz, R. (1971). Basic considerations in the psychotherapy of the depressed suicidal patient. *American Journal of Psychotherapy, 25,* 56–73.

Olin, H. S. (1976). Psychotherapy of the chronically suicidal patient. *American Journal of Psychotherapy, 30,* 570–575.

Robins, E., Murphy, G. E., Wilkinson, R. H., Jr., Gassner, S., & Kays, J. (1959). Some clinical considerations in the prevention of suicide based on a study of 134 successful suicides. *American Journal of Public Health, 49,* 888–899.

Roy, A. (1986). Suicide in schizophrenia. In Roy, A. (Ed.), *Suicide* (pp. 97–112). Baltimore: Williams & Wilkins.

Schwartz, D. A., Flinn, D. E., & Slawson, P. F. (1974). Treatment of the suicidal character. *American Journal of Psychotherapy, 28,* 194–207.

Shein, H. M., & Stone, A. A. (1969). Monitoring and treatment of suicidal potential within the context of psychotherapy. *Comprehensive Psychiatry, 10,* 59–70.

Siegel, K. (1986). Psychosocial aspects of rational suicide. *American Journal of Psychotherapy, 40,* 405–418.

Szasz, T. (1986). The case against suicide prevention. *American Psychologist, 41,* 806–812.

Chapter 16

The Ten Most Common Errors of Suicide Interventionists

Robert A. Neimeyer and Angela M. Pfeiffer

How prepared are medical and mental health professionals to manage suicidal crises in their patients? How skilled are they in selecting an appropriate response in counseling situations with potentially self-destructive clients, and to what extent does professional training help them to do so? Do common themes underlie various suboptimal responses? Most important, can the identification of such common themes be used to focus professional education in a way that redresses these weaknesses?

In this chapter, we provide at least some preliminary answers to these questions. Nearly 15 years of research on the suicide intervention skills of crisis-line staff (Neimeyer & Hartley, 1986; Neimeyer & MacInnes, 1981; Neimeyer & Neimeyer, 1984; Neimeyer & Oppenheimer, 1983), alcohol and drug counselors (Neimeyer & MacInnes, 1981), medical students (Neimeyer & Diamond, 1983), and master's-level counselors (Neimeyer & Bonnelle, 1994) have convinced us that competence in working with suicidal people is far from uniform among helping professionals, despite their best intentions in undertaking such work. This is not surprising, given the meager to nonexistent preparation in suicide assessment and intervention provided by training programs in such disciplines as clinical psychology (Bongar & Harmatz, 1991) and medicine (Dickinson, Sumner, & Fredrick 1992). Nonetheless, the shortcomings of interventionists are tragic, given the frequency with which suicidal people consult professional helpers before they attempt suicide (Wekstein, 1979).

THE DATA

To determine the common limitations of helping professionals in responding to distressed and self-injurious clients, we analyzed data provided by a reasonably large and representative group of interventionists representing two primary professions that come into frequent contact with suicidal people. A total of 215 interventionists participated in the study, comprising 121 medical residents and 94 master's-level counselors. Despite the fact that they were still in training, all participants were currently engaged in practicum or other work settings that required basic competence in the assessment and treatment of suicidal people. Approximately 51% of the respondents were female and 49% were male, and their mean age was 27.2 years.

The basic data for our analysis were participants' responses to the items on the Suicide Intervention Response Inventory (SIRI), a 25-item self-report instrument that assesses skill in selecting appropriate responses in hypothetical helping scenarios involving potentially suicidal individuals (Neimeyer & MacInnes, 1981). Several studies support the validity and reliability of the SIRI as a test of helpers' suicide intervention skills, whether they work in a telephone counseling or face-to-face treatment setting (for a review, see Neimeyer & Pfeiffer, 1994). Moreover, evidence indicates that responses to the SIRI are free of social desirability bias (Neimeyer & Bonnelle, 1994) and that the SIRI assesses counseling skills that are distinguishable from more abstract knowledge of factors associated with heightened lethality and intent (Inman, Bascue, Kahn, & Shaw, 1984).

We conducted an item analysis of participants' responses to the instrument with the goal of identifying frequently occurring errors, reflected on the SIRI by endorsement of the less appropriate or facilitative of two alternative caregiver responses to a particular client or patient presenting problem. Because one of the two response options for each item has been shown to be clearly superior to the other in the opinion of a select panel of highly expert suicidologists (Neimeyer & Bonnelle, 1994), we felt confident in interpreting selection of the incorrect alternative as indicative of a technical or strategic error in working with a distraught client. We then attempted to identify the underlying difficulties reflected in the most common errors. For example, in Item 24, an apparently dejected and vaguely paranoid client remarks, "I can't talk to anybody about my situation. Everyone is against me." In Option A, the helper replies, "That isn't true. There are probably lots of people who care about you, if you'd only give them a chance." In contrast, in Option B the helper replies empathically, "It must be difficult to find help when it's so hard to trust people." A total of 43 (20%) of the interventionists in the present sample selected the first option as the preferable one, suggesting a tendency toward defensiveness rather than acceptance of and

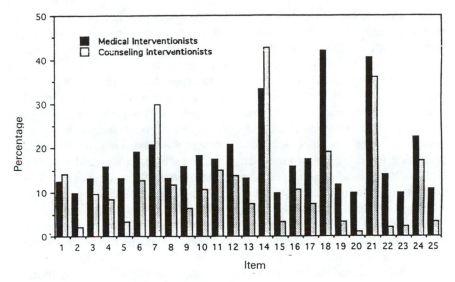

Figure 1 Percentage of interventionists (*N* = 215) who responded incorrectly to items on the Suicide Interventionist Response Inventory. Item content is identified in the Appendix.

attention to the client's feelings of despair and isolation. Ten recurring themes emerged in the analysis of the inadequate responses. By way of summary, the percentage of interventionists who selected the incorrect response to each item is presented in Figure 1. The items are identified in the Appendix, which presents Form 2 of the SIRI. The majority of participants in both disciplines selected the correct response to each item, but surprisingly high percentages of participants responded incorrectly on some items.

ERROR 1: SUPERFICIAL REASSURANCE

Given crisis interventionists' altruistic motivation to help others (Clary & Orenstein, 1991; Engs & Kirk, 1974), it is not surprising that they are frequently disposed to offer reassurance in response to a client's expression of acute distress and hopelessness. Sometimes, however, such attempts can be trivial or superficial, doing more harm than good to the process of counseling. For example, in the scenario in which a young, perturbed client indicates she feels systematically misunderstood and at times of misunderstanding experiences an impulsive need to cut herself, some would-be helpers in the present sample chose the response, "But you're so young and have so much to live for! How can you think of hurting yourself?" Although such responses are intended to emphasize more optimistic or positive aspects of the situation, they in fact risk alienating the client, whose sense of not being heard or taken seriously is reinforced by the interventionist's shock and implicit rejection of her communication. Ironically, such responses are anything but reassuring in their effect, often deepening clients' feelings that they are isolated in their distress.

Another form of trivial reassurance is the premature offering of a prepackaged meaning for the client's difficulties. Although this type of error is not the prerogative of any one group of respondents, helpers who themselves are highly committed to a particular philosophy of life (religious or secular) may be at higher risk for offering superficial reassurance of this kind. Thus, in the scenario presenting an angry client whose belief in God has been shaken by personal catastrophes, a number of interventionists chose the hackneyed response, "Well, God works in mysterious ways. Maybe this is His way of testing your faith." Although an exploration of the impact of personal tragedy on one's fundamental beliefs and values is fair game for therapy, automatic or badly timed interventions of this type seem likely to disrupt, rather than facilitate, the process of meaning reconstruction.

Perhaps the starkest expression of superficial reassurance takes the form of directly contradicting the client's protest of anguish and hopelessness. Faced with such a scenario, a surprisingly high percentage of the interventionists we studied were apt to respond, "Come on now. Things can't be all that bad." Such a response, however well intentioned, is unlikely to promote the working alliance between the client and therapist that is necessary for successful problem exploration and resolution. What seems required in such circumstances is a *credulous attitude* (Kelly, 1955), that is, a willingness to accept that *at least from the client's standpoint,* the situation is indeed critical and is to be taken seriously. This shared concern can provide a basis for mutual efforts at crisis definition and intervention.

ERROR 2: AVOIDANCE OF STRONG FEELINGS

An associated error committed by many of the helpers in our sample might be described as *the avoidance of strong feelings.* Confronted with a client's acute depression, fear, or grief, some interventionists retreated into the trivial reassurance described earlier or into professionalism, passivity, or advice giving. Quickly diverting discussion away from markers of powerful emotion and toward a more abstract or intellectualized exchange can serve the same purpose. For example, when interacting with a dejected client who feels no one cares whether he's alive or dead, some potential helpers shifted immediately to discussing why he believes no one cares, rather than first establishing an empathic bridge into the client's distress by reflecting his keen feelings of aloneness. Rather than deepening the level of therapy or counseling, such responses tend to keep the interaction on a purely cognitive level, preventing contact with the more profound feelings of distress whose exploration can hold the key to successful treatment (Greenberg & Safran, 1987).

Interventionists will sometimes pull back from strong emotion as if they are afraid of a contagion, as, for example, when a client's tears and sobbing are met with silence or pursuit of tangential issues, rather than a direct and sensitive articulation of the client's distress. In such cases, putting into words the feelings the client is mutely expressing (e.g., through responding, "With all the hurt you're feeling, it must be impossible to hold those tears in") can both help establish a real connection between the client and therapist and help the client verbalize feelings and issues that were previously only tacit or private. Such empathic interventions also help both the client and counselor hold the pain long enough to understand it, before rushing to its elimination.

ERROR 3: PROFESSIONALISM

Given the rigors of suicide and crisis intervention, it is not surprising that care-givers often find ways of insulating or protecting themselves from the sometimes brutal or exhausting realities of their clients' lives. One way interventionists may insulate themselves is by distancing or detaching themselves from the fellow human being who is seeking their help, for example, by seeking refuge in professionalism or the comfortable boundaries of role definition. Thus, in the scenario in which a client says her "thoughts are so terrible that I could never tell them to anybody," some interventionists in the present study responded, "You can tell me. I'm a professional, and I've been trained to be objective about these things." Although such a response may be calculated to put the reticent client at ease, this exaggerated air of objectivity and disinterest also carries the implicit message that the relationship is a hierarchical one, in which the penitent client is seeking the direction, forgiveness, or acceptance of a morally or emotionally superior being.

Although it may feel riskier to the interventionist, an alternative response that levels the interaction between the client and the therapist is probably more often facilitative of counseling. For example, in the preceding scenario, the helper might respond, "It sounds like some of your ideas are so frightening to you that you imagine others would be shocked to know what you are thinking." This opens the discussion to an exploration of both the content of the client's thoughts and the reactions the client imagines they would elicit in others, including the therapist. More important, an empathic reply of this kind avoids the implication of professional distance and allows the caregiver to use the relationship as a primary tool of therapy. In contrast, maintaining a distance from a more caring form of relating can limit the interpersonal learning that undergirds most forms of counseling and psychotherapy.

ERROR 4: INADEQUATE ASSESSMENT OF SUICIDAL INTENT

Whereas the foregoing errors can characterize any form of therapy, others are particularly relevant to work with the potentially suicidal client. One of these is the failure to conduct an adequate assessment of suicidal intent. This was surprisingly common among the physicians and master's-level counselors we studied, many of whom responded to hypothetical client's indirect expressions of suicide risk (e.g., "There just isn't anywhere left to turn" and "I'd be better off dead") with avoidance or reassurance, rather than with a more detailed evaluation of the level of the client's intent or plans (e.g., "You sound so miserable. Have you been thinking of hurting yourself?"). Even more strikingly, an equally high number of interventionists ignored or contradicted even *direct* client communications of self-injurious intent. In the scenario in which a client stated, "I decided to call in tonight because I really feel like I might do something to myself. I've been thinking about suicide," these counselors and physicians chose the response, "You say you're suicidal, but what is it that's *really* bothering you?" This implicit negation of the suicide threat not only precludes further assessment, but also erects potentially substantial barriers to the construction of a genuinely therapeutic relationship.

As detailed in other contributions to this volume (especially in Chapters 4 and 7), direct and indirect communications of suicidal threat should be taken seriously, with prompt and sensitive but thorough assessment of the level of intent, lethality, and perturbation associated with the client's plan.

ERROR 5: FAILURE TO IDENTIFY THE PRECIPITATING EVENT

A second and more subtle error that has special relevance to suicide intervention is the failure to identify a *precipitating event,* the specific occurrence or situation that prompted the client's decision to seek help. Pinpointing this trigger event not only can focus a time-limited therapy, but also can identify and prioritize issues in a way that a more abstract discussion cannot. In contrast, the failure to be specific complicates the formulation of relevant *action plans* that can begin to restore a client's sense of balance and equilibrium (Caplan, 1964).

Identification of a precipitating event need not take the form of a callous interrogation of a distressed client, but instead can represent an extension of the counselor's basic empathic concern. For instance, to the life-threatening client who complains at length that "life has been worthless" since the death of his wife several years before, the counselor might respond, "It sounds like everything just collapsed around you when your wife died. . . . But what has happened recently to make things even worse, to make you think that dying is the only way out?" This sort of inquiry might uncover the potential for some practical or immediate intervention to stabilize the client, and open up the opportunity for a longer term therapy for grief and loss.

ERROR 6: PASSIVITY

Particularly in the early stages of treatment with potentially suicidal people, the interventionist needs to be active, demonstrating engagement with the client through reflection of feelings, focused inquiry, and clear structuring of the interaction (see Chapter 4). However, a surprisingly high percentage of the counselors and physicians we studied tended to adopt an essentially passive, nonparticipatory role, even when the client clearly required higher levels of helper involvement. For example, in the scenario in which a client stammers that she needs help, at which point her voice breaks and silence ensues, fully a quarter of our sample preferred to respond rather clinically, "Go on. I'm here to listen to you talk," rather than joining with the client's distress by observing, "It must be very hard for you to talk about what's bothering you." In other situations, such passivity could literally break off the contact between the client and the helping individual or agency. For example, in the context of a crisis intervention phone call with a reluctant client whose problems have yet to be adequately assessed, the common suggestion by our respondents to "call back some other time when you can talk more easily" could terminate the connection at a potentially dangerous moment, with no clear plan for follow-up. Effective crisis intervention at such points may require a more energetic, involved stance, in which the counselor engages with the client through direct questioning, active listening, or other ways of maintaining and enhancing contact.

ERROR 7: INSUFFICIENT DIRECTIVENESS

A related error that was remarkably common among the professionals we studied was the tendency to be insufficiently directive in the management of suicidal crises. In a circumstance involving a telephone contact with a life-threatening adolescent, for example, more than one third of the sample responded to her bid to end the call with, "Okay, but if you keep feeling suicidal, remember you can always call back." In view of the dangerousness and unpredictability of the situation, a better alternative is to emphasize the importance of continuing their mutual problem-solving, or at minimum, to secure a verbal no-suicide contract until contact could be reestablished.

A roughly comparable number of interventionists displayed this lack of directiveness in a still more threatening scenario involving a highly perturbed caller who claims to have a gun pointed at his head and who threatens to pull the trigger unless he gets some help. In this case, a common error was to offer a weak reflection of the caller's feelings ("You seem to be somewhat upset"), rather than attempt to secure sufficient control over a potentially lethal situation to allow for the establishment of a helping contact (''I want you to put down the gun so we can talk''). Clearly, unless the interventionist is able to negotiate a safe structure for mutual problem exploration, he or she may never have a chance to engage in more subtle forms of helping behavior. Simply stated, effective crisis intervention often requires directive crisis management, particularly in terms of inserting some distance between a perturbed and impulsive client and means of self-injury.

ERROR 8: ADVICE GIVING

Like the crisis-line workers studied by Knowles (1979), some of the interventionists in our sample were drawn toward premature advice giving, choosing responses such as, ''Considering all you have going for you, your problems can't be all that serious. Try to focus more on the positive aspects of your situation.'' Unfortunately, this simplistic version of rational–emotive therapy (''Try not to worry about it'') is rarely effective, tending to convince the client that the counselor simply does not appreciate the gravity of the situation. Even when the advice goes beyond a blandly optimistic injunction to ''look on the bright side,'' it rarely provides a workable solution from the client's standpoint, because it is typically offered by an outsider who is unfamiliar with the actual or psychological constraints on the client that militate against taking the advice.

A more enlightened strategy is to work toward the formulation of a concrete action plan only *after* a thorough assessment of the particulars of the client's problem has been made, and then only if an adequate working alliance has been established to permit the client to take the interventionist's recommendations seriously. Such concrete agendas for client initiatives should be worked out collaboratively to have maximum impact, with the therapist prompting, shaping, and reinforcing the client's own tentative ideas, rather than giving authoritative advice. Suggestions arrived at in this way (''What would be one or two small steps you could take in the next few days to start to deal with this problem?'') are likely to arouse less resistance in the client and may even lead to novel interventions in the context of the client's life that the interventionist might not have envisioned.

ERROR 9: STEREOTYPIC RESPONSES

Especially in a crisis intervention setting, where contact with a client may be brief and mediated by the distance of a telephone line, counselors may be tempted to take shortcuts in exploring a client's experience of a problem by making unwarranted assumptions about the client's personality, pathology, or predicament. In the worst cases, these can border on stereotypic assumptions about a client of a certain gender, age, or racial group that can have a deleterious impact on subsequent interactions with the individual. An expression of this error in our sample was participants' tendency to respond to the scenario involving a tearful, apologetic male client with the response option, "Do you think that the reason it's hard for you to cry is because you're a man?" Whereas a discussion of sex role constraints might be appropriate at some future point in the therapy, in the crisis situation, such a response is likely to detract from the quality of the therapeutic relationship, representing a failure to track with sensitivity the client's emotional lead. As a safeguard against making such stereotypic responses, interventionists should focus on the individuality of each client, paying attention to the emotional nuances of his or her communications without trying to fit them into a typology of client problems.

ERROR 10: DEFENSIVENESS

One of the more difficult clinical situations for interventionists to negotiate is the angry or rejecting client, who may directly or indirectly rebuff the therapist's attempts to help. Granted, it may be difficult to find the optimal response to such clients, but interventionists who react to such provocations defensively or with a put-down only aggravate the problem, eroding whatever level of trust might be established in the relationship.

When the client challenges the interventionist's competence or willingness to understand, the caregiver might respond defensively. For example, in the scenario in which an angry client snaps, "How could you ever help me? Have you ever wanted to kill yourself?", helpers who reacted personally rather than therapeutically to this challenge responded, "Sure, I've thought about suicide sometimes. But I've always found more realistic solutions to my problems." The air of condescension and superiority in such a response can make the client feel not only even angrier but also belittled and rejected.

A similar error was made even more frequently by our sample in the scenario in which a foreclosed and vaguely paranoid client states that he couldn't talk to anyone about his situation because "everyone is against me." Many interventionists reacted with an outright rejection of the client's feelings, asserting the availability of social support in the client's life, despite the client's beliefs to the contrary. Whatever the reality of the client's social circumstances, it is unlikely that directly contradicting the client's impassioned protest will make the client more receptive to the helpfulness of others, the therapist included.

In a situation involving an angry or rejecting client, the more appropriate response on the part of the clinician would be to reflect empathically the client's feeling, in a way that opens a possible discussion of the implications of the client's beliefs for the working alliance (e.g., "It must be difficult to seek help when it's so difficult to trust people"). When client communications that are angry and rejecting occur *within* the therapy relationship, it is highly likely that they are (at some level) *about* the therapy relationship. For this reason, it is essential that the therapist explore them nondefensively if treatment is to get back on track. Alternative means of exploring a client's implicit anger at the therapist would be to make use of open-ended *inquiry* (e.g., "Does it seem to you that I'm having trouble understanding you as well?") or *disarming* responses (e.g., "You're absolutely right—we can't work together effectively unless I can earn your trust. Do you have any idea how we'd have to work together to achieve that?") (for a discussion of response skills to use in the face of criticism, see Burns, 1989). The key is not to respond in an automatic and self-protective fashion, by counterattacking, reacting sarcastically, apologizing, or making excuses, but instead to join with the client's concern through empathy, develop a common ground through honest establishment of points of agreement, and engage in mutual problem-solving through specific inquiry. When a gulf of misunderstanding or suspicion separates the client and therapist, it is the therapist's, not the client's, responsibility to cross the gulf and reestablish a working partnership.

SOME DISCIPLINARY DIFFERENCES

Although interventionists in both disciplines in our total sample committed the foregoing errors, clear differences did emerge between those with medical and those with counseling training in the *way they erred* when they did so (Figure 1). In general, when the medical residents erred, it was in reacting in a defensive, distancing, advice-giving, or essentially authoritarian fashion. For instance, the physicians were four times more likely than the counselors to respond to the scenario in which a client challenges their understanding with a defensive reply such as, "You're not giving me a chance. I've had a pretty rough life too; you're not the only one who's seen some hard times." Moreover, they were far more likely than the counselors to prefer formal and hierarchical interactions with distressed individuals. For example, in the scenario in which an upset client questions why the interventionist should care about him, some physicians chose to respond, "I've been trained to care about people. That's my job." Similarly, the physicians showed a greater tendency to gravitate toward reframing patient distress as mental illness or to refer the client for psychological testing, rather than having a more personal exchange oriented toward the feelings and meanings of the client in relation to his or her circumstances. In each scenario, the medical residents were three times more likely than their colleagues in counseling to select a professionalistic response.

The medical interventionists were also seven times more likely to dismiss client complaints with advice such as, "You've got to look on the bright side!" In a few extreme cases, such dismissal of client's feelings and concerns carried an authoritarian or admonishing overtone, as, for example, when a hypothetical client's statement of anger at his father was met with, "You shouldn't feel that way. After all, he is your father, and he deserves some respect." It is hard to imagine that such responses are effective in promoting either resolution of the patient's problems or the patient's attribution of competence and trustworthiness to the professional helper.

Finally, interventionists with a medical background were two or three times more likely than those with a counseling background to err in the direction of inadequately assessing suicidal intent, especially if the threat was vague or implicit. This was epitomized in the scenario in which a caller's voice on the telephone is slurred and unclear, in which a small percentage of the medical residents chose the response that instructed the caller to "get some sleep and call back in the morning." The failure to conduct a more thorough suicide assessment in such an instance (e.g., by asking, "Have you taken anything?") could well be a fatal error, one that comes uncomfortably close to the stereotyped portrayal of the doctor's habitual response to a troublesome patient: "Take two aspirin and call me in the morning." Needless to say, alertness to the subtler signs of potential self-injury is a prerequisite to any further attempts at suicide intervention.

When nonmedical counselors in our sample committed strategic errors, it was more often in the direction of excessive passivity or failing to structure the exchange with a reticent client. For example, they were less likely than their medically trained counterparts to prompt a silent client or to secure a no-suicide contract before terminating a session with a potentially life-threatening individual. In other words, when situations called for action, counselors were prone to overextend a basic posture of receptivity, to the point of ignoring the need for greater action or responsibility on their part. Whereas fading the initiative for change to the client may make sense in the context of longer term therapy, in the crucible of crisis intervention, the helping professional needs to be able to respond forcefully when indicated to establish an ongoing contact within which further assessment and intervention efforts can take place.

CONCLUSION

By concentrating on the common errors of suicide interventionists, we may have given the impression that the majority of the medical and nonmedical helpers in our study were grossly deficient in the clinical skills needed to treat self-destructive individuals. Fortunately, this was not the case—most members of both samples were generally competent in selecting facilitative therapeutic responses to a variety of crisis scenarios. Moreover, controlled research has indicated that helping professionals like those in our study typically are far more skillful in responding to individuals in crisis than are untrained psychology students (Neimeyer & MacInnes, 1981) or members of the general population (Neimeyer & Bonnelle, 1994). Thus, it would be erroneous to read these comments as an indictment of the proficiency of the interventionists in our study, many of whom were motivated to pursue their careers out of a genuine commitment to relieve human suffering.

That said, it was surprising that 10–40% of the interventionists in our study committed significant errors in the treatment of potentially self-destructive clients, including offering superficial reassurance, avoiding strong feelings, responding with professionalism, inadequately assessing suicide intent, failing to identify the precipitating problem, reacting passively, using insufficient directiveness in managing the emergency, giving unhelpful advice, engaging in stereotypic responses, and reacting defensively. The frequency with which these errors occurred in our sample is as much an indictment of professional education in these disciplines as it is a statement about the skill deficits of these generally well-intentioned helpers.

REFERENCES

Bongar, B., & Harmatz, M. (1991). Clinical psychology graduate education in the study of suicide: Availability, resources, and importance. *Suicide and Life-Threatening Behavior, 21,* 231–244.

Burns, D. L. (1989). *The feeling good handbook.* New York: William Morrow.

Caplan, G. (1964). *Principles of preventive psychiatry.* New York: Basic Books.

Clary, E., & Orenstein, L. (1991). The amount and effectiveness of help: The relationship of motives and abilities to helping behavior. *Personality and Social Psychology Bulletin, 17,* 58–64.

Dickinson, G. E., Sumner, E. D., & Frederick, L. M. (1992). Death education in selected health professions. *Death Education, 16,* 281–289.

Engs, R.C., & Kirk, R. H. (1974). The characteristics of volunteers in crisis intervention centers. *Public Health Reports, 89,* 458–464.

Inman, D. J., Bascue, L. O., Kahn, W. J., & Shaw, P. A. (1984). The relationship between suicide knowledge and suicide interviewing skills. *Death Education, 8,* 179–184.

Greenberg, L. S., & Safran, J. D. (1987). *Emotion in psychotherapy: Affect, cognition and the process of change.* New York: Guilford Press.

Kelly, G. (1955). *The psychology of personal constructs.* New York: Norton.

Knowles, D. (1979). Brief reports: On the tendency for volunteer helpers to give advice. *Journal of Counseling Psychology, 26,* 352–354.

Neimeyer, R. A., & Bonnelle, K. (1994). *The Suicide Intervention Response Inventory: A revision and validation.* Unpublished manuscript, Memphis State University, Memphis, TN.

Neimeyer, R. A., & Diamond, R. J. (1983). Suicide management skills and the medical student. *Journal of Medical Education, 58,* 562–567.

Neimeyer, R. A., & Hartley, R. E. (1986). Factorial structure of the Suicide Intervention Response Inventory. *Suicide and Life-Threatening Behavior, 16,* 434–447.

Neimeyer, R. A., & MacInnes (1981). Assessing paraprofessional competence with the Suicide Intervention Response Inventory. *Journal of Counseling Psychology, 28,* 176–179.

Neimeyer, R. A., & Neimeyer, G. J. (1984). Death anxiety and counseling skill in the suicide interventionist. *Suicide and Life-Threatening Behavior, 14,* 126–131.

Neimeyer, R. A., & Oppenheimer, B. (1983). Concurrent and predictive validity of the Suicide Intervention Response Inventory. *Psychological Reports, 52,* 594.

Neimeyer, R. A., & Pfeiffer, A. M. (1994). Evaluation of suicide intervention effectiveness. *Death Studies, 18,* 127–162.

Wekstein, L. (1979). *Handbook of suicidology.* New York: Brunner/Mazel.

APPENDIX 16-1: Suicide Intervention Response Inventory (Form 2)

The following items represent a series of excerpts from counseling sessions. Each excerpt begins with an expression by the client concerning some aspect of the situation he or she faces, followed by two possible helper responses to the client's remark.

You are to rate *each* response in terms of how appropriate or inappropriate you feel the reply is to the client's comment. In the blank, you should record a rating from -3 to $+3$, corresponding to the chart below. Be sure to respond to each item and try not to leave any blanks.

+ 3: Highly appropriate response
+ 2: Appropriate response
+ 1: Marginally appropriate response
  0: Neither appropriate nor inappropriate
− 1: Marginally inappropriate response
− 2: Inappropriate response
− 3: Highly inappropriate response

1. *Client:* I decided to call in tonight because I really feel like I might do something to myself . . . I've been thinking about suicide.

   _____ *Helper A:* You say you're suicidal, but what is it that's really bothering you?

   _____ *Helper B:* Can you tell me more about your suicidal feelings?

2. *Client:* And now my health is going downhill too, on top of all the rest. Without my husband around to care for me anymore, it just seems like the end of the world.

   _____ *Helper A:* Try not to worry so much about it. Everything will be alright.

   _____ *Helper B:* You must feel pretty lonely and afraid of what might happen.

3. *Client:* But my thoughts have been so terrible . . . I could never tell them to anybody.

   _____ *Helper A:* You can tell me. I'm a professional, and have been trained to be objective about these things.

   _____ *Helper B:* Some of your ideas seem so frightening to you, that you imagine other people would be shocked to know you are thinking such things.

4. *Client:* No one can understand the kind of pain I've been through. Sometimes I just feel like I have to hurt myself, so I cut my wrists.

_____ *Helper A:* It seems like you've been suffering so much that cutting your wrists is the only way you can make the pain go away.

_____ *Helper B:* But you're so young, you have so much to live for. How can you think of killing yourself?

5. *Client:* What are you anyway? Are you a doctor? How do you know what I've been going through? You've probably always had it pretty soft.

_____ *Helper A:* So you're wondering if I can understand how you feel.

_____ *Helper B:* You're not even giving me a chance. I've had a pretty rough life too; you're not the only one who's seen some hard times.

6. *Client:* My life has been worthless ever since my wife, Emma, died four years ago. The kids are grown and married now, and I've been retired from my job at the railroad for some time. It just seems that I'd be better off dead.

_____ *Helper A:* But try to think of what Emma would want for you. She'd want you to continue leading a productive life, wouldn't she?

_____ *Helper B:* It sounds like everything just collapsed around you when Emma died . . . But what has happened recently to make things even worse, to make you think that dying is the only way out?

7. *Client:* I really need help . . . It's just . . . [voice breaks: silence]

_____ *Helper A:* It must be hard for you to talk about what's bothering you.

_____ *Helper B:* Go on, I'm here to listen to you talk.

8. *Client:* When you sum up my problem like that, it makes it seem less confusing and not so scary.

_____ *Helper A:* See, it really isn't so bad after all. It certainly isn't anything you would think of killing yourself over, is it?

_____ *Helper B:* Sometimes talking about problems does make them a bit clearer. I think you realize how dangerous your suicidal feelings were, that's why you decided to contact me.

9. *Client:* You were suppose to help me, but you've only made things worse.

_____ *Helper A:* I'm sorry. I was only trying to help.

_____ *Helper B:* You sound pretty angry.

10. *Client:* How could you ever help me? Have you ever wanted to kill yourself?

_____ *Helper A:* It sounds like you're concerned abut whether I can understand and help you.

_____ *Helper B:* Sure, I've thought about suicide sometimes. But I always found more realistic solutions to my problems.

11. *Client:* I don't know . . . this whole thing with my wife really gets to me. [Sobs] I try so hard to keep from crying . . .

_____ *Helper A:* Do you think that the reason it's hard for you to cry is because you're a man?

_____ *Helper B:* With all the hurt you're feeling, it must be impossible to hold those tears in.

12. *Client:* How can I believe in God anymore? No God would ever let this happen to me; I've never done anything to deserve what's happened.

_____ *Helper A:* Things have gotten so bad, that it's difficult to see any meaning in the things that have happened to you.

_____ *Helper B:* Well, God works in mysterious ways. Maybe this is His way of testing your faith.

13. *Client:* I don't know why I'm calling you. My family is financially well off, and my husband spends plenty of time with me, even though he has a successful law career. Even my kids have been doing well. They get good marks at school and have lots of free time activities with their friends. But nothing seems to interest me. Life is just a bore . . .

_____ *Helper A:* Considering all you have going for you, your problems can't be all that serious. Try to focus more on the positive aspects of your situation.

_____ *Helper B:* So even though things seem to be going well at one level, life still seems pretty depressing, even if it's hard to say exactly why.

14. *Client:* I have to hang up now. My mother's coming home soon and I don't want her to know I've been talking to you.

_____ *Helper A:* Okay, but if you keep feeling suicidal, remember you can always call back.

_____ *Helper B:* All right, but first I want you to promise me you won't do anything to hurt yourself, until you call and talk to me. Will you repeat that promise?

15. *Client:* Is it really true, that many people feel this way? I thought I was the only one who had such dreadful, sinful ideas.

_____ *Helper A:* No, there are many people who suffer from mental illness. But with appropriate treatment by a qualified physician, some of these patients can be cured.

_____ *Helper B:* It is true. You're not the only one who has suicidal thoughts. And you can be helped to get through this crisis, just as others have been.

16. *Client:* I'm so lonely, so tired. [crying] There just isn't anywhere left to turn.

_____ *Helper A:* You seem so alone, so miserable. Have you been feeling suicidal?

_____ *Helper B:* Come on now. Things can't be all that bad.

17. *Client:* [over telephone] It's hard to talk here, with all these people.

_____ *Helper A:* Would it help if I asked questions?

_____ *Helper B:* Why don't you call back some other time when you can talk more easily?

18. *Client:* I have a gun pointed at my head right now, and if you don't help me. I'm going to pull the trigger!

_____ *Helper A:* You seem to be somewhat upset.

_____ *Helper B:* I want you to put down the gun so we can talk.

19. *Client:* Why should you care about me, anyway?

_____ *Helper A:* I've been trained to care about people. That's my job.

_____ *Helper B:* Because I think your death would be a terrible waste, and it concerns me that things are so that you are considering suicide. You need help to get through this critical period.

20. *Client:* I really hate my father! He's never shown any love for me, just complete disregard.

_____ *Helper A:* You must really be angry at him for not being there when you need him.

_____ *Helper B:* You shouldn't feel that way. After all, he is your father, and he deserves some respect.

21. *Client:* I don't think there's really anyone who cares whether I'm alive or dead.

_____ *Helper A:* It sounds like you're feeling pretty isolated.

_____ *Helper B:* Why do you think that no one cares about you anymore?

22. *Client:* I tried going to a therapist once before, but it didn't help . . . Nothing I do now will change anything.

_____ *Helper A:* You've got to look on the bright side! There must be something you can do to make things better, isn't there?

_____ *Helper B:* Okay, so you're feeling hopeless, like even a therapist couldn't help you. But has anyone else been helpful before—maybe a friend, relative, teacher, or clergyman?

23. *Client:* My psychiatrist tells me I have an anxiety neurosis. Do you think that's what's wrong with me?

_____ *Helper A:* I'd like to know what this means to you, in this present situation. How do you feel about your problem?

_____ *Helper B:* I'm not sure I agree with that diagnosis. Maybe you should seek out some psychological testing, just to be certain.

24. *Client:* I can't talk to anybody about my situation. Everyone is against me.

_____ *Helper A:* That isn't true. There are probably lots of people who care about you if you'd only give them a chance.

_____ *Helper B:* It must be difficult to find help when it's so hard to trust people.

25. *Client:* [Voice is slurred, unclear over telephone.]

_____ *Helper A:* You sound so tired. Why don't you get some sleep and call back in the morning?

_____ *Helper B:* Your voice sounds so sleepy. Have you taken anything?

SCORING KEY FOR THE ORIGINAL SUICIDE INTERVENTION RESPONSE INVENTORY

To score the original SIRI, simply tally 1 point for each of the 25 questions in which the respondent assigns a higher (more appropriate) rating to the more facilitative response, indicated for each item below. For example, the respondent would score 1 point if he or she assigned a higher value to Option B than to Option A on Item 1, and so on. No point is awarded for blanks or if the same number is given to each option within an item, because this reflects inability to discriminate a preferred from a nonpreferred response. Total scores can range from 0 to 25, the maximum tally of correct responses.

1. B	10. A	19. B
2. B	11. B	20. A
3. B	12. A	21. A
4. A	13. B	22. B
5. A	14. B	23. A
6. B	15. B	24. B
7. A	16. A	25. B
8. B	17. A	
9. B	18. B	

SCORING KEY FOR THE SUICIDE INTERVENTION RESPONSE INVENTORY FORM 2

To score the revised Suicide Intervention Response Inventory (SIRI-2), simply compute the difference (taking into account sign) between the respondent's rating for a particular item and the mean rating assigned by the criterion group of experts, as indicated in the following table. The total score on the SIRI-2, therefore, represents the total discrepancy between the individual and the panelist ratings across all items. Item 14 proved to be psychometrically ambiguous in our validation study, and we therefore recommend its exclusion from the SIRI-2. Unlike the original SIRI, whose scores range from 0 to 25, with larger scores representing greater degrees of competency, scores on the revised version span a much larger range, and represent degrees of variation from a hypothetically ideal score. Therefore, larger scores represent *less*, not more, competence in recognizing facilitative responses to a suicidal individual.

Mean Ratings (and Standard Deviations) of Appropriateness of Response Options in Items on the Suicide Intervention Response Inventory Form 2 by Panel of Experts

Response option	M	SD	Response option	M	SD
1A	− 2.71	.49	13A	− 2.57	.54
1B	1.86	.38	13B	2.29	.95
2A	− 2.71	.49	15A	− 2.57	.79
2B	1.86	.69	15B	2.14	.69
3A	− 2.14	1.07	16A	2.14	.69
3B	2.14	.38	16A	− 2.86	.38
4A	1.29	1.11	17A	1.57	1.27
4B	− 2.71	.49	17B	− 1.71	.95
5A	2.43	.54	18A	− 2.00	1.41
5B	− 2.71	.49	18B	1.43	1.72
6A	− 2.00	1.16	19A	− 2.29	.76
6B	2.57	.53	19B	1.57	.54
7A	2.00	.86	20A	2.00	1.41
7B	− 1.29	1.70	20B	− 2.86	.38
8A	− 2.29	.49	21A	1.86	1.35
8B	2.14	.90	21B	− 1.57	.79
9A	− 1.29	1.50	22A	− 2.71	.49
9B	1.29	1.80	22B	1.43	1.62
10A	2.29	.76	23A	1.57	1.40
10B	− 2.43	.98	23B	− 2.57	.54
11A	− 2.42	.54	24A	− 2.43	.79
11B	2.43	.79	24B	2.14	.69
12A	2.00	.82	25A	− 2.57	.79
12B	− 3.00	.00	25B	2.43	.79

Part VI

Applications to
the Case

In the general literature on psychotherapy, case consultations that provide alternative case conceptualizations are ubiquitous. Likewise, in treatment settings, discussions of suicidal patients are common. To date, however, little effort has been made to use a case history as a teaching tool for treatment of suicidal people. Part I of this book introduced readers to Arthur Inman, a deeply disturbed man whose pain became unbearable. Inman was a man who wrote voluminously, providing a unique historical view of a suicidal person. Throughout this book, the contributors have explored different aspects of suicide and its treatment. In Part VI, that knowledge is applied, in the form of two commentaries, to the case of Arthur Inman. Although such case consultations cannot provide a hands-on, practical approach to treatment, we attempt to raise some issues, with the purpose of allowing the reader to reflect on treatment possibilities for Inman. We hope that the learning experience represented by this exercise and the book of which it is a part will add to the reader's skill and sensitivity in formulating a framework for the treatment of suicidal people.

Chapter 17

The Inman Diary:
Some Reflections on Treatment

Antoon A. Leenaars
John T. Maltsberger

The case of Arthur Inman was presented in Chapter 1. Shneidman presented some excerpts from the diary that illustrate Inman's ruminations about suicide. There are many ways to analyze such personal documents. Here we return to the Inman case from the vantage point of the chapters on treatment in this volume. We, Leenaars and Maltsberger, will offer separate consultations on Inman's treatment. Thus, this chapter is not only a summary, but also an application of the findings presented in this volume to a single case study: Arthur Inman.

LEENAARS: A DEVELOPMENTAL PERSPECTIVE

Treatment of a suicidal person is best done within the context of a sound understanding of suicide. A developmental perspective is a significant aspect for such an understanding. By this I am not referring to the perspective of age as a demographic variable in suicide (although it may be a relevant one); I am referring to a genotypic view. From this perspective we learn that the suicidal person does not respond anew to each trauma in life, but rather reacts in ways that are largely consistent with previous reactions; I say largely consistent because at the same time there is change. In the suicidal person, as in all people, development is both continuous and discontinuous. This was certainly true for Arthur Inman.

His history is a key to understanding his multidimensional malaise and his recurrent suicidal solution.

A commonality about suicide is that there are abundant precursors to self-destruction in the suicidal person. Suicide has a history. In Inman's case, his early life is most significant. Although he did not begin the diary until the age of 24, his reflections on his early years are revealing. Inman himself was acutely aware about the essentials of such antecedents toward his self-destruction. Even about his birth he wrote, "My coming into the world was as arduous and painful as my life" (p. 19). His mother was very ill (something for which Inman never forgave her). Inman's birth and infancy were problematic. His mother described him as "fearfully detached." Inman's environment was equally detaching. His father was described as forceful, attempting to break Inman's will. Inman described his early home life as " a terrible thing." Even before birth he was rejected by his father, who had wanted a girl. His mother was described as no better, succumbing frequently to abuse. Of one such physical incident, Inman wrote, "My own mother had treated me unfairly, so unfairly that there was no excuse for her." He saw the physical abuse as "heartless," adding, however, "that real cruelty always lurked behind the cruel words she often said" (p. 32). Inman's early years were traumatic. Obviously, even then treatment for the family would have been necessary, yet little of such help was available in those days. Indeed, in the early part of this century, the medical profession explained all illnesses with a few basic concepts, and psychotherapy, as we know it, was virtually unknown.

Much of Inman's childhood was unbearably painful because he felt insufficiently loved by his parents. Still, he ambivalently adored his mother, despite her ordering, pleading, and cajoling. This was not so with his father. Inman resented and despised his father, experiencing no love for him. Needless to say, the relationship between Inman's parents was dysfunctional; it is likely that they stayed in the marriage because Inman's mother feared that a divorce would destroy her social position, a prime value in Atlanta at that time.

Inman's school years were no better. He was shipped off to Haverford School against his will. In 1910 he wrote to his mother,

> The boys here are awful; you can't even stay in your own room much without them messing everything up. One of them took my hockey stick Saturday and busted it; one of them has taken away my cap, and all I have left is a thin summer cap. I hope I won't have to go here next year, because I don't see how I can stand it. (p. 81)

Inman felt abandoned. His anguish was deep, and, despite his plea, he spent 5 years at Haverford School, developing even more ills that would last a lifetime. He had few friends. After Haverford School, Inman spent 2½ years at Haverford College, where, in February 1916, he collapsed. Of this, he wrote in the diary, "If I could have foreseen ahead, I would have killed myself" (p. 131).

From my perspective, crisis intervention would have been necessary at this time. Inman, however, was taken to a German doctor who diagnosed autotoxic poisoning and subjected Inman to what Inman called "the German stuffing treatment." The collapse, I believe, marks a critical point in Inman's development, much of the rest of which was to be continuous . . . elliptical. He was painfully depressed. His history explains much of what we learned abut him in Chapter 1. He had a life of unbearable pain and, as we see in our patients, the early history is the beginning to a suicidal solution.

Suicide occurs in the lives of many people of various ages. At the time Inman was a child, children were considered to be uniquely immune to suicide. Inman's case reveals an archival fact: Children are not immune. Recent research (Pfeffer, 1993) documents self-destructive behavior in children, showing that these youngsters have serious developmental problems. That was true for Inman by the age of 5 or 6 (Aaron, 1985). Adolescent suicide, on the other hand, has been documented for centuries. Although suicide in youth is already a multi-dimensional event, familial dysfunction has been identified as a critical factor (Berman & Jobes, 1991; Leenaars & Wenckstern, 1991). Characteristics of such developmental traumas include separation, anxiety, inflexible systems, communication disturbances, symbiotic parent-child relationships, and long-term disorganization (within the context of ever-recurrent traumas, like Inman's experiences at home and school) (Leenaars & Wenckstern, 1991). All of these symptomatic features were evident in the Inman family. Inman's pain was, according to his own perception, related to the upheavals in his family.

How could a clinician have intervened? What treatment would have helped Inman? I will limit my comments to a few directions, based on the recommendations of the contributors to this volume, beginning with Shneidman's quoting of Maltsberger in Chapter 1:

A tenable working hypothesis would be that the hate, now displaced onto Jews, Roosevelt, blacks, and whoever else, arose from some bitter childhood disappointment in someone from whom the patient had longed to be given much but had received little. The best guess is his father.

As we have seen, that is true! His earliest attachments were suicidogenic. Thus, regarding treatment, Shneidman concludes,

I would hope that some *therapeutic alliance* with Inman would have been possible. Had that occurred, I suspect that he might have been helped. (emphasis added)

The alliance would be essential. Attachment needed to have been introduced early in Inman's life, well before the collapse. I wonder what Dr. Boris Sidis, the therapist whom Inman saw in Boston, did. Why did Inman steadfastly resist therapeutic help? Inman's mother also resisted Sidis's help—why? Was it possible to develop a relationship with Inman and his parents? Maybe McLean and Taylor's observations about family therapy in Chapter 6 need to be considered. Family help was needed. Would the family, however, have entered such a risk? The mother colluded against Sidis and clung to Inman, and the father was ostracized from interviewing. Why was such dysfunction needed?

McLean and Taylor write, "Many family therapies . . . share common goals, such as restoration of communication and reduction of demoralization." The Inman family was dysfunctional. To address Inman's unbearable pain as a youth, the clinician would need to address the rejection and demoralization by his father and his mother. The family's communication, if it existed, was toxic. Inman was hopeless and helpless by an early age, maybe the situation was before he was born.

Assessment is complex, as Kral and Sakinofsky show in Chapter 2. Yet it is possible. Many of the signposts for treatment discussed throughout this book are evident in Inman's diary. Inman was suicidal. As Shneidman indicated, this was true at an early age. Shneidman's recapitulation of Inman's statements, like a suicide note, reveals Inman's malaise and are clear reflections of his pain and suicidal risk. Over time in the diary, one reads in the protocols: high perturbation and lethality. In the clarity of clinical hindsight, his writings consistently were focused on his suicidal solution. The diary speaks for itself. There is no doubt in my mind that, as Allport, Murray, and Shneidman have argued, personal documents—i.e., communication, ideation—are invaluable in understanding the suicidal person and have direct implications for treatment. Whether in the form of individual therapy with Inman's parents before his birth, child therapy for Inman, or family therapy while Inman was a youth, early treatment was imperative.

Would medication have helped? In Chapter 11, Slaby offers directions. Would antidepressants have restored Inman's stability after his collapse in 1916 to allow further intervention? What about hospitalization? Goldblatt and Sederer in this volume provide some sound intense plans for Arthur's treatment. By the time of Arthur's collapse, hospitalization may have been necessary. As Sederer notes in Chapter 13, the patient's past history is still the best predictor of suicide risk. By the time Inman collapsed, more intense treatment than weekly outpatient therapy—perhaps hospitalization—should have been considered. Such treatment should have begun with crisis intervention (with the family's participation). How did Inman construe his circumstances? What was critical? How did the collapse have adjustive value? What needs were blocked? How could the perturbation be alleviated? What were the options? Who was available to help? How could Inman's parents be included in the treatment? Etc. Once the level of perturbation was lowered, however, the clinician would have needed to move toward more in-depth treatment—psychotherapy, hospitalization, and medication should have been considered.

I would like to close my few observations in line with my outline of Inman's life until the collapse, by repeating an observation Berman and Jobes made in Chapter 7: "It is axiomatic that the adolescent identified to be at risk for suicide or suicidal behavior needs help." Yet, by the time of his collapse (and even more so in later years), Inman was "notoriously reluctant to seek help," something Berman and Jobes note is true of many adolescents and, I would add, young adults. After Sidis, Inman hated therapists. Of course, such transferences are not unusual. Many of my adolescent and young adult patients transfer hate onto me. But that too is treatable. Could someone have helped Inman? To conclude, if I had full control of Inman's treatment, I would have recommended treatment for Inman's parents years before Inman's birth.

MALTSBERGER: PSYCHIATRIC COMMENT

The critical moment was 1916, the year in which Arthur Inman, chronically unhappy throughout adolescence, collapsed into a major depressive episode at the age of 21, and embarked on a lifelong career of hypochondriacal misery that ended in suicide 47 years later.

There can be little doubt about the 1916 diagnosis—in his junior year at Haverford, Inman was suffering crying fits, profound loss of energy, difficulty sleeping, loss of appetite, and morbidly low self-respect. He had been troubled by diverse physical aches and pains since the previous year. Hustled into a hospital and treated by a gastroenterologist, he improved enough to be discharged to the care of his well-meaning but befuddled parents, whereupon began a morbid regression in which he and his mother clung together, consulted endless physicians, excluded the father, rejected psychiatric treatment, and ultimately settled on a course of osteopathic treatment that lasted the rest of his unhappy life (Aaron, 1985).

He strained a muscle climbing in the gymnasium a year before the breakdown. Inman was convinced that he had seriously injured himself, attributing the depressive symptoms that developed subsequently to this minor strain. He repudiated any suggestion that his difficulties were at heart psychological, and, over time, supported by the osteopaths he consulted (he had six osteopaths making house-calls in 1942), he developed near-delusional, or delusional, ideas about his body.

His mother appears to have been neurasthenic; Inman identified with her and amplified her complaints as she hovered about his bed in a dark room during 1916. They made each other frantic.

> Mother came in my room to try to help me. Once there she was too ill to leave. She had the feeling that once she left me she would die before reaching her own room

and that she preferred to stay with me. She absolutely believed what she said. So did I. (p. 167)

Only when Arthur's long-suffering father managed to separate mother and son in 1917 did Arthur begin to improve, but by that time he had acquired the first of numberless successive paid attendants who catered to his whims and indulged his selfish crotchets.

Inman was rarely free of depressive symptoms after 1916. Sometimes these deepened dangerously. We know of two suicidal overdoses before he finally shot himself, one taken in 1941 and another in 1963. Contemporary psychiatrists would diagnose a narcissistic personality disorder complicated by a chronic affective (depressive) disorder. In the absence of good treatment, Inman's condition worsened. After the 1930s he was a heavy drinker, and took large quantities of barbiturates as well. The evidence that he was chronically poisoned by large doses of bromides is strong. Although there are no suggestions of frank psychosis in the diary (with the possible exception of delusional ideas about his body, which were supported by his cadre of osteopaths) until just before his death, there is a strong suggestion that he shot himself in a state of acute visual hallucinosis that verged on delirium tremens. What a friend witnessed the day before Inman shot himself is consistent with a state of acute alcohol–barbiturate withdrawal possibly complicated by bromide poisoning:

> Kathy Connor stepped into Arthur's room and found him agitated to the extreme. He told her of horrid shapes with deformed hands stretching out to seize him, creatures with tongues protruding from their ears, eyes glaring out of foreheads, bursts of intensely colored fire. When she touched him he screamed with pain and asked her to leave. (p. 1598)

Although admittedly severe, had Inman's psychiatric illness received good treatment at the beginning, the downward spiral in which he was trapped might have been interrupted. The regression into which he was pitched in 1916 had a strong oedipal color to it, with he and his mother clinging together as misunderstood sufferers and the father excluded as an insensitive brute. When the eminent psychiatrist Dr. Boris Sidis saw Inman in 1916 and suggested that mother and son should be separated and Inman admitted to a sanitarium, a violent paranoid devaluation of Sidis followed:

> The door opened at last, and in he came, a compact Lucifer figure of a Jew. With his entrance some malign influence seemed to permeate the room. He requested (like an order, that request) that Mother leave us alone. She did so. The man pulled a chair close to mine, sat down, turned his black eyes full into mine. I cannot in mere words express the sensation of horror that overwhelmed me. Here was evil incarnate. (p. 150)

What Inman demanded, and what he got, was to be treated with the prerogatives of a small child. The strong, seemingly benign, fatherlike Dr. Cyrus R. Pike, who was willing to indulge Inman's demands, became principal osteopath after 1917 and remained in this position until he died in 1949. Pike was as idealized as Sidis was debased; Inman viewed him as an unconquerable fighter and leader. Inman adopted a passive homosexual attitude toward Pike from the beginning, and their relationship was to some extent one of dominance and submission. Various enemas were part of his osteopathic routine, and Pike frequently had to manipulate his patient's "intestines" to get them into place.

Inman's narcissism was formidable. Because his intimidated father provided him a generous flow of funds enabling him to live as he pleased, it deepened. He appears to have been incapable of sustaining friendship, but paid an array of servants to keep him company, type his diary, and run his errands. Others mattered only to the extent that boosted his sense of self-importance, catered to his physical comfort, and relieved his loneliness. He married in 1923 and treated his masochistic wife, Evelyn, in the same way, beating her and pulling her hair when she displeased him.

> I love people in direct proportion to how sweetly or how quickly they give me my way. When they instantaneously, unfairly or prolongedly cross me, no matter how deeply I love them, for the time being I hate their guts. I like to get my own way. (p. 1341)

Exploitative in the extreme, Inman was an actual as well as psychological voyeur, and probably an actual as well as psychological exhibitionist as well. He paid women and young girls small sums of money over many years to visit him in a darkened bedroom where he "probed" for their experiences, especially sexual ones, and induced many to "pet" with him. He did not bother to conceal these activities from Evelyn and actively promoted an intimate relationship between her and Pike that recapitulated the original childhood triangle of himself and his parents. His fantasies were grandiose; he fancied himself an expert on world affairs, pleased himself with daydreams of becoming Emperor of the United States, and wished he could become invisible and could instantly transport himself anywhere simply by wishing it. He dreamed that he was an endangered baby Jesus or Moses. He was a shameless sneak and manipulator and repeatedly wished that his long-suffering and execrated father would die so he could get his money. His dreams repeatedly reflected oedipal themes of competition with devalued other men for forbidden sexual intimacies.

Inman's relationships with others, his sexual attitudes, his triangular preoccupations, and his grandiosities point strongly to a fixation at the psychological development of a boy between the ages of 3 and 5 years. Like boys of that age, he lacked a stable sense of himself in general, and enduring adult masculine ideals in particular. He failed to form a perdurable identification with his father, or with a father substitute, and, as a consequence, never escaped the sense that he was a special, helpless, misunderstood child. The want of a sturdy, realistic inner masculine ideal (psychoanalytically speaking, Inman suffered from incomplete ego-ideal development) left him vulnerable on a number of counts (Freud, 1914/1974; Murray, 1964).

First, he responded subserviently to certain other idealized men in a most unrealistic way. His relationship with Pike was the most egregious instance of this; in consequence of his devotion to his osteopath, Inman's poor physical and psychological health were made much worse. Second, good self-esteem cannot stabilize and perdure in the absence of a stable, realistic ego-ideal system; grandiose, unattainable self-expectations persevered from Inman's childhood (he longed to be "a great man") and perpetually cast him into disappointment. Without such structures, mood regulation is unstable and depressive fluctuations expectable. Third, because he had no adult conscience, Inman's relationships with others around him were exploitative and selfish in the extreme. Consequently, he was left emotionally alone and isolated as he grew older. Furthermore, his deep sense of personal worthlessness and profound narcissistic rage (Kohut, 1972) invited compensatory devaluation of others (e.g., Jews, blacks, and political leaders) that must have made him even more repellent to those close to him than to those who slog their way through the swamp of his diary.

Inman's suicide was a preventable one. He had taken a dangerous overdose 9 months before he shot himself. Evelyn knew he had a gun. When he took the first suicidal overdose in 1941, she waited for hours before summoning medical aid; he might have died. Although Aaron gives few details about Inman's last few days, it seems clear that had help been summoned and treatment administered for what appears to have been a withdrawal psychosis, he would probably have survived—at least for a while. His mistreated and ambivalent wife appears to have cooperated in his demise.

The character problem that underlay Inman's depression (i.e., his profound narcissism, disturbed relationships to others, and lack of a stable sense of self) just might have been treatable in 1916 or 1917 had the patient not succeeded in persuading his parents to support him in the gratifying life of a neurasthenic invalid, surrounded by complicit servants and osteopaths. His enjoyment of primitive pleasures was great; Inman would not have wished to surrender them. We know that when narcissistic, exploitative trends in a patient's relationships to others come under psychotherapeutic scrutiny, intense anger is likely to result. The therapeutic alliance is likely to break down at such moments unless the therapist can protect, fortify, and use the positive themes of the transference and of the real relationship. Inman scorned psychiatrists and psychoanalysts; it seems unlikely that he would have persevered in any treatment very long when invited to look honestly at how he abused and exploited other people. I would expect such an outpouring of rage and devaluation against the therapist that the treatment would have ended at once.

The chances of Inman's obtaining effective treatment fell sharply after 1917 as he snuggled into his invalidism. Although there were some psychoanalysts in Boston in the 1920s, the phenomena of character pathology and narcissism were not then well understood. The Boston Psychoanalytic Society and Institute was not organized until 1933. Sidis might have helped; after one encounter, however, he was dismissed as a devil-Jew. In 1926, Evelyn checked out Dr. Morton Prince, a respected Boston practitioner; she and Arthur dismissed him scornfully.

> I really believe that the whole tribe of psychoanalysts [sic; Prince was not a psychoanalyst] are more interested in effecting acquiescence of the patient to themselves than in effecting a cure. Dr. Prince asserted violently that Dr. Pike should be in jail, that he was a scoundrel as were all osteopaths. Evelyn walked out. (p. 299)

At some juncture, Inman consulted Stanley Cobb, a kindly and highly sophisticated psychoanalyst widely respected in Boston, a nationally respected expert on psychosomatic illnesses. Cobb was dismissed as "a dud and dumb" (p. 1517). About to be visited by a psychologist, Dr. Brainard, after the 1941 suicide attempt, Inman recorded a dream reflecting the inevitable latent hostile transference, clearly revealing his paranoid style of projected hostility and arrogance, a formidable character defense:

> I dreamed last night that this new doctor turned up with a prescription made out before he had seen me (which he refused to explain) and a supercilious contempt for my ideas and assumptions. (p. 1048)

Had Inman the good fortune to get into treatment with a highly skilled therapist early on, there remains the slight possibility he might have been able to repair the fatal character flaws that led to his suicide. By 1963 it was too late for that. Inman at age 68 was an old man who had nothing to look back upon except a life of selfish indulgences and exploitations. Unloved, alcoholic, and corrupt, he shot himself to avoid the intolerable depressive emptiness that finally caught up with him.

REFERENCES

Aaron, D. (1985). *The Inman diary*. Cambridge, MA: Harvard University Press.

Berman, A., & Jobes, D. (1991). *Adolescent suicide: Assessment and intervention*. Washington, DC: American Psychiatric Press.

Freud, S. (1974). On narcissism. In J. Strachey (Ed. & Trans.), *The standard edition of the complete psychological works of Sigmund Freud* (Vol. 14, pp. 67–102). London: Hogarth Press. (Original work published in 1914).

Kohut, H. (1972). Thoughts on narcissism and narcissistic rage. *Psychoanalytic Study of the Child, 27,* 360–400.

Leenaars, A., & Wenckstern, S. (1991). Suicide in the school-age child and adolescent. In A. Leenaars (Ed.), *Life-span perspectives of suicide* (pp. 95–120). New York: Plenum.

Murray, J. M. (1964). Narcissism and the ego-ideal. *Journal of the American Psychoanalytic Association, 12,* 477–528.

Pfeffer, C. (1993). Suicidal children. In A. Leenaars (Ed.), *Suicidology: Essays in honor of Edwin Shneidman* (pp. 175–185). Northvale, NJ: Jason Aronson.

Index